Data Protection and Compliance in Context

The British Computer Society

BCS is the leading professional body for the IT industry. With members in over 100 countries, BCS is the professional and learned Society in the field of computers and information systems.

BCS is responsible for setting standards for the IT profession. It is also leading the change in public perception and appreciation of the economic and social importance of professionally managed IT projects and programmes. In this capacity, the Society advises, informs and persuades industry and government on successful IT implementation.

IT is affecting every part of our lives and that is why BCS is determined to promote IT as the profession of the 21st century.

Joining BCS

BCS qualifications, products and services are designed with your career plans in mind. We not only provide essential recognition through professional qualifications but also offer many other useful benefits to our members at every level.

BCS membership demonstrates your commitment to professional development. It helps to set you apart from other IT practitioners and provides industry recognition of your skills and experience. Employers and customers increasingly require proof of professional qualifications and competence. Professional membership confirms your competence and integrity and sets an independent standard that people can trust. Professional Membership (MBCS) is the pathway to Chartered IT Professional (CITP) Status.

www.bcs.org/membership

Further Information

Further information about BCS can be obtained from: BCS, First Floor, Block D, North Star House, North Star Avenue, Swindon, SN2 1FA, UK.
Telephone: 0845 300 4417 (UK only) or + 44 (0)1793 417 424 (overseas)
Email: customerservice@hq.bcs.org.uk
Web: www.bcs.org

Data Protection and Compliance in Context

Stewart Room, LLM
Barrister & Solicitor
Chairman, National Association of Data Protection
and Freedom of Information Officers
Proprietor, DPA Law
Partner, Rowe Cohen Solicitors & Head of Information
Law Unit

The British Computer Society
Publishing and Information Products
First Floor, Block D
North Star House
North Star Avenue
Swindon
SN2 1FA
UK

www.bcs.org

ISBN 1-902505-78-6
ISBN13 978-1-902505-78-7

British Cataloguing in Publication Data.
A CIP catalogue record for this book is available at the British Library.

 captured, authored, published, delivered and managed in XML
CAPDM Limited, Edinburgh, Scotland   www.capdm.com

Printed by Biddles Ltd.

For Samantha and Annabel,
with all my love

Contents

List of Figures and Tables

Author

Barrister and solicitor Stewart Room is a partner at Rowe Cohen Solicitors, where he heads the Information Law Unit and the firm's London office. He has previously been in private practice at the Bar. His clients include EMC^2, Computer Associates, Dell, Novell, Hitachi, Fujitsu, the Chartered Institute of Public Finance and Accountancy, the Direct Marketing Association, the Federation of Small Businesses, Veredus, UNICEF, the National Theatre and the International Cricket Council. Stewart Room is the National Chair of the National Association of Data Protection and Freedom of Information Officers (NADPO) and a member of the BCS Information Privacy Expert Panel. He is also a visiting lecturer on Computer and Communications Law, Queen Mary, the University of London, and the proprietor of DPA Law, a leading online resource on data protection and privacy.

Acknowledgements

I do have some very important acknowledgements to make. First and foremost I wish to thank my wife, Samantha, for all of her encouragement and support throughout the writing of this book and in the six years leading up to it. If it was not for Samantha I would not have been confident enough, or sufficiently informed, to tackle this project. Thank you Samantha, I owe you everything.

My partners at Rowe Cohen Solicitors are also very deserving of mention, for giving me the space, time and encouragement I needed to grow our position in the data protection legal market place. Particular thanks are due to Ian Lewis, Graham Small and Simon Cohen.

I also wish to acknowledge my peers in data protection, from whom I have learned so much. They have all contributed to this book in some way. First, my colleagues at the National Association of Data Protection and Freedom of Information Officers (NADPO), who have accorded me the very great privilege of electing me to the Chair of this most impressive organization. I do encourage others to join NADPO and to take a role in its new National Council. Dr Ian Walden, at the Centre for Commercial Law Studies, Queen Mary, is also owed a debt of gratitude. He has been a great inspiration.

I would like to thank two other great supporters. First, my pupil master, Charles Joseph of Tanfield Chambers, who nurtured me as a young barrister and has been a great help to me ever since. Second, my assistant, Emily Chantzi, an excellent data protection lawyer in her own right and a good friend whose value cannot be overstated.

I would also like to thank Hugh Small, for giving me a comfortable and quiet place to work.

Finally, thanks to Matthew Flynn, Florence Leroy and Suzanna Marsh at the BCS, my colleagues on the BCS Information Privacy Expert Panel, the BCS itself and my copy editor Sarah Price, of Sprite Documentation Services, and my proofreader Barbara Eastman, who have helped to make sense of my ramblings.

Abbreviations

ATCSA	Anti-terrorism, Crime and Security Act 2001
BCR	Binding Corporate Rules
DPA	Data Protection Act 1998
DPEC	Directive on Privacy and Electronic Communications
EC	European Community
ECHR	European Convention for the Protection of Human Rights and Fundamental Freedoms of 1950
EEA	European Economic Area
EEC	European Economic Community
EU	European Union
FAQ	Frequently asked question
FSA	Financial Services Authority
GCHQ	Government Communications Headquarters
HR	Human resources
HRA	Human Rights Act 1998
IFA	Independent financial advisor
NSA	National Supervisory Authority
OECD	Organisation for Economic Co-operation and Development
Ofcom	Office of Communications
PDA	Personal digital assistant
PNR	Passenger name record
RIPA	Regulation of Investigatory Powers Act 2000

Glossary

Anonymization The removal of personal identifiers so that information no longer identifies a living individual.

Article 29 Working Party An independent body with advisory status that is constituted under Article 29 of the Data Protection Directive. It is composed of representatives of the national supervisory authorities for data protection and European Community (EC) officials. Its duties require it to examine the operation of the Data Protection Directive and to provide opinions and advice to the European Commission.

Binding Corporate Rules A scheme approved by a Decision of the European Commission for making lawful the transfer of personal information within a group of companies, covering the situation where information is transferred from a company situated within the European Economic Area (EEA) to a company situated in a country outside of the EEA.

Blagging A colloquialism for the unlawful obtaining of personal information by a person who conceals their true identity by pretending to be a person with a lawful entitlement to the information sought.

Bluetooth technologies Bluetooth is a an industrial specification for wireless personal area networks, used to connect Bluetooth enabled devices such as personal digital assistants (PDAs), mobile telephones and laptop computers.

Convergence The term given to the harmonization in 2002 of EC laws regulating communications by telecommunications, internet and broadcasting media.

Council of Europe An intergovernmental human rights organization that was founded after the Second World War, now with 46 Member States.

Council of Europe Data Protection Convention 1981 The first and only European treaty on data protection.

Data For the purposes of the Data Protection Act 1998, (i) information that is being processed by automated equipment; (ii) information that is recorded with the intention that it will be processed by automated equipment; (iii) information that is recorded as part of a relevant filing system or with the intention that it should form part of a relevant filing system; (iv) information that forms part of an accessible record; and (v) recorded information held by a public authority.

Data controller A person or organization with the power to control the purpose or manner of processing of personal data.

Data processor A person or organization that processes personal data on behalf of a data controller.

Data protection principles For the purposes of the Data Protection Act 1998 a series of eight rules for the fair, lawful, legitimate and safe processing of personal data. It is the data controller's duty to comply with the data protection principles.

Data subject A person who is the subject of personal data.

Digital safe A colloquialism for a storage device for digital information that provides highly robust security.

EC Data Protection Directive 1995 A legal instrument of the EC implemented in the UK by the Data Protection Act 1998. The Data Protection Directive protects the fundamental rights and freedoms of natural persons, particularly their right to privacy with respect to the processing of personal data. The Directive also outlaws prohibitions and restrictions on the flow of personal data between EC Member States for reasons connected with the protection of fundamental rights and freedoms.

Electronic shredding A colloquialism for the process by which digital information is permanently deleted from a storage device by repeated overwriting with new binary code.

European Community (EC) Part of the European Union established in 1957 as the European Economic Community by the Treaty Establishing the European Community.

Fair processing A key requirement within the data protection principles. Personal data must be processed fairly, meaning, among other things, that personal data must be collected by a fair method and that the data subject should be provided in most cases with the data controller's identity, a description of the purposes for which the data are intended to be processed and information about any unusual or non-obvious circumstances.

Firewall A logical barrier that is designed to prevent unauthorized or unwanted communications between parts of a computer network.

Information Commissioner The national supervisory authority for the UK, established for the purposes of ensuring compliance with the requirements of Article 28 of the Data Protection Directive.

Information Tribunal (Data Protection Tribunal)   The tribunal established under the Data Protection Act 1998 for hearing appeals from information and enforcement notices served by the Information Commissioner.

Informational privacy   A key element within a state of privacy describing the right that individuals enjoy to control the flow of information about themselves.

Lifecycle   As in information lifecycle, the period between the initial collection of data and its final deletion or destruction.

Necessity test   A precondition of many of the conditions for making the processing of personal data and sensitive personal data legitimate is that the processing should be necessary for the particular purpose.

Non-adequate country   A country situated outside the EEA that does not ensure an adequate level of protection for personal data undergoing processing.

Organisation for Economic Co-operation and Development (OECD)
An intergovernmental organization that provides a forum for the governments of 30 leading market democracies to discuss and develop policies to meet the challenges of globalization.

Personal data   Information relating to an identified or identifiable living individual.

Recipient   Any person to whom personal data are disclosed in the course of processing done by, or on behalf of, the data controller, apart from persons who receive personal data as a result of a particular inquiry made in exercise of legal powers, such as the Information Commissioner or the police.

Relevant filing system   A highly structured manual file containing personal data. Such a file must be structured by reference to criteria relating to living individuals so as to give easy access to the personal data within.

Safe harbor   A scheme approved by a decision of the European Commission for making lawful the transfer of personal information from within the EEA to commercial undertakings in the US that have declared their compliance with the safe harbor principles.

Subscriber   A person or organization that subscribes to a publicly available electronic communications service.

Substantive privacy   A key element within a state of privacy describing the right that individuals enjoy to take substantive decisions about how they live their lives.

Technological measures   In order to protect personal data, it is a requirement of the Data Protection Directive and the Data Protection Act that data controllers should take technological measures to guard against accidental loss and damage to personal data and unauthorized use. Technological measures include firewalls, anti-virus software and other privacy enhancing technologies.

Technological threats   Technological threats to personal data include malicious software, spyware, adware, ransomware and cookies.

Teleworking   A working arrangement in which employees enjoy flexibility in their place of work, hours of work and means of work. Rather than attending the workplace they connect to the workplace through electronic communications networks.

Third party   Anyone other than the data controller, the data subject or the data processor. A third party can be a natural person or legal persons, such as companies.

Transborder data flows   The movement of personal data across national boundaries.

User (in the context of user and subscriber)   A person who uses an electronic communications service.

Value added service   Any electronic communications service that requires the processing of traffic data or location data beyond what is necessary for the transmission of an electronic communication or its billing.

White list   A colloquialism for the group of countries situated outside the EEA whose laws, according to decisions made by the European Commission, ensure an adequate level of protection for personal data that are undergoing processing.

Useful Websites

Council of Europe	www.coe.int
DPA Law	www.dpalaw.co.uk
European Court of Human Rights	www.echr.coe.int/echr
European Union	www.europa.eu
European Commission	www.ec.europa.eu/index_en.htm
European Commission data protection website	www.ec.europa.eu/justice_home/fsj/privacy
Council of the European Union	http://ue.eu.int/cms3_fo/index.htm
European Court of Justice	http://curia.europa.eu
European Parliament	www.europarl.europa.eu
European Data Protection Supervisor	www.edps.eu.int
UK Information Commissioner	www.ico.gov.uk/eventual.aspx
Information Tribunal	www.informationtribunal.gov.uk
Office of Public Sector Information	www.opsi.gov.uk
Organisation for Economic Co-operation and Development	www.oecd.org
Office of the United Nations High Commissioner for Human Rights	www.ohchr.org/english/
US Department of Commerce safe harbor pages	www.export.gov/safeharbor/index.html
US Federal Trade Commission	www.ftc.gov/privacy

Preface

My publisher, Matthew Flynn at the British Computer Society, set a very challenging brief for this book. Taking account of the intended price, a modest 100,000 word allowance and a nine-month time limit, the idea was to write a book on data protection that will be of the greatest use to our target readers who are data protection officers and other professionals working in data protection, including consultants, training course providers and lawyers.

We hope that this book will also be of some assistance to people studying on data protection courses, but I should clarify at the outset that we did not set out to write a course book for the ISEB certificate in data protection, although I would estimate that we have covered about three quarters of the ISEB syllabus. I readily accept that the complete novice to data protection might struggle with the style and contents, but I will be publishing more penetrable summaries of the chapters on my website www.dpalaw.co.uk to act as companion guides for these readers.

The core of this book consists of a walk through and analysis of the Data Protection Act 1998 and related legislation supported by references to case law, European law and official guidance issued by the Information Commissioner and the Article 29 Working Party (an official body established by the Data Protection Directive) as appropriate. Of course, due to the constraints of space I have not been able to include everything, so I would encourage readers to regularly check my website for updates and more detailed references.

Chapter 1, 'Introduction to Data Protection', endeavours to put the Data Protection Act into context. I have tried to explain the history of data protection and how the law has developed, showing the wider international and European aspects of the law and the relationship with the right to privacy. I have also tried to identify the key aspects of data protection laws, including their aims and objectives, which involved tackling the main words, phrases and definitions, such as 'data controller', 'data subject', 'data processor', 'data', 'personal data' and 'processing'. If all of this can be distilled down to one sentence, I would suggest that data protection laws have been formulated at intergovernmental level to achieve a balance between the right to privacy and the wider economic, political and social interest in ensuring that flows of personal information between countries are maintained.

Chapter 2, 'Transparency', is more thematic, drawing together a series of issues that are connected by one common thread. I have called this common thread 'transparency', because the law contains a multifaceted framework that requires the data controller to give the data subject and the Information Commissioner adequate information about its processing operations, that is, the data controller must be transparent about these operations. Thus, Chapter 2 discusses consensual processing, fair processing, processing purposes, notification, the right of access and information notices. There are exceptions to the transparency provisions, however, which are identified. Subject to these exceptions, it might be fair to say that data protection laws require data controllers to adopt a 'cards-up' approach.

Chapter 3, 'General Rules on Lawfulness', identifies and analyses the basic processing standards required of data controllers, another key aspect of data protection laws, and contains the main discussion of the 'data protection principles'. There are eight data protection principles in the Data Protection Act and in combination with the transparency provisions they provide the foundations upon which data protection laws are built. At this junction I should highlight the fact that the first and second data protection principles are also discussed within Chapter 2. Thus it can be said that transparency is part of lawfulness as well as being a standalone topic in its own right. Again, there are exceptions.

Chapter 4, 'The Right to Object', discusses the circumstances in which the data subject can prevent the data controller from processing their personal data. The right to object empowers the data subject to take control over their personal data and is a vital compliance mechanism in its own right.

Chapter 5, 'Transborder Data Flows', discusses the law concerning the movement of personal data between countries. In summary, European Community data protection laws prevent the flow of personal data to countries outside of the European Economic Area that do not offer adequate protection for privacy, although this rule can be overcome by use of certain approved devices, such as model contractual clauses endorsed by the European Commission, and in special circumstances, such as when the data subject consents to the transfer. Within the Data Protection Act it is the eighth data protection principle that contains the key provisions.

Chapter 6, 'Privacy and Electronic Communications', is concerned with the modified data protection rules that regulate the processing of personal data over electronic communications networks, such as the internet or by telephone.

Chapter 7, 'Enforcing Data Protection Laws', looks at the powers vested in the data subject, the Information Commissioner and the courts that can be used to enforce the requirements of the laws. The role of the criminal law is discussed, as is the right of the data subject to seek compensation for damage and distress. The regulatory tools at the disposal of the Information Commissioner are all identified.

Chapter 8, 'Compliance', aims to provide data controllers with some practical guidance on how they can start to make their processing operations legally compliant. Of course, the topic of compliance could fill a book of this size all by itself, so compromises in the coverage are inevitable I am afraid.

However, I hope that this chapter provides data protection officers with some inspiration. This chapter will be expanded upon on my website.

Stewart Room, May 2006.

1 Introduction to Data Protection

Data protection is a topic of global importance. Data protection laws can be found in all the major industrialized nations, they are being developed for developing nations and they are the focus of significant intergovernmental cooperation. International organizations, such as the United Nations,[1] the Organisation for Economic Co-operation and Development,[2] the Council of Europe and the European Community (EC), have invested heavily in data protection, issuing guidance and laws that are remarkably consistent in terms of their aims, objectives and requirements.

DATA PROTECTION IN THE UK – THE DATA PROTECTION ACT 1998

In the UK the framework piece of legislation is the Data Protection Act 1998, or 'DPA' for short. The DPA repealed and replaced its predecessor, the Data Protection Act 1984, in order to give effect to the requirements of the EC Data Protection Directive 1995. The DPA also gives effect to the requirements of the Council of Europe's Data Protection Convention 1981. The DPA is supplemented and supported by many other pieces of legislation, which will be introduced at appropriate places.

The DPA describes itself as being an Act that makes 'new provision for the regulation of the processing of information relating to individuals'. This statement is worth thinking about, for it has massive ramifications. Putting it simply, the processing of information relating to individuals is something that we all do. Every government body processes information relating to individuals, as does every public authority, every business and every person with a PC.

Processing personal data – information relating to data subjects

However, it is only the processing of information relating to identifiable living individuals that is regulated by the DPA. The DPA does not regulate the processing of information relating to unidentified or unidentifiable living individuals, or the processing of information relating to the deceased or the processing of information relating to companies, non-incorporated organizations (such as clubs and societies), public authorities, charities or similar bodies. Information relating to identifiable living individuals is known as 'personal data' and the people whose personal data are processed are known as 'data subjects'.

Automated and manual processing by data controllers and data processors

The Act regulates both automated processing of personal data, that is, processing done by computers, and limited kinds of manual processing of personal data, but only where the processing is performed by 'data controllers' and 'data processors'. The data controller, who is characterized by having the power to determine the purpose of the processing or the manner of the processing, carries most of the obligations under the DPA. A data processor processes personal data on behalf of a data controller, but is not an employee (for the purposes of the DPA employees of data controllers form part of the data controller). The data controller is ultimately responsible for ensuring that the data processor's activities are compliant with the DPA.

The concept of processing

The concept of processing is extremely wide, covering every conceivable act that can be done on or towards personal data, from its initial collection right through to its final deletion or destruction. Acts of processing include organization, adaptation or alteration of data, retrieval, consultation or use of data, disclosure of data by transmission and dissemination and the alignment, combination, blocking, erasure or destruction of data.

Summary – the key things to remember

A person who is interested in data protection should remember the following things:

- Data protection laws regulate the processing of personal data by data controllers and data processors. The DPA also concerns 'third parties' and 'recipients'. A third party is anyone other than the data controller, the data subject or the data processor and can include legal persons, such as companies, as well as individuals. A recipient is any person to whom personal data are disclosed in the course of processing done by or on behalf of the data controller, apart from persons who receive personal data as a result of a particular inquiry made in exercise of legal powers, such as the Information Commissioner or the police.
- The fairness, lawfulness and legitimacy of data processing are benchmarked against the 'data protection principles'. There are eight data protection principles in the DPA.
- The Information Commissioner is the UK's supervisory authority, responsible for promoting the following of good practice by data controllers and for enforcing compliance with the DPA.
- Personal data is information relating to living individuals and includes opinions about living individuals and indications of the data controller's intentions towards living individuals.
- Within Europe, the most important laws are the European Convention for the Protection of Human Rights and Fundamental Freedoms, the Data Protection Convention[3] and the Data Protection Directive.[4]

- Within Europe, the main law-making bodies are the Council of Europe, the EC, the Article 29 Working Party, the national governments, the national supervisory authorities and the courts.
- The aims of data protection laws are twofold: they protect privacy and they support the free flow of personal data between data controllers and between countries.
- The DPA replaced and repealed the Data Protection Act 1984, in order to give effect to the requirements of the Data Protection Directive 1995. The DPA also gives effect to the requirements of the Data Protection Convention 1981.

OVERVIEW AND HISTORY OF DATA PROTECTION LAWS

The DPA forms part of a comprehensive and harmonized European legal framework for the regulation of the processing of personal data. This framework is a consequence of work done by the Council of Europe and the EC. Of course, data protection laws can be found outside of Europe too.

The two principal aims of data protection laws

Wherever they are found, data protection laws have two principal aims. These are:

- The protection of privacy during the processing of personal data.
- The maintenance of free flows of personal data between countries. This requires the elimination of obstacles to the free flow of personal data between countries that are based solely on the protection of privacy.

These dual aims certainly appear to be in conflict (privacy of personal information v. the free flow of it), but data protection laws have to deal with the realities of modern life, which include the fact that free flows of personal information are vital to the economy and to the effective performance of public functions, hence they must be maintained. Maintaining free flows of personal data obviously interferes with personal privacy, so the law compensates for the interference by requiring a high level of protection for the privacy of personal data undergoing processing. The high level of protection is that prescribed by data protection laws themselves, which put in place strong mechanisms to prevent unfair or unlawful processing. Ensuring a high level of protection for the privacy of personal data that is undergoing processing is a prerequisite to the continuance of free flows of personal data.

Putting the same point differently, the law will allow a person to transfer data to another person or to another country provided that the transferor meets the minimum standards prescribed by the law.

Laws in Europe should be in harmony – the reason for Council of Europe and EC activity

The Council of Europe and the EC are the two organizations responsible for the development of data protection laws in Europe. These organizations are separate and distinct. The Council of Europe, founded in 1949, is essentially a human rights organization consisting of 46 European Member States. The other organization, the EC, started life as the European Economic Community in 1957 and it currently has 25 Member States. The UK, like all other EC Member States, is a member of both organizations and the DPA gives effect to the requirements of the data protection laws of both organizations, namely the Data Protection Convention and the Data Protection Directive.

The Council of Europe and the EC have taken the lead in the development of data protection laws within Europe due to the fact that European governments recognize that there need to be harmonized data protection laws across Europe in order to achieve the two principal aims of data protection, namely the protection of privacy and the maintenance of free flows of personal data.

The need for harmonization of laws is explained by the fact that a key theory within data protection laws is that differences in the levels of protection for privacy offered by national laws can cause obstacles to the free flow of personal data between countries, that is, a country with a high level of protection for privacy could impede the flow of personal data to a country with weaker protection. The harmonization of laws addresses this problem, because where laws are harmonized the scope for differences between countries on fundamental issues is removed.

It would be a mistake to fall into the trap of thinking that the harmonization process requires the national laws of the countries within the area of harmonization to be exactly the same. Harmonization is not meant to achieve exactness in the laws of each participating country. In fact, despite harmonization, participating countries have a wide margin for manoeuvre, with the result that differences in national laws are still being detected. For instance, penalties for breach of data protection laws differ from country to country.

The protection of privacy

Privacy is a very wide concept. It includes the private space (such as the home), private items (such as letters and photographs), private relationships (such as sexual relationships) and private information (such as information about people).

The right to respect for personal privacy is a recognized human right. Within Europe the principal human rights law is the European Convention for the Protection of Human Rights and Fundamental Freedoms of 1950 (or the 'ECHR' for short). The ECHR has been incorporated into UK law by the Human Rights Act 1998.

Article 8 of the ECHR protects the right to privacy and provides the founding principles upon which European data protection laws are built. It says:

> (1) Everyone has the right to respect for his private and family life, his home and his correspondence.
>
> (2) There shall be no interference by a public authority with the exercise of this right except such as is in accordance with the law and is necessary in a democratic society in the interests of national security, public safety or the economic well-being of the country, for the prevention of disorder or crime, for the protection of health or morals, or for the protection of the rights and freedoms of others.

It often comes as a surprise to learn that neither the DPA, nor the Data Protection Convention or the Data Protection Directive have tried to define the meaning of the word privacy. Thus, we need to look elsewhere for a definition.

Concepts within privacy – informational and substantive privacy

One early definition of privacy that still holds well is that it is a 'right to be let alone'.[5] This definition is supported by two newer concepts, 'substantive privacy' and 'informational privacy'. The theory behind substantive privacy is that people should be free to make substantive decisions about how they lead their lives, free from interference by the State or by others. The theory behind informational privacy is that people should be able to control the flow of information about them. These two concepts are interconnected and a state of informational privacy is often a prerequisite to enjoyment of substantive privacy.

To illustrate, imagine a country passing a law to ban the practice of a particular religion. Such a ban interferes with substantive privacy, that is, the freedom of individuals to choose to practice the religion. The State's interference with substantive privacy will not be enough to completely eradicate the religion, however, as devotees will practice in private, out of view of the State. If the State really wants to eradicate the religion, it will also need to identify who is practising the religion, which means interfering with informational privacy.

Privacy versus other rights and interests

The right to privacy is not an absolute right in the sense that it does not transcend all other rights and interests. Instead, the right to privacy is one of many competing interests and it is the law's job to find an appropriate balance between them. This is why Article 8.2. of the ECHR allows interference with the right to privacy by public authorities where the interference 'is in accordance with the law and is necessary in a democratic society in the interests of national security, public safety or the economic well-being of the country, for the prevention of disorder or crime, for the protection of health or morals, or for the protection of the rights and freedoms of others'.

Another competing interest is freedom of expression, which is also a human right. Freedom of expression is a powerful friend of journalists and publishers who rely upon its terms to justify the publication of personal information, with the justification being that a free press is in the public interest. Article 10 of the ECHR says the following about freedom of expression:

> **Everyone has the right to freedom of expression. This right shall include freedom to hold opinions and to receive and impart information and ideas without interference by public authority and regardless of frontiers.**

Recent cases on the meaning of privacy

Although there is no universally agreed definition of privacy, in most cases the difficulty does not lie in deciding whether information is private, but, rather, whether the interference with privacy was lawful. Indeed, in a very important case, *A v. B & C*,[6] Lord Woolf said:

> **the question of whether there is an interest capable of being the subject of a claim for privacy should not be allowed to be the subject of detailed argument . . . In those cases in which the answer is not obvious, an answer will often be unnecessary.**

The difficult issue, whether the interference with privacy is lawful, is the issue to which data protection laws are addressed; that is, they seek to strike a balance between the privacy rights of the individual and the rights and interests of data controllers as far as the processing of personal data is concerned.

The following series of recent cases stand to illustrate the fact that a wide variety of information can be said to be private:

- In 2003 the European Court of Human Rights decided in the case of *Peck v. United Kingdom*[7] that CCTV footage showing Mr Peck attempting to commit suicide in the street contained private information. This was despite the fact that his suicide attempt was in a public place.
- In 2004 the UK House of Lords decided in the case of *Campbell v. Mirror Group Newspapers*[8] that covertly taken photographs showing the claimant outside premises where a Narcotics Anonymous meeting was held contained private information. This was despite the fact that the defendant enjoyed a legitimate press right to publish a story about the claimant's attendance at Narcotics Anonymous in light of her previous denials of drug abuse.
- In 2004 the European Court of Human Rights decided in the case of *Von Hannover v. Germany*[9] that covertly taken photographs of the

claimant in a French restaurant with a companion contained private information.

- In 2005 the UK Court of Appeal held in the case of *Douglas v. Hello! Ltd (No 2)*[10] that covertly taken photographs at the claimants' wedding contained private information, despite the fact that the claimants were under contract with a magazine for publication of wedding photographs.

In the case of *Douglas v. Hello! Ltd (No 2)* Lord Phillips addressed the question 'what is the nature of private information'. His answer was:

> What is the nature of 'private information'? It seems to us that it must include information that is personal to the person who possesses it and that he does not intend shall be imparted to the general public. The nature of the information, or the form in which it is kept, may suffice to make it plain that the information satisfies these criteria.

The relationship between the ECHR and the DPA, including protections for manual data

It is important to recognize that the connection between the ECHR and European data protection laws is inviolable. Data protection laws are best regarded as modified privacy laws, in the sense that they build upon the right to respect for privacy contained in Article 8 of the ECHR, in order to provide clearer protections for the privacy of personal data undergoing processing. In the UK because of the Human Rights Act 1998, the courts and the Information Commissioner are obliged when interpreting the DPA to ensure that their interpretations are compatible with the ECHR. Every court case commenced under the DPA can also be brought under the Human Rights Act.

If data protection laws are viewed in their wider context it will be seen that despite the limitation they place on the protections for the manual processing of personal data, privacy in manual data is generally protected due to the right to privacy within Article 8 of the ECHR. In the UK a breach of confidence action can be used to protect the right to privacy if in the circumstances of the case the data subject has a reasonable expectation of privacy. UK law has moved on significantly since the introduction of the Human Rights Act and clarification of the fact that the protections in Article 8 of the ECHR extend to threats from the private sector.

The emergence of European data protection laws – law making to protect privacy

The first European data protection law was a regional law passed by the German State of Hesse in 1970 (the first national data protection law was introduced by Sweden in 1973), but the movement towards European data protection laws actually began in the late 1960s after it had become appreciated that scientific and technological advances, particularly the invention of the semi-conductor chip and increasing computerization within the private sector, posed new threats to personal privacy; it was foreseen that computers would be able to automatically process personal data in unprecedented ways, in unprecedented volumes and at unprecedented speeds. The passage below, taken from a Council of Europe Recommendation from 1968[11] provides a fascinating insight into the nature of the concerns at the beginning of the development of data protection laws:

> newly developed techniques such as phone-tapping, eavesdropping, surreptitious observation, the illegitimate use of official statistical and similar surveys to obtain private information, and subliminal advertising and propaganda are a threat to the rights and freedoms of individuals and, in particular, to the right to privacy ...

These new threats led to calls for new laws to protect privacy within the context of the automated processing of personal data stemming from worries about the adequacy of the protection for privacy afforded by Article 8 of the ECHR. To explain, while it is clear that Article 8 guarantees respect for private and family life, the home and correspondence, in the late 1960s, governments were not sure that the wording of Article 8 extended to computer processing or to threats to privacy emerging from the private sector. A Resolution issued by the Council of Europe in 1974[12] reported that:

> A survey, conducted in 1968–70 by the Committee of Experts on Human Rights of the Council of Europe, on the legislation of the Member States with regard to human rights and modern scientific and technological developments has shown that the existing law does not provide sufficient protection for the citizen against intrusions on privacy by technical devices. Generally, the existing laws touch upon the protection of privacy only from a limited point of view, such as secrecy of correspondence and telecommunications, inviolability of the domicile, and so on. Moreover, the ramifications of the concept of privacy have never been established. It is also doubtful whether the European Convention on Human Rights, of which Article 8 (1) guarantees to everyone 'the right to respect for his private and family life, his home and his correspondence', offers satisfactory safeguards against technological intrusions into privacy. The Committee of Experts on Human Rights has noted, for example, that the Convention takes into account only interferences with private life by public authorities, not by private parties.

Privacy and the private sector

It is now settled that the right to privacy contained in the ECHR does apply to the private sector as well as to activities of the State and the public sector. This is despite the fears expressed in the early years of development of data protection laws. For example, in the case of *Douglas v. Hello! Ltd (No 2)* Lord Phillips explained that:

> the European court has recognised an obligation on Member States to pro-
> tect one individual from an unjustified invasion of private life by another
> individual and an obligation on the courts of a Member State to interpret
> legislation in a way which will achieve that result.

Thus, the State will protect an individual's right to privacy from invasion
by another individual, which includes private sector and voluntary sector
companies and organizations. This is the effect of the decisions in *Campbell
v. Mirror Group Newspapers* and *Von Hannover v. Germany*.

The late 1960s and early 1970s – the initial work undertaken by the Council of Europe: Data protection rules to protect privacy

The Council of Europe is an intergovernmental human rights organization
that was established after the end of the Second World War. Its most famous
legal instrument is the ECHR. The Council of Europe commenced its work
in the field of data protection in 1968, at a time when a small number of
its Member States were considering the introduction of national laws on
data protection. In this year a Council of Europe Parliamentary Assembly
issued Recommendation 509, which required the Council's Committee of
Experts on Human Rights to examine whether 'having regard to Article 8 of
the Convention on Human Rights, the national legislation in the Member
States adequately protects the right to privacy against violations which may
be committed by the use of modern scientific and technical methods' and,
if not, 'to make recommendations for the better protection of the right of
privacy.'

The efforts of the Committee of Experts on Human Rights resulted in the
Council's Committee of Ministers addressing two Resolutions to the Member
States on the protection of privacy. The first Resolution, in 1973,[13] concerned
the protection of privacy in the context of private sector 'electronic data
banks'. The second Resolution,[14] in 1974, concerned public sector electronic
data banks.

Both of these Resolutions are based around a series of 'principles' that
address the key privacy concerns within data protection, such as the accuracy of electronic personal data, the security of electronic personal data, the
purposes for which electronic personal data are processed and the right of
access. These principles have remained remarkably stable and consistent
over the years and they can now be found, almost unchanged, within Schedule 1 of the DPA.

The Resolutions required the Council of Europe Member States to take all
necessary steps to give effect to the principles. These Resolutions therefore
represent the true beginnings of European data protection laws.

The UK's first tentative steps towards data protection – the 1970s

The UK was one of the Council of Europe Member States that considered
data protection at this initial stage of development of the law. In 1972 the

'Report of the Committee on Privacy' (sometime called the 'Younger Report', after its Chair, Kenneth Younger), published 10 principles for the handling of personal information by computers. In 1975 this Report was followed by two government white papers, which indicated plans for legislation on private sector and public sector computer use. These white papers were followed by the establishment of the Data Protection Committee in 1976, chaired by Sir Norman Lindop. The 'Report of the Committee on Data Protection' was published in 1978, recommending rules that mirror modern data protection laws.

Data protection between 1980 and 1990 – from privacy to maintaining free flows of personal data (transborder data flows)

The 10 years between 1980 and 1990 saw thinking on data protection laws develop and mature. While the primary focus of concerns in the late 1960s and early 1970s was the protection of privacy within the context of automated processing of personal data, the 1980s saw the emergence of the second aim of data protection laws, the removal of obstacles to the free flow of personal data between countries (sometimes called 'transborder data flows').

The transborder flow of personal data is of fundamental economic and societal importance. The global economy cannot survive without the movement of personal data between countries and across continents and the effective performance of vital public functions, such as law enforcement and the prevention and detection of crime, is often totally reliant upon data sharing between different countries.

Although the transborder flow of personal data is of fundamental economic and societal importance, it involves very obvious privacy implications arising from the fact that the person's personal data leaves the borders of their country of residence, making it much harder to protect.

One foreseeable consequence of the drive to protect the privacy of personal data undergoing processing is that transborder data flows could be hindered, or prevented altogether, because of understandable fears that personal data will not be adequately protected when processed abroad. This consequence was addressed during the second phase of data protection laws, with the accepted solution being that once data protection laws were harmonized between countries it would be unlawful for one country to hinder or prevent data flows to another country within the harmonized area on the sole ground of protection of privacy; within the area of harmonization the right to privacy is adequately protected.

1980 – the OECD deals with transborder data flows

The first organization to address this issue was the Organisation for Economic Co-operation and Development (OECD). The OECD, which was originally established in 1947 as the Organisation for European Economic Co-operation, provides a forum for the governments of 30 leading market democracies to discuss and develop policies to meet the challenges of globalization. One of these challenges is the maintenance of transborder flows of personal data.

In 1980 the OECD published its own data protection guidelines.[15] The preface to these guidelines is highly illuminating of the issues:

> The development of automatic data processing, which enables vast quantities of data to be transmitted within seconds across national frontiers, and indeed across continents, has made it necessary to consider privacy protection in relation to personal data. Privacy protection laws have been introduced, or will be introduced shortly, in approximately one half of OECD Member countries (Austria, Canada, Denmark, France, Germany, Luxembourg, Norway, Sweden and the United States have passed legislation. Belgium, Iceland, the Netherlands, Spain and Switzerland have prepared draft bills) to prevent what are considered to be violations of fundamental human rights, such as the unlawful storage of personal data, the storage of inaccurate personal data, or the abuse or unauthorised disclosure of such data.
>
> On the other hand, there is a danger that disparities in national legislations could hamper the free flow of personal data across frontiers; these flows have greatly increased in recent years and are bound to grow further with the widespread introduction of new computer and communications technology. Restrictions on these flows could cause serious disruption in important sectors of the economy, such as banking and insurance.
>
> For this reason OECD Member countries considered it necessary to develop Guidelines which would help to harmonise national privacy legislation and, while upholding such human rights, would at the same time prevent interruptions in international flows of data.

The Guidelines contain a series of principles that echo those found in the Council of Europe's initial 1973 and 1974 Resolutions, addressing issues such as the lawfulness of processing, the accuracy and security of personal data and transparency in processing. In respect of transborder flows of personal data, the Guidelines prefer a test of 'equivalent protection' saying that:

> a Member country should refrain from restricting transborder flows of personal data between itself and another Member country except where the latter does not yet substantially observe these Guidelines or where the re-export of such data would circumvent its domestic privacy legislation. A Member country may also impose restrictions in respect of certain categories of personal data for which its domestic privacy legislation includes specific regulations in view of the nature of those data and for which the other Member country provides no equivalent protection.

1981 – the Council of Europe's Data Protection Convention (Europe gets serious)

In 1981 the Council of Europe opened for signature the Data Protection Convention,[16] the first and only European Treaty on data protection. The principal reason for the Data Protection Convention was the Member States' failure to respond to the 1973 and 1974 Resolutions in a consistent manner.

The Data Protection Convention represents a watershed for European data protection laws, being the moment when data protection moved from an aspiration to a fundamental goal. Like the OECD Guidelines, the Data Protection Convention echoed the principles contained in the 1973 and 1974 Resolutions and preserved the importance of free flows of personal data, saying that the Member States 'shall not, for the sole purpose of the protection of privacy, prohibit or subject to special authorization transborder flows of personal data going to the territory of another Party'. Thus, the Data Protection Convention cemented the second principal aim of data protection laws within Europe, namely the removal of obstacles to the free flow of personal data between countries.

1984 – the UK's first Data Protection Act

In 1984 the UK Parliament passed the Data Protection Act 1984, to give effect to the UK's obligations under the Data Protection Convention. The 1984 Act regulated the 'processing' and the 'disclosure' of 'personal data' 'recorded in a form in which it can be processed by equipment operating automatically', that is, the processing of personal data by computers. Manual files were not regulated, a substantial omission rectified by the DPA.

From 1990 – the rise to prominence of the EC

In 1957 a small group of European countries created the European Economic Community (EEC) through the signing of the Treaty Establishing the European Economic Community, otherwise known as the Treaty of Rome. In 1997 the EEC was renamed the EC. The EC forms part of the European Union (EU) and it currently consists of 25 Member States. As stated earlier, the EC and the Council of Europe are separate entities.

During the first phase in the development of European data protection laws, from the late 1960s to the mid 1970s, the EEC played only a peripheral role. This was because the thinking behind the law in the first stage was focused upon the protection of privacy, which, as a human right, fell more naturally within the sphere of competence of the Council of Europe. However, the EEC was supportive of the developments in the field and in 1981 the European Commission issued a Recommendation[17] addressed to the EEC Member States saying:

> The Commission recommends those Member States of the Community which have not already done so to sign, during the course of 1981, the Council of Europe convention for the protection of individuals with regard to automatic processing of personal data, and to ratify it before the end of 1982.

While the EEC was content to let the Council of Europe take the lead, its 1981 Recommendation also contained a statement of future intent, warning the EEC member states that if they did not act promptly in signing and ratifying the Data Protection Convention, an EEC instrument could follow. This is what the Recommendation said:

> **The Commission of the European Communities accordingly welcomes the Council of Europe convention for the protection of individuals with regard to automatic processing of personal data. It is of the opinion that this convention is appropriate for the purpose of creating a uniform level of data-protection in Europe. If, however, all the Member States do not within a reasonable time sign and ratify the convention, the Commission reserves the right to propose that the Council adopt an instrument on the basis of the EEC Treaty.**

Unfortunately, by the end of the 1980s only a few of the EEC Member States had ratified the Data Protection Convention. Therefore, in 1990 the European Commission formally proposed the introduction of the Data Protection Directive.[18] This proposal marked the starting point of the EC's leadership in European data protection and the relative downgrading of the importance of the Data Protection Convention. The Data Protection Directive was formally approved in 1995.[19]

The EC, the Data Protection Directive and free movement

The Data Protection Directive is a very important harmonization measure that was introduced under the Internal Market provisions of the Treaty of Rome, to protect human rights and to maintain transborder flows of personal data. A recent report by the European Commission[20] has said:

> [The Data Protection] Directive ... enshrines two of the oldest ambitions of the European integration project: the achievement of an Internal Market (in this case the free movement of personal information) and the protection of fundamental rights and freedoms of individuals. In the Directive, both objectives are equally important.

By way of background, the Treaty of Rome sets out the legal powers of the EC and at this moment in time the EC is unable to make standalone human rights laws, unlike the Council of Europe. Instead, it must base its laws on a specific power within the Treaty, hence the reason for the introduction of the Data Protection Directive as a harmonization measure under the Treaty's Internal Market provisions, as is now explained.

The Treaty of Rome describes the Internal Market as 'an area without internal frontiers in which the free movement of goods, persons, services and capital is ensured'. In order to create the Internal Market, the Treaty requires 'the abolition, as between Member States, of obstacles to the free movement of goods, persons, services and capital'. If it is not already clear, free movement is one of the principal goals of the EC, highly cherished by politicians, businesses and EU citizens. Free movement entails many powerful rights and entitlements allowing, for example, workers to take up offers of employment from other EC Member States and enabling companies to set up offices abroad. Free movement improves the competitiveness of the European economy and benefits the consumer.

EXAMPLE

A London-based company wants to open an office in Paris. The ability to do this is based upon the free movement of services, capital and workers. It is highly likely that in this scenario there will be movement of persons, as the London-based company will no doubt want to send key management personnel to Paris to oversee the opening, which requires movement of information about these persons. Indeed, in the present scenario the movement of personal information between the London and Paris offices is inevitable. Typical incidents of transfer of personal information between the two offices will occur in the transfer of personnel records. However, if privacy laws could prevent the transfer of personal data from one country to the other, the business would soon grind to a halt and the rights of free movement would fail.

By 1990, when the creation of the Data Protection Directive was formally proposed, the EC (like the Council of Europe and the OECD) had long realized that differences (actual and potential) in the Member States' national laws for the protection of privacy with respect to the processing of personal data could act as obstacles to free movement; a Member State with a high level of protection for privacy could ban the flow of personal data from within its borders to a Member State that provided a low level of protection for privacy, which would have obvious implications for free movement in the example.

Therefore, the EC decided that it was necessary to take action to bring the Member States' national laws into line, based upon the provisions contained in the Data Protection Directive, a process known as harmonization. As mentioned earlier, the Directive's provisions were designed to ensure a high level of protection for the fundamental rights and freedoms of natural persons, particularly the right to privacy. In addition, the Directive outlawed all national measures that restricted or prohibited the free flow of personal data between EC Member States for reasons connected with the protection of fundamental rights and freedoms. Based on this reasoning, the EC has been able to introduce the Data Protection Directive, which is clearly a human rights law, under the guise of protecting the Internal Market. Article 1 of the Directive, which describes its objectives, says:

> (1) In accordance with this Directive, Member States shall protect the fundamental rights and freedoms of natural persons, and in particular their right to privacy with respect to the processing of personal data.
>
> (2) Member States shall neither restrict nor prohibit the free flow of personal data between Member States for reasons connected with the protection afforded under paragraph 1.

The EC has been able to overcome the prohibition against standalone human rights law making due to a number of factors. In addition to the factual connection between the protection of human rights and the proper functioning of the Internal Market, respect for human rights forms part of the general principles of EC law as well as part of the national laws of the EC Member States (the UK has the Human Rights Act 1998). It is also noteworthy that the EC is a signatory to the ECHR.

In conclusion, the thinking at the very heart of the Data Protection Directive connects the protection of privacy with free movement. The essence of the thinking is:

- Free movement of goods, persons, services and capital is impossible without free movement of personal data.
- Differences in national laws for the protection of privacy in personal data undergoing processing can act as obstacles to free movement.
- Differences in national laws can be overcome through a process of harmonization.
- Once national laws are harmonized, obstacles to free movement disappear.

The structure of the Data Protection Directive

The Data Protection Directive consists of 72 recitals and 34 articles. The recitals explain the theories behind the law and the motivations of the law makers, providing a vital aid to interpretation. The articles are arranged in seven chapters. The chapters are titled:

(1) general provisions;

(2) general rules on the lawfulness of the processing personal data;

(3) judicial remedies, liability and sanctions;

(4) transfer of personal data to third countries;

(5) codes of conduct;

(6) supervisory authority and working party on the protection of individuals with regard to the processing of personal data; and

(7) community implementing measures.

As it is a harmonization measure the Data Protection Directive's provisions leave EC Member States with much room for manoeuvre. Instead of prescribing in detail the obligations of the Member States, the Directive sets general principles and leaves the Member States to implement national measures in the form and manner of their choosing. Due to this wide margin of discretion vested in the Member States there are still many differences in national laws and between national views and the EC's view of how data protection laws should be.

Because it sticks to the general principles it is not surprising to see that certain concepts and phrases keep reappearing throughout the Directive. These will be encountered time and time again during an analysis of data protection laws and data protection in practice.

A very prominent concept within the Directive is 'necessity'. This is because many of the grounds for making processing lawful are prefaced by the requirement that the processing should be necessary. Another prominent concept is 'adequacy', as the Directive prevents the flow of personal data from the EC Member States to other countries that do not offer adequate protection for personal data. A third prominent concept is 'suitability', as the Directive requires EC Member States to adopt 'suitable measures' to ensure the full implementation of its provisions. Collectively, these concepts provide the Member States with considerable discretion over the detail of their national laws.

The Data Protection Directive and the processing of manual data

A major advance made by the Data Protection Directive when compared to the Data Protection Convention was the extension of the law to cover manual data. While the Data Protection Convention gave Council of Europe Member States the option to regulate the manual processing of personal data, this was not compulsory. The Data Protection Directive changed this for EC Member States, making the regulation of manual processing compulsory where personal data are held in a 'personal filing system' (the DPA calls these 'relevant filing systems').

The Data Protection Directive and the European Economic Area

The Data Protection Directive is a legal instrument of the EC, but its protections extend to an area known as the 'European Economic Area' (EEA). The EEA is the combined area of the EC Member States and Iceland, Liechtenstein and Norway. The EEA was created by the Agreement on the European Economic Area in 1992.

The right to privacy in the UK

It has already been explained that the right to respect for privacy contained in Article 8 of the ECHR has been incorporated into UK law by the Human Rights Act 1998 (HRA). Due to the obligations placed on Member States by the ECHR it can now be said with certainty that the right to privacy will be protected by the UK courts, both from interferences by the State and by other individuals.

The HRA contains two key provisions that are central to the development of the law in this area. First, section 2 of the HRA requires courts and tribunals to take into account decisions of the ECHR when determining a question that has arisen in connection with an ECHR right. Second, because of section 6 it is unlawful for courts and tribunals in their capacity as public bodies to act in a way that is incompatible with an ECHR right.

In the case of *Campbell v. Mirror Group Newspapers*[21] Baroness Hale explained the court's position. She said:

> The 1998 Act does not create any new cause of action between private persons. But if there is a relevant cause of action applicable, the court as a public authority must act compatibly with both parties' Convention rights.

The court's obligation is to do justice between the parties and as a public authority it must perform this duty in a manner that is compatible with the Convention rights. The logical effect of these obligations is that the court should consider always whether a Convention right, like the right to privacy, is engaged in the case before it and this may often require a more detailed enquiry than merely asking the parties for their views. If the right to privacy is engaged the court will have to protect it and, if necessary, balance it against other interests, such as freedom of expression.

If an individual wishes to start a court action to protect their privacy, their claim is determined in accordance with the law of confidence, with private information being treated as confidential information. The individual will be successful if they can show that the person threatening their privacy knows or ought to know that the individual has a reasonable expectation that their information will remain private. In the case of *Douglas v. Hello! Ltd (No 2)*[22] Lord Philips explained the law following a decision of Lord Woolf in *A v. B & C*.[23]

> Lord Woolf then laid down guidelines which a court should follow when considering a similar application. These include the proposition that in the great majority of, if not all, situations where the protection of privacy is justified in relation to events after the 1998 Act came into force, an action for breach of confidence will provide the necessary protection. As to interests capable of being subject to a claim for privacy, these will usually be obvious. A duty of confidence will arise whenever a party subject to the duty is in a situation where he knows or ought to know that the other person can reasonably expect his privacy to be protected. If there is an intrusion in a situation where a person can reasonably expect his privacy to be respected then that intrusion will be capable of giving rise to an action for breach of confidence unless the intrusion can be justified.

The state of the UK law concerning the right to privacy is that this will be protected by the courts in a claim for breach of confidence. A data subject claiming a breach of the DPA may also rely upon the law of confidence in a court action to enforce their rights.

The future of data protection laws

The Data Protection Directive is now 10 years old, which represents nearly one-third of the total lifespan of data protection laws. The key thinking upon which the Directive itself is built will soon reach its 40th anniversary.

The nature of the threats to privacy has changed substantially since the Council of Europe took its first steps, which presents new challenges. Furthermore, experience of the laws in action, plus some unusual court decisions, have led to calls for revision of the Data Protection Directive. Two important areas of concern are:

- the omnibus approach to regulation favoured by the Data Protection Directive;
- the failure to eradicate divergences in national laws.

Problems with the omnibus approach and alternative solutions, including the Lindqvist case

Subject to some exemptions the Data Protection Directive requires regulation of every act of data processing irrespective of the extent of the threat to privacy or the threat to the Internal Market. The fact that this can lead to harsh results was revealed in a recent case heard by the European Court of Justice, *Bodil Lindqvist v. Åklagarkammaren i Jönköping.*[24] The case in question concerned the activities of a Swedish lady, Bodil Lindqvist, who built a website to help her fellow parishioners who were preparing for their confirmation. Mrs Lindqvist's website contained information about parishioners living in her village, Alseda, including names and other personal data, such as the fact that one person was off work with an injured foot. Mrs Lindqvist published this information without consent and without having notified under the Swedish law. She was prosecuted and convicted, receiving a criminal record and a fine. The Swedish appeal court referred the case to the European Court of Justice for a determination as to whether the Data Protection Directive applied to Mrs Lindqvist's activities. The European Court of Justice held that the Directive did apply, despite making a finding that Mrs Lindqvist's activities were 'not economic but charitable and religious'.

Regarding the nature of the information published by Mrs Lindqvist, while it fell within the categories of private information identified earlier, there was no evidence that the publication of this information caused any negative effect for the persons concerned. As regards the link with the Internal Market, the best that can be said is that the link was indirect.

Lindqvist is the type of case that could bring the law into disrepute; it might be thought that it trivializes the subject matter, causes a drain on the scarce resources of the regulators and the courts and places an unjustifiable burden on ordinary persons. However, potentially harsh results are the natural consequences of the omnibus approach, where nearly everything is regulated.

An alternative to the omnibus approach is the sectoral approach favoured in the US. Rather than regulating everything, the sectoral approach identifies the areas of utmost concern and prioritizes regulatory action by reference to seriousness. For these reasons the US has introduced data protection and privacy legislation in the medical field (see the Health Insurance Portability and Accountability Act 1996), in the financial services field (see the Financial Services Modernization Act 1999), to prevent spam (see the Controlling the Assault of Non-Solicited Pornography and Marketing Act 2003) and to protect the privacy of children using the internet (see the Children's Online Privacy Protection Act 1998) as well as in other key areas. However, there is no general privacy law in the US.

There is evidence that the EC is becoming more favourably disposed to the sectoral approach and it remains possible that the law will develop more along the lines of the US model rather than continue along the current path. For instance, in 1997 the EC approved a separate Directive on data protection in the telecommunications sector,[25] which was replaced in 2002 by the Directive on Privacy and Electronic Communications.[26] The EC has also periodically considered a possible Directive on worker's data protection and in December 2005 the European Parliament approved a Directive on the Retention of Communications Data,[27] which was endorsed by the Ministers of Justice and Home Affairs in February 2006. In addition, the Working Party constituted under Article 29 of the Data Protection Directive regularly issues opinions and working documents on sectoral issues within data protection, which have addressed many diverse issues, such as data protection and genetic research,[28] data protection and direct marketing,[29] data protection and use of the internet[30] and data protection and the use of airline passenger information by law enforcement agencies.[31]

Another alternative might be to require evidence of a substantial negative privacy effect or evidence of a substantial negative Internal Market effect before serious sanctions can be imposed, an approach that may weed out trivial cases from the full scope of the regulatory regime.

The beginnings of this approach have already been detected within domestic law. In a landmark case in 2002, *Durant v. Financial Services Authority*,[32] the Court of Appeal delivered a judgment that is widely considered to have significantly curtailed the DPA. By way of background, the Court of Appeal was asked to rule on the meaning of personal data. It has effectively introduced a privacy filter into domestic law, saying that for information to be personal data it has to be information that 'affects (the data subject's) privacy', with the implication being that there is a threshold level of negative effect that is required before the DPA applies. Of course, the problem with this approach is that the data subject might be unable to learn the extent of the privacy effect without having a guaranteed legal right of access to information about processing, the use of which is not conditional upon prior proof of a negative effect. *Durant* almost creates a chicken and egg circular argument about which comes first, the right of access in section 7 or the need to satisfy the *Durant* definition of personal data?

Continuing divergences – the failure of harmonization?

The EU introduced the Data Protection Directive in order to harmonize the national laws of the EU Member States. Although all of the Member States have introduced national data protection laws, worrying differences still exist, as a recent report by the EC has identified.[33] The continuance of differences stems from the fact that the Directive gives the Member States a very wide margin for manoeuvre. It does not specify the precise detail required of national laws.

This very wide margin for manoeuvre enables the UK to take a rather lax attitude to sanctions, penalties and enforcement with the result that a prosecution in the circumstances described in the *Lindqvist*[34] case is inconceivable in this country. Even now, 10 years after the introduction of the Data Protection Directive, there is very little legal action commenced against data controllers in this country. This is not because domestic data controllers are particularly fastidious about legal compliance. Rather, it is a result of a weak legal regime and, perhaps, a cultural resistance to privacy issues.

The potential for continuing divergences was fully revealed by *Durant v. FSA*.[35] The Court of Appeal's 'privacy filter', discussed above, surprised commentators and is considered to have put the UK out of kilter with mainland Europe. Indeed, the decision is so problematic that the European Commission is reported to have asked the UK government to justify certain aspects of the DPA, particularly whether, in light of *Durant*, the right of access is guaranteed within the UK as the Data Protection Directive requires.

Future direction, including the Charter of Fundamental Rights of the European Union

An important distinction has already been made between the human rights law-making powers of the Council of Europe and those of the EC, with the core point being that the EC does not currently have standalone human rights law-making powers. For this reason the Data Protection Directive is constructed as an Internal Market measure. Of course, the reality of the situation is that the EC embraces human rights law making and it wishes to see its competence grow in this field.

Thus, in 2000 the EU 'proclaimed' the Charter of Fundamental Rights of the European Union. At the moment the legal status of the Charter is ambiguous, but if the proposal for an EU Constitution is adopted, the Charter will be directly incorporated into the Constitution, making it part of EU law. Articles 7 and 8 of the Charter provide as follows:

> Article 7
> Respect for private and family life
> Everyone has the right to respect for his or her private and family life, home and communications.

> Article 8
> Protection of personal data
>
> (1) Everyone has the right to the protection of personal data concerning him or her.
>
> (2) Such data must be processed fairly for specified purposes and on the basis of the consent of the person concerned or some other legitimate basis laid down by law. Everyone has the right of access to data which has been collected concerning him or her, and the right to have it rectified.
>
> (3) Compliance with these rules shall be subject to control by an independent authority.

It is moot whether the Charter will make much difference to the law in the UK, but it does send out a very important message about the relative importance of privacy laws and data protection laws.

KEY ASPECTS WITHIN DATA PROTECTION LAWS

When data protection laws are properly analysed the following key aspects become apparent:
(1) The processing of personal data must be transparent.
(2) The processing must comply with the general rules on lawfulness.
(3) The data subject must be given a right to object.
(4) Transborder flows of personal data are allowed, subject to a test of adequacy.
(5) There must be appropriate remedies, sanctions and penalties.

However, there are some powerful exceptions. For example, the transparency provisions will not apply if they would defeat the purpose of the processing.

The data protection principles

European data protection laws are structured around key principles, which the DPA calls the 'data protection principles'. The DPA contains eight data protection principles and these are found in the first schedule to the Act.

The principles and the data controller

The DPA places the obligation to comply with the data protection principles on the data controller, who is the person or entity with the power to determine the manner of processing and its purpose. Section 4(4) of the DPA says that 'it shall be the duty of a data controller to comply with the data protection principles in relation to all personal data with respect to which he is the data controller'. This obligation also extends to ensuring that data processors (persons or organizations processing personal data on behalf of data controllers) comply with the seventh data protection principle. Data controllers who take advantage of model contractual clauses to render lawful transfers of personal data to non-adequate countries outside the EEA also carry an obligation tantamount to ensuring that the data importer complies with the principles.

The principles and the interpretation

The data protection principles are supported by interpretation contained in Schedule 1, Part II of the DPA. Section 4(2) says 'those principles are to be interpreted in accordance with Part II of Schedule 1'.

Key aspect – transparency (including the first and second data protection principles)

The need for transparency in processing, while not quite sacrosanct, is one of the most important aspects of data protection laws. Putting the matter bluntly, a real respect for privacy means being open about one's processing activities. Of course, there are times when transparency will be counterproductive or harmful to other interests (for example, in the fight against serious crime), but these instances are limited in number and are subject to strict rules.

The DPA's approach to the issue of transparency is complex and multifaceted, but the essential elements can be categorized as follows:

- **The promotion of consensual processing**: The DPA encourages processing operations that are conducted with the data subject's consent, wherever this is possible. For example, the first criterion for making the processing of personal data legitimate is that the data subject has given consent.
- **Fair processing**: The first data protection principle requires processing to be fair and lawful. This is a complicated requirement because the first data protection principle merges a series of separate requirements within the Data Protection Directive, namely those contained in Articles 6, 7, 8, 10 and 11. As far as fairness is concerned, processing must be generally fair (the equivalent provision is contained in Article 6 of the Data Protection Directive) and must be specifically fair in the sense that the data subject should be supplied with information about the data controller and the processing prior to the commencement of processing (see Articles 10 and 11 of the Data Protection Directive for

the equivalent provisions). Furthermore, the data subject should not be deceived or misled about the processing purpose, requirements that are not actually contained in the Data Protection Directive.

- **Obtaining for specified purposes**: The second data protection principle requires personal data to be obtained for specified, lawful purposes. This requires the data controller to notify the data subject of the purpose prior to collection of the personal data. The notice can be given direct to the data subject or it can be included within the data controller's notification.

- **Notification**: Most data controllers are obliged to register with the Information Commissioner prior to the commencement of processing, a process known as notification. In summary, this process involves the data controller supplying the Information Commissioner with information about itself and its data processing activities, which the Information Commissioner then enters on a publicly accessible register. Where the obligation to notify exists (there are some exemptions from the obligation), it is a criminal offence to process personal data without having notified. It is also a criminal offence to fail to keep notifications accurate and up to date. Additionally, in certain cases where the obligation to notify is exempted the data subject may serve a written request on the data controller for 'the relevant particulars', which form the bulk of the information that would be provided if the obligation to notify existed.

- **The right of access to personal data**: Data subjects are generally allowed access to their information and access to information about the data controller's activities. Where the right of access applies the information usually has to be supplied within 40 days. The right of access is one of the DPA's 'subject information provisions'.

- **Information notices**: The Information Commissioner is empowered to serve information notices on data controllers requiring them to furnish him with key information about their processing activities.

Key aspect – general rules on lawfulness (the first to fifth data protection principles)

Chapter II of the Data Protection Directive is titled 'general rules on the lawfulness of the processing of personal data'. These general rules consist of nine sections including:

(1) principles relating to data quality;

(2) criteria for making data processing legitimate; and

(3) special categories of processing.

The general rules on the lawfulness of the processing of personal data also include the transparency provisions, identified above, and the right to object, discussed later.

The Data Protection Directive's principles relating to data quality are incorporated in the DPA's data protection principles, which are contained in the first schedule of the Act. The criteria for making data processing legitimate are contained in the second and third schedules. For comparative purposes Table 1.1 shows the critical parts of the data quality principles as they appear in the Data Protection Directive and the DPA.

TABLE 1.1   *Data quality*

Data Protection Directive 1995 See Article 6.1. Personal data must be:	Data Protection Act 1998 See Schedule 1, Part I Personal data shall be:
(a) Processed fairly and lawfully.	1. Processed fairly and lawfully and, in particular, shall not be processed unless – (a) at least one of the conditions in Schedule 2 is met, and (b) in the case of sensitive personal data, at least one of the conditions in Schedule 3 is also met.
(b) Collected for specified, explicit and legitimate purposes and not further processed in a way incompatible with those purposes.	2. Obtained only for one or more specified and lawful purposes, and shall not be further processed in any manner incompatible with that purpose or those purposes.
(c) Adequate, relevant and not excessive in relation to the purposes for which they are collected and/or further processed.	3. Adequate, relevant and not excessive in relation to the purpose or purposes for which they are processed.
(d) Accurate and, where necessary, kept up to date; every reasonable step must be taken to ensure that data which are inaccurate or incomplete, having regard to the purposes for which they were collected or for which they are further processed, are erased or rectified.	4. Accurate and, where necessary, kept up to date. *Note*: The DPA gives the data subject the right to have inaccurate data rectified, blocked, erased or destroyed, but this right is contained in section 14 of the Act and not in the principles.
(e) Kept in a form which permits identification of data subjects for no longer than is necessary for the purposes for which the data were collected or for which they are further processed.	5. Not be kept for longer than is necessary.

Within the Data Protection Directive the criteria for making processing legitimate apply only to personal data that does not fall within one of the 'special categories'. The special categories are the processing of personal data revealing racial or ethnic origin, political opinions, religious or philosophical beliefs or trade-union membership and the processing of data concerning health or sex life. Following the approach of Table 1.1, the critical parts of the criteria for making the processing of personal data legitimate are shown in Table 1.2.

The Data Protection Directive and the DPA both prohibit the processing of the special categories of personal data, or 'sensitive personal data' as the DPA prefers, unless the processing satisfies one of the specified conditions. For

TABLE 1.2   *Criteria for making processing legitimate*

Data Protection Directive 1995 See Article 7	Data Protection Act 1998 See Schedule 2
Member States shall provide that personal data may be processed only if:	Conditions for the processing of personal data referred to in the first data protection principle:
(a) The data subject has unambiguously given his consent.	1. The data subject has given his consent to the processing.
(b) Processing is necessary for the performance of a contract to which the data subject is party or in order to take steps at the request of the data subject prior to entering into a contract.	2. The processing is necessary – (a) for the performance of a contract to which the data subject is a party, or (b) for the taking of steps at the request of the data subject with a view to entering into a contract.
(c) Processing is necessary for compliance with a legal obligation to which the controller is subject.	3. The processing is necessary for compliance with any legal obligation to which the data controller is subject, other than an obligation imposed by contract.
(d) Processing is necessary in order to protect the vital interests of the data subject.	4. The processing is necessary in order to protect the vital interests of the data subject.
(e) Processing is necessary for the performance of a task carried out in the public interest or in the exercise of official authority vested in the controller or in a third party to whom the data are disclosed.	5. The processing is necessary – (a) for the administration of justice, (b) for the exercise of any functions conferred on any person by or under any enactment, (c) for the exercise of any functions of the Crown, a Minister of the Crown or a government department, or (d) for the exercise of any other functions of a public nature exercised in the public interest by any person.
(f) Processing is necessary for the purposes of the legitimate interests pursued by the controller or by the third party or parties to whom the data are disclosed, except where such interests are overridden by the interests for fundamental rights and freedoms of the data subject.	6. The processing is necessary for the purposes of legitimate interests pursued by the data controller or by the third party or parties to whom the data are disclosed, except where the processing is unwarranted in any particular case by reason of prejudice to the rights and freedoms or legitimate interests of the data subject.

completeness, Table 1.3 shows the grounds upon which the special categories of personal data may be processed.

It is important to note that if sensitive personal data are processed, the data controller will need to satisfy a criterion for legitimacy from Schedule 2 and a criterion from Schedule 3.

Key aspect – the right to object (preventing processing)

The right to object enables the data subject to exert control over their personal data. The DPA provides the data subject with a right to prevent processing likely to cause damage or distress, a right to prevent processing for

TABLE 1.3 *Criteria for the processing of the special categories of personal data (sensitive personal data)*

Data Protection Directive 1995 See Article 8.2.	Data Protection Act 1998 See Schedule 3
The prohibition against the processing of the special categories of personal data shall not apply where –	
(a) The data subject has given his explicit consent to the processing of those data, except where the laws of the Member State provide that the prohibition may not be lifted by the data subject's giving his consent.	1. The data subject has given his explicit consent to the processing of the personal data.
(b) Processing is necessary for the purposes of carrying out the obligations and specific rights of the controller in the field of employment law in so far as it is authorised by national law providing for adequate safeguards.	2. (1) The processing is necessary for the purposes of exercising or performing any right or obligation which is conferred or imposed by law on the data controller in connection with employment. (2) The Secretary of State may by order – (a) exclude the application of sub-paragraph (1) in such cases as may be specified, or (b) provide that, in such cases as may be specified, the condition in sub-paragraph (1) is not to be regarded as satisfied unless such further conditions as may be specified in the order are also satisfied.
(c) Processing is necessary to protect the vital interests of the data subject or of another person where the data subject is physically or legally incapable of giving his consent.	3. The processing is necessary – (a) in order to protect the vital interests of the data subject or another person, in a case where – (i) consent cannot be given by or on behalf of the data subject, or (ii) the data controller cannot reasonably be expected to obtain the consent of the data subject, or (b) in order to protect the vital interests of another person, in a case where consent by or on behalf of the data subject has been unreasonably withheld.
(d) Processing is carried out in the course of its legitimate activities with appropriate guarantees by a foundation, association or any other non-profit-seeking body with a political, philosophical, religious or trade-union aim and on condition that the processing relates solely to the members of the body or to persons who have regular contact with it in connection with its purposes and that the data are not disclosed to a third party without the consent of the data subjects.	4. The processing – (a) is carried out in the course of its legitimate activities by any body or association which – (i) is not established or conducted for profit, and (ii) exists for political, philosophical, religious or trade-union purposes, (b) is carried out with appropriate safeguards for the rights and freedoms of data subjects (c) relates only to individuals who either are members of the body or association or have regular contact with it in connection with its purposes, and (d) does not involve disclosure of the personal data to a third party without the consent of the data subject.
(e) Processing relates to data which are manifestly made public by the data subject or is necessary for the establishment, exercise or defence of legal claims.	5. The information contained in the personal data has been made public as a result of steps deliberately taken by the data subject.

6. The processing –
(a) is necessary for the purpose of, or in connection with, any legal proceedings (including prospective legal proceedings),
(b) is necessary for the purpose of obtaining legal advice, or
(c) is otherwise necessary for the purposes of establishing, exercising or defending legal rights.

7. (1) The processing is necessary –
(a) for the administration of justice, (aa) for the exercise of any functions of either House of Parliament,
(b) for the exercise of any functions conferred on any person by or under an enactment, or
(c) for the exercise of any functions of the Crown, a Minister of the Crown or a government department.
(2) The Secretary of State may by order –
(a) exclude the application of sub-paragraph (1) in such cases as may be specified, or
(b) provide that, in such cases as may be specified, the condition in sub-paragraph (1) is not to be regarded as satisfied unless such further conditions as may be specified in the order are also satisfied.

8. (1) The processing is necessary for medical purposes and is undertaken by –
(a) a health professional, or
(b) a person who in the circumstances owes a duty of confidentiality which is equivalent to that which would arise if that person were a health professional.
(2) In this paragraph 'medical purposes' includes the purposes of preventative medicine, medical diagnosis, medical research, the provision of care and treatment and the management of healthcare services.

9. (1) The processing –
(a) is of sensitive personal data consisting of information as to racial or ethnic origin,
(b) is necessary for the purpose of identifying or keeping under review the existence or absence of equality of opportunity or treatment between persons of different racial or ethnic origins, with a view to enabling such equality to be promoted or maintained, and
(c) is carried out with appropriate safeguards for the rights and freedoms of data subjects.
(2) The Secretary of State may by order specify circumstances in which processing falling within sub-paragraph (1)(a) and (b) is, or is not, to be taken for the purposes of sub-paragraph (1)(c) to be carried out with appropriate safeguards for the rights and freedoms of data subjects.

10. The personal data are processed in circumstances specificed in an order made by the Secretary of State for the purposes of this paragraph.

direct marketing purposes and, in certain circumstances, a right to prevent automated decision taking.

Key aspect – transborder data flows (including the eighth data protection principle)

As mentioned earlier, the removal of obstacles to the free flow of personal data is one of the two principal aims of data protection laws. This aim provides the legal basis for the Data Protection Directive itself. To recap, the Directive considers free flows of personal data to be integral components of the rights of free movement that are central to the Internal Market's proper functioning.

The Directive's starting point is that transborder flows of personal data between the EC Member States may not be restricted or prohibited on the sole ground of protection of privacy (see Article 1.2.). However, transfers to countries outside the EU may only take place if the third country offers an 'adequate' level of protection for personal data.

The DPA adopts a similar approach, saying at the eighth data protection principle that 'personal data shall not be transferred to a country or territory outside the European Economic Area unless that country or territory ensures an adequate level of protection for the rights and freedoms of data subjects in relation to the processing of personal data'.

Both the Directive and the DPA explain how the adequacy of third countries is measured. They both also contain derogations from the general rule so that in certain circumstances transfers to non-adequate third countries are allowed.

Key aspect – enforcement (remedies, sanctions and penalties)

The Data Protection Directive requires the EC Member States to provide every person with a right to 'a judicial remedy for any breach of the rights guaranteed him by the national law applicable to the processing in question' (Article 22) and an entitlement to 'receive compensation from the controller for [any] damage suffered' as a result of 'an unlawful processing operation or of any act incompatible with the national provisions adopted' (Article 23). In addition, it is stated that 'Member States shall adopt suitable measures to ensure the full implementation of the provisions of this Directive and shall in particular lay down the sanctions to be imposed in case of infringement of the provisions adopted' (Article 24). Finally, the Member States are required to establish completely independent supervisory authorities endowed with sufficient investigative powers, effective powers of intervention, the power to engage in legal proceedings and the power to hear complaints from data subjects (Article 28).

Taking these obligations in reverse order, the independent supervisory authority under the DPA is the Information Commissioner. Using their powers under the DPA, the Information Commissioner can commence criminal proceedings against data controllers, they can serve 'enforcement notices', 'information notices' and 'special information notices', they can conduct proceedings in the Information Tribunal, they can assess processing for legal compliance upon the request of the data subject and, with a warrant, they can enter upon premises to inspect, examine, operate or test processing equipment and to seize documents or materials containing evidence.

The DPA also creates a small series of primary criminal offences, by which it is meant that a criminal prosecution can be commenced directly by the Information Commissioner or the Director of Public Prosecutions upon the obtaining of evidence of a breach of the rule concerned. However, it is important to note that all breaches of the DPA can ultimately lead to criminal prosecutions, although the notice procedures have to be followed first in the majority of cases.

The data subject may commence civil proceedings for compensation where damage is suffered as a result of a breach of the DPA. If distress is suffered as well, a claim for compensation can be maintained for that harm, but there is no standalone right to sue for compensation for distress where no damage is caused, except where the processing is done for journalistic, artistic or literary purposes.

The data subject may also commence civil proceedings to enforce the right or access or the right to object.

The sixth, seventh and eighth data protection principles

As mentioned earlier, the DPA contains eight data protection principles. For completeness, the sixth, seventh and eighth data protection principles say the following:

> 6. Personal data shall be processed in accordance with the rights of data subjects under this Act.
>
> 7. Appropriate technical and organisational measures shall be taken against unauthorised or unlawful processing of personal data and against accidental loss or destruction of, or damage to, personal data.
>
> 8. Personal data shall not be transferred to a country or territory outside the European Economic Area unless that country or territory ensures an adequate level of protection for the rights and freedoms of data subjects in relation to the processing of personal data.

KEY WORDS AND PHRASES – DATA, PERSONAL DATA AND PROCESSING

It is the processing of personal data by data controllers and data processors that is regulated by the DPA. To recap, the person whose personal data are processed is known as the data subject, the data controller is the person with the power of control over the purpose or manner of the processing and the data processor is the person who processes personal data on behalf of a data controller. While the status of data subject is reserved for living individuals only, data controllers and data processors can be living individuals or organizations, such as companies, public bodies, clubs, associations and charities.

What are data?

The DPA is concerned with two kinds of data, electronic data and manual data. During the first phase in the development of European data protection laws, from the late 1960s to the mid-1970s, the focus was electronic data. However, by the start of the 1980s it was recognized that manual processing of data caused problems too. Thus, the definition of 'personal data' within the OECD Guidelines of 1980[36] is 'any information relating to an identified or identifiable individual', although the Guidelines left the regulation of manual processing optional. The Data Protection Convention also gave its signatory countries the option of regulating manual processing (the UK declined this option, restricting the Data Protection Act 1984 to electronic data).

The Data Protection Directive takes a different line, making compulsory the regulation of certain kinds of manual files known as 'personal data filing systems' as well as manual processing that is connected to automated processing. The DPA has given effect to the Directive's requirements in respect of personal data filing systems through its rules on 'relevant filing systems'. The DPA has also extended coverage to other kinds of manual data thereby going further than the Directive's mandatory requirements.

For the purposes of the DPA, 'data' are special kinds of information, namely information that falls within one of the five categories described in section 1(1) of the DPA. It can be said that all data are information, but not all information is data. The five categories of data are:

(1) Information that is being processed by means of equipment operating automatically in response to instructions given for that purpose. It is important to note the tense preferred by the DPA, which is the present tense. The DPA does not talk about information that was processed by means of equipment operating automatically. The present tense is repeated in all of the categories.

(2) Information that is recorded with the intention that it should be processed by means of equipment operating automatically in response to instructions given for that purpose.

(3) Information that is recorded as part of a relevant filing system, or with the intention that it should form part of a relevant filing system.

(4) Information that does not fall into any of the first three categories but forms part of an 'accessible record'.

(5) Information that is recorded information held by a public authority that does not fall into any of the first four categories.

These definitions are complex, but in a nutshell they are describing two kinds of information, electronic information and manual information. The first category is electronic information processed by computers and computerized equipment. Categories 3, 4 and 5 are manual information. The second category can be either electronic or manual information.

The relationship between information and data

It was stated earlier that all data are information but not all information is data. This statement needs further explanation because an understanding of the relationship and distinction between information and data is an imperative within a proper understanding of the DPA.

Information will become data when it is processed in the manner described in one of the five categories above. Thus, when information enters a computer, or a relevant filing system or an accessible record, it becomes data for the purposes of the DPA. Information will also become data prior to its entry into a computer or one of the regulated manual files, if it is recorded with the intention that it should enter them.

Perhaps the more complicated issue is the status of information that is extracted from data, as occurs when an electronic file is printed, or a page from a regulated manual file is removed and photocopied. Such information will still be treated as data due to the fact that the definition of processing includes the use of data and the disclosure of data. According to section 1(2) of the DPA, using or disclosing data includes using or disclosing the information contained in the data. This means that information extracted from data will be regulated by the DPA provided, of course, that the data are personal data. The effect of this is as follows:

- If information is recorded with the intention that it will enter a computer, or one of the regulated manual files, it is treated as data for the purposes of the DPA and for the definition of processing.
- Once information enters a computer, or one of the regulated manual files, it is also treated as data.
- Information that leaves a computer or one of the regulated manual files is also treated as data.

The first category of data – electronic information

Equipment that operates automatically in response to instructions given for that purpose is computerized equipment and includes PCs, mobile telephones, PDAs, voice dictation machines and telephone answering machines. For this reason the first category of data is usually referred to as electronic data.

In order for information to fall within this category it must be being processed by automated equipment, because of DPA's use of the present tense. If information is no longer being processed by automated equipment it cannot fall within this category, which is the effect of the decision of Mr Justice Laddie in *Smith v. Lloyds TSB Bank Plc*.[37] Conversely, information that is extracted from electronic data, such as printed copy, will be treated as data as confirmed by the Court of Appeal in *Campbell v. Mirror Group Newspapers*[38] and in *Johnson v. Medical Defence Union*[39] provided that the electronic form continues to exist.

The second category of data – electronic or manual information

The second category of data can be either electronic information or manual information, depending upon the circumstances. Two common examples of the second category of data can help with understanding of this point.

EXAMPLES

(1) A customer telephones a call centre to complain about a product. The telephonist who answers the call is required to type details of complaints received into a computer database, for record-keeping purposes. Because of a temporary technical fault, the telephonist cannot access the database, so they jot down details on a pad of paper, so that they can enter them later, when the fault is corrected. In this example information is recorded, a requirement of the second category of data, albeit manually. As the telephonist's intention is to enter the information into a computer database it can be said that the manual information is recorded with the intention that it will be processed by equipment operating automatically, making the manual information fall into the second category of data.

(2) A person copies an electronic file from a PC to a CD, for backup purposes. The PC is later destroyed in a fire, but the CD is kept safe. The information in the CD is clearly electronic information but it cannot fall within the first category of data, because it is not being processed by equipment operating automatically (it is merely being held in electronic form, in a carrier for electronic information). Therefore, it must be information falling within the second category of data, because it is recorded with the intention that it will be processed by equipment operating automatically at a later date.

The third category of data – highly structured manual information

The third category of data covers highly structured information, namely information that forms part of a relevant filing system and information that is recorded with the intention that it will form part of a relevant filing system. The definition of relevant filing system is also contained in section 1(1) of the DPA and means:

> any set of information relating to individuals to the extent that, although the information is not processed by means of equipment operating automatically in response to instructions given for that purpose, the set is structured, either by reference to individuals or by reference to criteria relating to individuals, in such a way that specific information relating to a particular individual is readily accessible.

The meaning of relevant filing system expressly excludes information that is processed by equipment operating automatically and, logically, any information that may be processed by such equipment (if manual information is recorded with the intention that it will be processed by equipment operating automatically, it will fall within the second category, as explained above). Thus, there can be no doubt that a relevant filing system can consist only of manual information.

The Durant case – manual files

That a relevant filing system is highly structured arises from the fact that the structure makes specific information relating to a particular individual 'readily accessible'. According to the Court of Appeal in the case of *Durant v. Financial Services Authority*,[40] this means that the structure of the file should 'enable easy location' of the personal data within it, which is only possible within highly structured files. Indeed, and as the Court of Appeal rightly observed, the Data Protection Directive says that relevant filing systems enable 'easy access' to the personal information within them. In fact, the Court of Appeal said that 'the required "easy" access to such data must be on a par with that provided by a computerised system'.

So, what type of manual file will meet the definition of relevant filing system? The starting point is to consider the Court's description of the manual files held by the Financial Services Authority (FSA), as these provide the best example of files that fail to meet the definition. The following description is taken from the judgment of Lord Justice Auld:

> The first [category of manual file] was the Major Financial Groups Division systems file ('the MFGD Systems file'). It was a file, in two volumes, relating to the systems and controls that Barclays Bank was required to maintain and which was subject to control by the FSA. The file, which was arranged in date order, also contained a few documents relating to part of Mr Durant's complaint against the Bank, which concerned such systems and controls.
> The second category of file was 'the MFGD Complaints file' – relating to complaints by customers of Barclays Bank about it to the FSA – the subdividers being ordered alphabetically by reference to the complainant's name, containing behind a divider marked 'Mr Durant' a number of documents relating to his complaint, filed in date order.
> The third category of file was the Bank Investigations Group file ('the B.I.G file'), maintained by the FSA's Regulatory Enforcement Department, relating and organised by reference to issues or cases concerning Barclays Bank, but not necessarily identified by reference to an individual complainant. It contained a sub-file marked 'Mr Durant', containing documents relating to his complaint. Neither the file nor the sub-file was indexed in any way save by reference to the name of Mr Durant on the sub-file itself.
> The fourth category of file was the Company Secretariat papers, a sheaf of papers in an unmarked transparent plastic folder held by the FSA's Company

> Secretariat, relating to Mr Durant's complaint about the FSA's refusal to dis-
> close to him details and the outcome of its investigation of his complaints
> against Barclays Bank, not organised by date or any other criterion.

While it is clear that the definition of relevant filing system applies to only highly structured manual information, the question remains whether only highly structured manual information can fall within the third category of data.

Taking the third category literally, it would seem that it can consist of both highly structured manual information (relevant filing systems) and manual information that is not highly structured (or not structured at all). This is because the third category refers to two types of information: (i) information that forms part of a relevant filing system; and (ii) information that is recorded with the intention that it will form part of a relevant filing system, that is, information that will form part of a relevant filing system at some point in time after its recording.

EXAMPLE

A Human Resources (HR) Director conducts an annual appraisal of one of the work force. In advance of the appraisal the HR Director explains to the worker that they may submit a short manuscript statement describing their achievements in the period under review, which will be inserted into the worker's personnel file at the end of the appraisal process. When this happens an entry will be made in the index at the front of the file identifying the document, its location and page number. In this example the statement itself is not part of a relevant filing system but when it is written, the intention exists that it will form part of a relevant filing system at a later date.

The fourth category of data – manual data of specific character

The fourth category of data can only be manual, because the fourth category excludes the first and second categories, but it cannot be a relevant filing system or recorded with the intention that it will form part of a relevant filing system, because the fourth category excludes the third category. Information falling within the fourth category is known as an 'accessible record', which is defined in section 68 of the DPA. According to section 68 there are three kinds of accessible records: (i) 'health records'; (ii) 'educational records'; and (iii) 'accessible public records'.

Health records are defined in section 68(2) of the DPA and they have two essential characteristics. The first characteristic is that they consist of 'information relating to the physical or mental health or condition of an individual'. The second characteristic is that they are made by or on behalf of a 'health professional' in connection with the care of the individual con-cerned. The meaning of health professional is contained in section 69 of the

DPA and includes health professionals working in the public and private sectors, such as registered medical practitioners, registered dentists, registered opticians and registered pharmaceutical chemists (see section 69 of the DPA for the full list).

Educational records are defined in Schedule 11 of the DPA. The meaning of educational record is different for each part of the UK, although there is one element that is common to all areas, namely that records prepared by teachers solely for their own use are not educational records.

Accessible public records are defined in Schedule 12 of the DPA. The public bodies covered by Schedule 12 differ within the UK, but the nature of the records is the same; they are records about public sector residential tenancies and records held for social work purposes.

The fifth category of data – public sector manual information

This category of data, recorded information held by a public authority that does not fall within any of the other categories, was introduced into the DPA as a result of an amendment made by the Freedom of Information Act 2000. The fifth category can only be manual data.

Recorded information falls into two categories, structured and unstructured. The definition of structured data is very similar to the definition of relevant filing system but, of course, structured data and relevant filing systems are not the same thing. The definitions are shown in Table 1.4.

TABLE 1.4   *Structured data and relevant filing systems*

Structured data See DPA section 9(A)(1)	Relevant filing system See DPA section 1(1)
. . . information which is recorded as part of, or with the intention that it should form part of, any set of information relating to individuals to the extent that the set is structured by reference to individuals or by reference to criteria relating to individuals.	. . . any set of information relating to individuals to the extent that, although the information is not processed by means of equipment operating automatically in response to instructions given for that purpose, the set is structured, either by reference to individuals or by reference to criteria relating to individuals, in such a way that specific information relating to a particular individual is readily accessible.

Both definitions refer to sets of information, sets of information relating to individuals and structuring by reference to individuals or criteria relating to individuals. The key difference is that in relevant filing systems the structure makes specific information relating to a particular individual readily accessible. Structured public sector manual data falling within the fifth category lacks the necessary ingredient of ready accessibility found within relevant filing systems.

Consequences of the definitions of data

The cumulative effect of the five categories of data has some very important consequences depending upon whether the data controller is part of the private sector or part of the public sector. The key point is that the DPA applies to a wider variety of information in the public sector than in the private sector, as Table 1.5 shows.

TABLE 1.5   *Data in the public and private sectors*

Category of data	Public sector	Private sector
First – electronic information processed by automated equipment	Applies	Applies
Second – electronic information to be processed by automated equipment	Applies	Applies
Second – manual information to be processed by automated equipment	Applies	Applies
Third – relevant filing system	Applies	Applies
Fourth – accessible records	Applies	Applies, but to a lesser extent
Fifth – public sector recorded information	Applies	Does not apply

The main point to be drawn from Table 1.5 is that manual data undergoing processing are subject to greater protection in the public sector than in the private sector. However, due to the ECHR, incorporated into UK law by the Human Rights Act, privacy in manual data is generally protected in both the private and public sectors.

Personal data

Understanding the meaning of personal data is vital to a proper understanding of the DPA and the implementation of compliance strategies. Table 1.6 shows how the definition has evolved from the Data Protection Convention through to the Data Protection Directive and to the DPA.

TABLE 1.6   *The meaning of personal data*

Convention	'personal data' means any information relating to an identified or identifiable individual ('data subject');
Directive	'personal data' shall mean any information relating to an identified or identifiable natural person ('data subject'); an identifiable person is one who can be identified, directly or indirectly, in particular by reference to an identification number or to one or more factors specific to his physical, physiological, mental, economic, cultural or social identity;
DPA	'personal data' means data which relate to a living individual who can be identified – (a) from those data, or (b) from those data and other information which is in the possession of, or is likely to come into the possession of, the data controller, and includes any expression of opinion about the individual and any indication of the intentions of the data controller or any other person in respect of the individual;

Personal data under the DPA

Information falling within one of the five categories of data can only be personal data in two circumstances:

- if the data relate to a living individual and that individual can be identified from those data;
- if the data relate to a living individual and that individual can be identified from those data and any other information that is in the possession of the data controller or is likely to come into the possession of the data controller.

The meaning of personal data also includes expressions of opinion about the data subject and any indication of the data controller's intention in respect of the data subject, or any indication of another person's intention in respect of the data subject.

Thus, there are two key issues within the meaning of personal data. First, does the data identify a living individual? Second, does the data relate to the identified living individual?

Identification of the living individual

The requirement of identification stems from the fact that data protection laws are intended to protect the privacy of personal data undergoing processing. Information that cannot and does not identify a person cannot be said to affect someone's privacy. This means that information about anonymous people that is undergoing processing will not be regulated.

The second definition of personal data covers the situation where an anonymous person can be identified when the anonymous information is combined with other information in the data controller's possession or other information that is likely to come into the data controller's possession.

EXAMPLE

A supermarket introduces a loyalty card scheme. Each loyalty card has a unique number. The current series of numbers in circulation are recorded in an electronic master file. A second electronic file contains the names and contact details of the persons to whom the loyalty cards have been allocated. In this example the electronic master file of the current series of loyalty card numbers does not identify any individuals when it is read in isolation. However, if the reader of the electronic master file can gain access to the second electronic file, the ability to identify people from their loyalty card numbers becomes immediately achievable. Thus, the electronic master file contains personal data and is regulated by the DPA.

On a practical level, this has important implications for persons and organizations that wish to avoid the DPA by anonymizing files. This technique will only work if there is complete and effective anonymization. Merely applying codes and ciphers will not work if they can be broken or deciphered with the use of other information in the data controller's possession.

The Durant case – does the information 'relate to' a living individual?

A thorny question is can a document refer to an identified living individual without relating to that person for the purpose of the definition of personal data? This question was examined by the Court of Appeal in *Durant v. Financial Services Authority*.[41]

Durant v. Financial Services Authority is a controversial case but, for the time being at least, it should be regarded as being the definitive case on the meaning of personal data. As it is a decision of the Court of Appeal it binds all courts below, including the High Court, the County Court and the Information Tribunal. The case is controversial due to the fact that it is considered to put English and Welsh law into conflict with the laws of other European countries. In a nutshell, *Durant* is considered to unduly restrict the operation of the DPA.

Of course, not everyone will agree that *Durant* is a bad decision. In fact, many data controllers, particularly commercial operators in the private sector, had good cause to celebrate when the decision was announced, because it relieves them of many burdens of regulation.

The background to *Durant* is long and complicated, but it is clear that Mr Durant was once a customer of Barclays Bank. Unfortunately, a dispute arose between him and Barclays that could not be resolved. Thus, Mr Durant commenced litigation against Barclays, which ended in failure in 1993. Following this Mr Durant embarked upon a long battle to reopen his case, which included making complaints to the FSA. In 2001 he sought disclosure of his personal data held by the FSA, using his right of access contained in section 7 of the DPA. The FSA gave disclosure of some electronic records, but it refused to disclose a series of manual files. Therefore, Mr Durant commenced a court action under section 7(9) of the DPA, to obtain an order enforcing his right of access. One of the questions identified by the court was 'what makes "data", whether held in computerized or manual files, "personal" within the meaning of the term "personal data" in section 1(1) of the 1998 Act so as to entitle a person identified by it to its disclosure under section 7(1) of the Act?'

The Court of Appeal identified the key issue to be the 'meaning of the words "relate to" in the opening words of the definition [of personal data], in particular to what extent, if any, the information should have the data subject as its focus, or main focus'.

Mr Durant argued that the words 'relate to' have a very broad meaning covering 'any information retrieved as a result of a search under his name, anything on file which had his name on it or from which he could be identified or from which it was possible to discern a connection with him'. The FSA argued the opposite, saying that the words 'relate to' have a narrow meaning, that they imply a 'more or less direct connection with an individual'.

The Court of Appeal preferred the FSA's argument. The leading judgment in the case was given by Lord Justice Auld, who said:

> not all information retrieved from a computer search against an individual's name or unique identifier is personal data within the Act. Mere mention of the data subject in a document held by a data controller does not necessarily amount to his personal data. Whether it does so in any particular instance depends on where it falls in a continuum of relevance or proximity to the data subject as distinct, say, from transactions or matters in which he may have been involved to a greater or lesser degree.

In amplification of this Lord Justice Auld identified two concepts, biographical significance and focus, which, in simple terms, means that information will only be personal data if it affects the privacy of the individual. He said:

> The information should have the putative data subject as its focus rather than some other person with whom he may have been involved or some transaction or event in which he may have figured or have had an interest, for example, as in this case, an investigation into some other person's or body's conduct that he may have instigated. In short, it is information that affects his privacy, whether in his personal or family life, business or professional capacity.

In light of this case, it is now clear that a document can refer to a living individual without 'relating to' that person for the purposes of the DPA. The mere mention of a person in a document does not make that document personal data.

Of course, from time to time data controllers will find it difficult to apply the concepts of biographical significance and focus. In an attempt to provide assistance on the proper application of the concepts, in October 2004 the Information Commissioner published a guidance paper on the impact of *Durant*.[42] In this paper the Information Commissioner suggests in 'cases where it is not clear whether information relates to an individual' the data controller 'should take into account whether or not the information in question is capable of having an adverse impact on the individual'. This seems to be a fair restatement of the Court of Appeal's decision that personal data is information that affects the person's privacy, but it also draws attention to the significant problem within the *Durant* formulation, which is how much adverse effect is required for information to be personal data? Helpfully the Information Commissioner uses the guidance paper to give some examples of what is and what is not personal data. Examples of personal data are:

- marketing lists containing a name and contact details (e.g. address, telephone number, email);
- information about an individual's medical history;
- information about an individual's salary;

- information about an individual's tax liabilities;
- information within an individual's bank statements;
- information about individuals' spending habits.

Examples of what are not personal data are:

- the mere reference to a person's name where the name is not associated with any other personal information;
- incidental mention in the minutes of a business meeting of an individual's attendance in an official capacity;
- where an individual's name appears on a document or email indicating only that it has been sent or copied to that particular individual.

For the purposes of legal compliance by data controllers the real importance of the Information Commissioner's guidance paper lies in the fact that it shows his thinking and hints at a regulatory approach that is based on some kind of proof of an adverse privacy effect. In borderline cases this might discourage the Information Commissioner from taking regulatory action against a data controller. This approach to regulation was confirmed by the Information Commissioner on 22 November 2005, at the Annual Conference of the National Association of Data Protection Officers, when a new enforcement strategy was announced.[43]

Legitimate criteria for the processing of personal data

In order to render the processing of personal data legitimate, the first data protection principle says that the data controller must satisfy one of the conditions in Schedule 2. These are shown in Table 1.2.

Sensitive personal data

Reference has already been made to the 'special categories' of personal data. The DPA calls the special categories 'sensitive personal data' (section 2 of the DPA). Sensitive personal data are personal data consisting of information as to the data subject's:

- racial or ethnic origin;
- political opinions;
- religious beliefs or other beliefs of a similar nature;
- membership of a trade union;
- physical or mental health or condition;
- sexual life;
- commission or alleged commission of any offence, including any proceedings commenced and the disposal of such proceedings or the sentence of the court.

In addition to satisfying one of the conditions in Schedule 2 the first data protection principle requires the data controller to satisfy one of the conditions contained Schedule 3 of the DPA in order to make the processing of sensitive personal data legitimate. The conditions within Schedule 3 are shown in Table 1.3.

Other criteria for making the processing of sensitive personal data legitimate are contained in an important order made under the DPA.[44] This order provides a framework for the processing of sensitive personal data in the absence of explicit consent, for example where the processing is in the substantial public interest and is necessary for the purposes of the prevention or detection of any unlawful act.

Processing

The concept of processing is very wide, covering every single act that can be done on or towards data, from its initial capture right through to its final deletion or destruction. Table 1.7 shows how the definition has evolved since the Data Protection Convention.

TABLE 1.7   *The meaning of processing*

Convention	'automatic processing' includes the following operations if carried out in whole or in part by automated means: storage of data, carrying out of logical and/or arithmetical operations on those data, their alteration, erasure, retrieval or dissemination;
Directive	'processing of personal data' ('processing') shall mean any operation or set of operations which is performed upon personal data, whether or not by automatic means, such as collection, recording, organisation, storage, adaptation or alteration, retrieval, consultation, use, disclosure by transmission, dissemination or otherwise making available, alignment or combination, blocking, erasure or destruction;
DPA	'processing', in relation to information or data, means obtaining, recording or holding the information or data or carrying out any operation or set of operations on the information or data, including –
	(a) organisation, adaptation or alteration of the information or data,
	(b) retrieval, consultation or use of the information or data,
	(c) disclosure of the information or data by transmission, dissemination or otherwise making available, or
	(d) alignment, combination, blocking, erasure or destruction of the information or data;
	In this Act, unless the context otherwise requires –
	(a) 'obtaining' or 'recording', in relation to personal data, includes obtaining or recording the information to be contained in the data, and
	(b) 'using' or 'disclosing', in relation to personal data, includes using or disclosing the information contained in the data.

The Johnson case, other cases and the meaning of processing

Although the definition of processing is extremely wide, this does not mean that everyone agrees its scope. In the case of *Johnson v. Medical Defence Union*,[45] the defendant unsuccessfully argued for a narrowing definition, saying that where computer data are concerned there will only be processing if every operation is automated. Mr Justice Rimer, the judge in the case, summarized the defendant's argument as follows:

> Here, he says, Dr Roberts was not engaging in any 'automatic' processing of Mr Johnson's data. In relation to the four electronic files, she was not making her selection by any automatic process. She made it by applying her own, non-automatic judgment to a computer database. In relation to the manual files, they do not come into the picture at all because they are not part of a 'relevant filing system'. There was, therefore, no relevant processing at all of Mr Johnson's personal data.

This was a difficult argument for the defendant, for two reasons. First, most computers are not fully automated; the existence of the keyboard and the mouse proves this. This point was made by the Data Protection Tribunal in *CNN Credit Systems Ltd v. The Data Protection Registrar*,[46] a 1991 decision concerning the first data protection principle in the Data Protection Act 1984. The Tribunal said:

> We do not see the function of the Act as being the regulation of computers in the sense of fully automatic machines behaving automatically. Rather it is designed to regulate the use of such machines by human beings who feed information into them, extract information from them, and instruct machines what do to by computer programs or keyboard or other instructions.

Second, the law on the meaning of processing was clarified by the Court of Appeal in the case of *Campbell v. MGN Ltd.*[47] In *Campbell* Lord Phillips said:

> The Directive and the Act define processing as 'any operation or set of operations'. At one end of the process 'obtaining the information' is included, and at the other end 'using the information'. While neither activity in itself may sensibly amount to processing, if that activity is carried on by, or at the instigation of, a 'data controller', as defined, and is linked to automated processing of the data, we can see no reason why the entire set of operations should not fall within the scope of the legislation. On the contrary, we consider that there are good reasons why it should.

In this part of his judgment Lord Phillips was saying that manual processing by a data controller that is linked to automated processing will be processing for the purposes of the Data Protection Directive and the DPA.

Mr Justice Rimer followed Lord Phillips' judgment, dismissing the defendant's argument. In order to understand the full effect of this case, it is necessary to understand a little about the processing operations performed by the Medical Defence Union (MDU). By way of background, the MDU provides members of the medical profession with a discounted professional indemnity insurance policy, as well as associated advisory services. Mr Johnson was a member of the MDU for over 10 years during which time he had 17 contacts with the organization, including about complaints. These contacts resulted in the creation of 17 files, some electronic and some manual. Although he was never the subject of a clinical negligence claim, the MDU decided to terminate his membership as he presented an unacceptable risk. A significant factor in the MDU's decision was the number of contacts that Mr Johnson had with the organization.

When assessing whether or not to terminate his membership a member of the MDU's staff, Dr Roberts, completed a series of documents on her computer, one of which summarized the information in the 17 files relating to Mr Johnson. Twelve of these files were manual files, three were computer files, one was on CD and one was on microfiche. The computer summary was then printed and circulated to the persons involved in the decision-making process.

The MDU's legal team objected to this being treated as processing, because the selection of the information from the 17 files was not done automatically, but by a human being. Therefore, they said, this could not be processing and nor could the resulting hard copies of the computer summary. Mr Justice Rimer rejected the MDU's argument, holding that there was automated processing by reason of the inputting of data into the computer on which the summary was created. He said:

> I accept, therefore, that Dr Roberts's selection of material from the various manual and microfiche files and their inputting into a computer amounted to 'processing' within the meaning of the definition of 'processing' in section 1(1) [DPA] as expanded in section 1(2)(a) [DPA]; and that it makes no difference that none of such files was or formed part of a 'relevant filing system'. I accept also that her selection of information from the computerised files for inputting into the computer similarly amounted to 'processing' within the meaning of that definition as elaborated in section 1(2)(a) and/or (b) [DPA].

The Smith case and the meaning of processing

There are limits to the meaning of processing, however, as clarified in the case of *Smith v. Lloyds TSB Bank Plc*.[48] In this case the claimant's barrister unsuccessfully tried to develop an argument that he called the 'once processed always processed' point. In fact, a variant of this argument was first presented by the same barrister in the first hearing in *Johnson v. MDU*, in 2004[49] again unsuccessfully. The 'once processed always processed' argument says that if information was processed by the data controller on automatic equipment it will become data and will remain data even if the automatic equipment ceases to exist. The judge in *Smith v. Lloyds TSB Bank Plc*, Mr Justice Laddie, summarized the argument as follows:

> Thus, for example, if a series of letters about the data subject were typed on word processors and thereafter retained on computer hard discs, they would have been processed, i.e. held, on relevant automatic equipment. Even if the data controller has wiped all the hard discs clean some years ago and only retains hard copies of the documents in unstructured files, they still contain data within the meaning of the 1998 Act because, once processed always processed.

Mr Justice Laddie, who also tried the first hearing in *Johnson v. MDU*, did not like this argument. He said:

> I do not accept this argument. Even if s 1 of the 1998 Act is treated as including the words from Article 3, it does not help Mr Smith. As I said in Johnson, the question of whether information is data has to be answered at the time of the data request. [The] argument involves a subtle sleight of hand. What he is saying is that because the information was held on automatic equipment but now is not, this means that it is partly so held. However this runs together two situations which are separated by time. What is relevant for the 1998 Act is whether, at the time of the data request, the information is wholly or partly held by means of equipment operating automatically. That is not the position here. As of 2001 Lloyds did not hold information relating to Mr Smith either wholly or partly on automatic equipment. Rewriting the section makes no difference.

Mr Justice Laddie's rejection of the 'once processed always processed' argument is entirely consistent with Lord Phillips' judgment in *Campbell v. MGN*, but this does not mean that the argument is totally devoid of merit. Indeed, when Article 3.1. of the Data Protection Directive is considered, which sets the Directive's scope, it is possible to interpret it to mean that the Directive does not require synchronous automatic and manual processing for the manual by-products of automatic processing to be regulated. If this observation is correct, then the 'once processed always processed argument' may also be regarded as being consistent with Lord Phillips' judgment in *Campbell v. Mirror Group Newspapers*. For completeness, Article 3.1. of the Data Protection Directive says:

> This Directive shall apply to the processing of personal data wholly or partly by automatic means, and to the processing otherwise than by automatic means of personal data which form part of a filing system or are intended to form part of a filing system.

There is another variant of the 'once processed always processed' argument that has not yet been presented in argument before the court. This variant concerns deleted electronic data, in the sense that deletion as understood by most computer users does not actually delete the data, but merely removes references to it in the file allocation tables against which a computer searches when data are sought to be retrieved. True deletion can only be accomplished by a process colloquially known as electronic shredding, which consists of the repeated overwriting of the data to be deleted with new binary code. If electronic data are not shredded in this fashion, they may be retrievable despite deletion. Consequently, in many cases where the data controller claims that only manual records exist it could be possible to disprove this assertion provided that the original processing equipment exists. In *Harper v. The Information Commissioner*, a recent Information Tribunal case brought under the Freedom of Information Act 2000, it was confirmed that a public authority's duty to disclose information under an access request made under section 8 of the Freedom of Information Act can extend to deleted data.[50]

The special purposes – journalism, art and literature

Section 3 of the DPA refers to the 'special purposes', which means processing for the purposes of journalism, for artistic purposes and for literary purposes. The special purposes are acknowledged in the DPA due to their long-standing importance within the freedom of expression. Processing for the special purposes benefit from significant exemptions contained in section 32 of the DPA.

THE DPA – IMPORTANT MISCELLANY

The DPA achieved Royal Assent on 16 July 1998 and the majority of its provisions came into force on 1 March 2000. This repealed and replaced the Data Protection Act 1984, but it is subject to some important transitional provisions that are designed to ensure a smooth transition from the 1984 Act to the DPA. Most of the transitional provisions expired on 24 October 2001, but a few still remain:

- Until 24 October 2007 'eligible manual data', which are manual data that were first held by a data controller before 24 October 1998, and 'accessible records', which are certain kinds of health records, educational records and public records, are exempt from most of the data protection principles as well as from the data subject's right to seek a court order for the rectification, blocking, erasure or destruction of inaccurate personal data.
- Until 24 October 2007 'recorded information held by a public authority' are exempt from the DPA's rules about accuracy.
- There is a limited, permanent exemption for processing of personal data for historical research purposes.

The jurisdiction of the DPA

The Data Protection Directive required EC Member States to apply its national laws where 'the processing is carried out in the context of the activities of an establishment of the controller on the territory of the Member State' (Article 4).

In order to work out whether they are regulated by the DPA, data controllers need to consider the provisions contained in section 5 of the Act, which can be distilled down to three primary questions:

- Are they processing personal data?
- Are they established in the UK?
- Are they processing personal data in the context of the UK establishment?

If the answer to all of these questions is yes, the DPA will apply, subject to some important exemptions described in Part IV of the Act.

However, if the data controller is not established in the UK nor in any other country within the EEA, the DPA will still apply if the data controller 'uses equipment in the United Kingdom for processing the data otherwise than for the purposes of transit through the United Kingdom' (section 5(1)(b) of the DPA). In these cases the data controller must nominate a representative established in the UK (section 5(2) of the DPA).

Figure 1.1 shows the issues in sequence.

The meaning of establishment

A data controller who is an individual will be established in the UK for the purposes of the DPA if he is ordinarily resident in the UK. In the recent case of *Skjevesland v. Geveran Trading Co Ltd*[51] it was decided that whether a businessman with residences in several countries including the UK was ordinarily resident for the purposes of the Insolvency Act 1986 was a question of fact and degree and it was necessary to look at the cumulative effect of the evidence.

A data controller that is a company will be established in the UK if the company is incorporated under the law of any part of the UK. A data controller that is a partnership or an unincorporated body will be established in the UK if it is formed under the law of any part of the UK.

Further assistance with the meaning of establishment is provided by an Article 29 Working Party working document,[52] which explains:

> The notion of establishment is relevant in Article 4(1)c of the directive in the sense that the controller is not established on Community territory. The place, at which a controller is established, implies the effective and real exercise of activity through stable arrangements and has to be determined in conformity with the case law of the Court of Justice of the European Communities. According to the Court, the concept of establishment involves the actual pursuit of an activity through a fixed establishment for an indefinite period. This requirement is also fulfilled where a company is constituted for a given period.

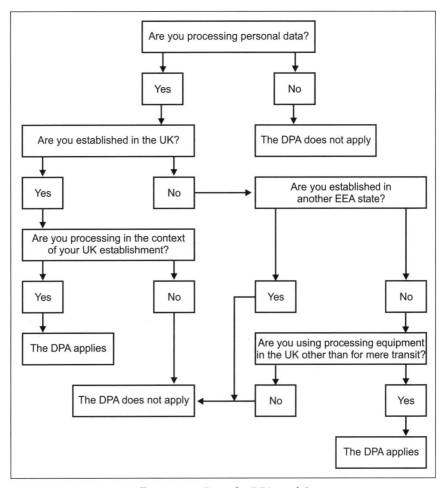

FIGURE 1.1 *Does the DPA apply?*

Establishment in more than one EC Member State

Data controllers established in more than one EC Member State will be subject to the data protection laws of each country of establishment. This point is dealt with in Article 4.1.(a) of the Data Protection Directive, which says:

> When the same controller is established on the territory of several Member States, he must take the necessary measures to ensure that each of these establishments complies with the obligations laid down by the national law applicable . . .

The Article 29 Working Party's working document says:

> When the same controller is established on the territory of several Member States, each of the establishments must comply with the obligations laid down

> by the respective law of each of the Member States for the processing carried out by them in course of their activities . . . where the controller chooses not to have only one, but several establishments, he does not benefit from the advantage that complying with one law is enough for his activities throughout the whole Internal Market. This controller then faces the parallel application of the respective national laws to the respective establishments.

Data controller not established in the EC

If the data controller is not established anywhere in the UK, this is not the end of the matter. In these situations the data controller needs to ask whether they are using equipment situated within the UK other than for the purposes of transiting data through the UK. This issue arises often in internet transactions.

Before addressing the substantive issues it needs to be asked when is equipment used only for transit? Again, the Article 29 Working Party's working document provides assistance, saying:

> A typical case where equipment is used for transit only are the telecommunications networks (back bones, cables etc.), which form part of the Internet and over which Internet communications are traveling from the expedition point to the destination point.

For the purposes of the Data Protection Directive a website based outside the EC may make use of equipment situated in the UK to process personal data, although it is important to recognize, as the Article 29 Working Party says, that 'not any interaction between an Internet user in the EU and a web site based outside the EC leads necessarily to the application of EU data protection law'. In order for the law to apply, it seems necessary for the foreign website to make use of the internet user's computer in such a fashion that it can be said that the computer is under the control of the foreign website. Of course, this taking of control element needs to involve the processing of personal data for the Data Protection Directive to apply. The Article 29 Working Party says:

> The Working Party considers that the concept of 'making use' presupposes two elements: some kind of activity undertaken by the controller and the intention of the controller to process personal data.

The Article 29 Working Party's working document also gives some examples of the kind of activities that can result in the application of the Data Protection Directive. These are:

- the use of cookies;
- the use of JavaScript;
- the use of spyware.

The location and nationality of the data subject

An important question is does the data subject need to be located in the EC, or be a national of an EC Member State for the Data Protection Directive to apply? The answer to this question is no. Again, the Article 29 Working Party's working document is of help:

> It is worth noting that it is not necessary for the individual to be an EU citizen or to be physically present or resident in the EU. The directive makes no distinction on the basis of nationality or location because it harmonises Member States laws on fundamental rights granted to all human beings irrespective of their nationality. Thus, in the cases that will be discussed below, the individual could be a US national or a Chinese national. In terms of application of EU data protection law, this individual will be protected just as any EU citizen. It is the location of the processing equipment used that counts.

Exemptions to the DPA

The DPA contains a complex framework of exemptions and restrictions. The main ones are contained Part IV of the DPA, the full list of which is as follows:

- national security (section 28);
- crime and taxation (section 29);
- health, education and social work (section 30);
- regulatory activity (section 31);
- journalism, literature and art (section 32);
- research, history and statistics (section 33);
- manual records held by public authorities (section 33a);
- information available to the public by or under an enactment (section 34);
- disclosures required by law or made in connection with legal proceedings (section 35);
- parliamentary privilege (section 35a);
- domestic purposes (section 36).

Only the domestic purposes exemption is a full exemption, so that where personal data are processed by an individual only for the purposes of that individual's personal, family or household affairs (including recreational purposes) the DPA will not apply. The national security exemption can act as a complete exemption, but first a government minister needs to sign a certificate to that effect. All the other exemptions are partial exemptions. Some of them are fleshed out in subordinate legislation made under the DPA.

There are other exemptions within Schedule 7 of the Act. These exemptions concern the right of access and the supply of prior information, which both form part of the DPA's transparency safeguards. The obligation to supply prior information forms part of the first data protection principle. The DPA refers to the right of access and the obligation to supply prior information as the 'subject information provisions' (section 27(2)).

Staying with transparency, the right of access and the obligation to notify are themselves both subject to exemptions.

Finally, section 38 of the DPA allows the Secretary of State to make further exemptions.

2 Transparency

INTRODUCTION

The DPA contains a series of provisions that can be grouped together under the title 'transparency'. These transparency provisions provide the foundations of data protection laws providing a fundamental level of protection for the privacy of personal data undergoing processing. It might seem obvious, but it is worth saying it all the same; an individual's privacy is better protected when the individual is properly informed about the data controller's activities.

The DPA's principal transparency provisions were identified in the previous chapter. To recap, they are:

- the promotion of consensual processing;
- the requirement of fair processing;
- the requirement for specified processing purposes;
- notification;
- the right of access to personal data;
- information notices.

CONSENSUAL PROCESSING (INCLUDING THE FIRST DATA PROTECTION PRINCIPLE)

The DPA's promotion of consensual processing is compelling. In respect of the first data protection principle consent is the first criterion for making the processing of personal data legitimate (Schedule 2 of the DPA) and explicit consent is the first criterion for making the processing of sensitive personal data legitimate (Schedule 3 of the DPA). The data subject's consent can also overcome the general prohibition against the transfer of personal data to countries outside the EEA that do not provide an adequate level of protection for the privacy of personal data undergoing processing (see Schedule 4 of the Act).

However, while the promotion of consent is compelling, there is considerable confusion about the meaning of consent, what needs to be done to obtain consent and how the obtaining of consent can be proved. This has caused the Information Commissioner to caution against relying immediately upon consent as the criterion for making processing legitimate. The Information Commissioner's 'Legal Guidance'[53] says:

> The Commissioner's view is that consent is not particularly easy to achieve and that data controllers should consider other conditions in Schedule 2 (and

Schedule 3 if processing sensitive personal data) before looking at consent. No condition carries greater weight than any other. All the conditions provide an equally valid basis for processing. Merely because consent is the first condition to appear in both Schedules 2 and 3, does not mean that data controllers should consider consent first.

It is impossible to be sure of the quality of this opinion, as it purports to rely upon an unknown statistical basis for its authority. Data controllers may therefore wish to treat this part of the Information Commissioner's 'Legal Guidance' with some caution; data controllers rely upon consent on a daily basis for literally billions of processing operations without any difficulties, because, with the exercise of proper thought and consideration, systems can be designed to obtain verifiable consent of the required quality.

Although the DPA does not define the meaning of consent the Data Protection Directive does. It says that 'the data subject's consent' means 'any freely given specific and informed indication of his wishes by which the data subject signifies his agreement to personal data relating to him being processed'. It is undoubtedly the case that freely given, specific and informed consent requires data controllers to be transparent about their activities. Nothing else could satisfy this definition of consent.

When the Directive's definition of consent is split down into its core components the following requirements are identified:

- The data subject's consent must be freely given.
- The data subject's consent must be specific.
- The data subject's consent must be informed.
- The data subject's consent must be communicated to the data controller.

Freely given consent

The requirement that consent must be freely given clearly excludes any consent that is forced from the data subject, for example through duress. It is also considered that where there is significant inequality of bargaining power between the data subject and the data controller any consent obtained will not be freely given.

An obvious example of an unequal bargaining position that invalidates consent is an arrest situation where the police obtain personal information from a person suspected of committing a crime. It would be most inappropriate and unrealistic to consider that consent is given freely in this situation. Thus, the police will rely upon a different criterion for legitimacy, such as those relating to the exercise of public functions.

Specific and informed consent

These requirements are very closely linked. Together they require the data controller to supply the data subject with sufficiently detailed information about the processing activities, which the data subject will respond to. Naturally, the information should be supplied before the personal data are collected or otherwise first processed.

Communication of consent

The starting point is that the data controller cannot assume consent. Furthermore, valid consent cannot be obtained through the data subject's silence. Instead, the data subject must be seen to actually do something to communicate consent, such as signing a document or completing and returning a form. Of course, obtaining the data subject's signature to a document that identifies the processing activities in sufficient detail will provide the best evidence of communication of consent.

Consent can be obtained through a variety of means. A common approach is the use of opt-out boxes, where the data subject is asked to tick a box if they do not agree to the list of processing activities identified within the document. Subject to some special rules on direct marketing, an opt-out can secure valid consent in cases where the data subject returns the document without ticking the opt-out box.

The difference between consent and explicit consent

The explicit consent criterion for making the processing of sensitive personal data legitimate is clearly meant to mean something different from the consent criterion for making the processing of personal data legitimate, of this there can be no doubt. The difficult task is working out the scope of the difference between explicit consent and consent.

The Information Commissioner's 'Legal Guidance'[54] says:

> There is a distinction in the Act between the nature of the consent required to satisfy the condition for processing and that which is required in the case of the condition for processing sensitive data. The consent must be 'explicit' in the case of sensitive data. The use of the word 'explicit' and the fact that the condition requires explicit consent 'to the processing of the personal data' suggests that the consent of the data subject should be absolutely clear. In appropriate cases it should cover the specific detail of the processing, the particular type of data to be processed (or even the specific information), the purposes of the processing and any special aspects of the processing which may affect the individual, for example, disclosures which may be made of the data.

It is implicit within the Information Commissioner's discussions of the meaning of explicit consent that those data controllers who are relying upon explicit consent as the criterion for making the processing of sensitive personal data legitimate will have a thorough understanding of the data processing operations carried out on their behalf. Achieving the required thorough understanding needs a DPA compliant environment within the data controller's organization.

Cases on consent

Four decisions of the Data Protection Tribunal under the Data Protection Act 1984 give assistance on the meaning of consent. These cases, *Innovations (Mail Order) Ltd v. The Data Protection Registrar,*[55] *Linguaphone Institute Ltd v. The Data Protection Registrar,*[56] *British Gas Trading Ltd v. Data Protection Registrar*[57] and *Midlands Electricity Plc v. The Data Protection Registrar*[58] are discussed in the section 'Cases on fairness', below.

FAIR PROCESSING (THE FIRST DATA PROTECTION PRINCIPLE)

The first data protection principle within Schedule 1, Part I of the DPA says:

> **Personal data shall be processed fairly and lawfully and, in particular, shall not be processed unless –**
> **(a) at least one of the conditions in Schedule 2 is met, and**
> **(b) in the case of sensitive personal data, at least one of the conditions in Schedule 3 is also met.**

The concept of fairness within the first data protection principle is actually an amalgam of three parts of the Data Protection Directive, plus one part that is not contained in the Directive. The first reference to fairness is actually extracted from Article 6.1.(a) of the Data Protection Directive, which says personal data must be 'processed fairly and lawfully', and forms part of the Directive's principles relating to data quality (see Table 1.1). Fairness for these purposes requires consideration of the fairness of the processing purpose, the processing manner and the processing operations performed.

Fairness also has to be viewed from the perspective of the interpretation within Schedule 1, Part II of the DPA. The interpretation does two things. First, at paragraph 1 it introduces the concept of fair obtaining of data, requiring an examination of the method used to obtain data, including whether the data subject was deceived or misled as to the processing purpose. This part of the concept of fairness is the part that is not contained in the Directive. Second, paragraph 2 of the interpretation implements Articles 10 and 11 of the Directive and it is these provisions that are specifically part of the transparency provisions as categorized by this book, as they require, for processing to be fair, data controllers to provide data subjects with information about their processing activities, referred to later as 'the supply of prescribed information'.

So that there is no ambiguity, in any given case a proper analysis of fair processing requires consideration of the following questions:

(1) Is the processing purpose fair?

(2) Is the processing manner fair?

(3) Is the processing operation fair?

(4)   Has the information been fairly obtained?

(5)   Has the data controller supplied the prescribed information?

Questions 1, 2 and 3 express the issues within the fairness component of Article 6.1.(a) of the Data Protection Directive, implemented within the first line of the first data protection principle ('personal data shall be processed fairly and lawfully'). The fourth question expresses the issue within paragraph 1 of the interpretation, fair obtaining. The fifth question expresses the issue within paragraph 2 of the interpretation, which implements Articles 10 and 11 of the Data Protection Directive.

Fairness generally, including the Johnson case

As mentioned above, fair processing is about much more than the supply of the prescribed information required by paragraph 2 of the interpretation. This point is excellently illustrated by the case of *Johnson v. Medical Defence Union*,[59] where the judge, Mr Justice Rimer, divided his analysis of fairness into three parts. First, he analysed fairness from the perspective of the requirements contained in paragraph 2 of the interpretation, namely the supply of prescribed information. Second, he analysed the question 'was the processing anyway unfair', which involved looking at the processing purpose, which was the assessment of risk for insurance purposes. Third, he analysed whether there was any element of unfairness within the actual processing operation, namely the creation of a document containing a summary of information originally contained in 17 separate files. The second and third parts of his analysis are, to all intents and purposes, an analysis of the fair processing component within Article 6.1.(a) of the Data Protection Directive.

As the concept of fairness is much wider than the supply of the prescribed information it follows that the supply of the prescribed information does not of itself provide the data controller with a guarantee that its processing is fair. This point was clearly acknowledged by Mr Justice Rimer, who said, after completing his analysis of the Articles 10 and 11 requirements implemented by paragraph 2 of the interpretation, that:

> the exclusion of [paragraph 2 of the interpretation] from consideration . . . only closes one route by which Mr Johnson might have been able to demonstrate an element of presumed unfair processing for the purposes of the first data protection principle. There remains the more general question of whether – even though I have held those paragraphs do not apply – the processing of Mr Johnson's personal data was anyway fair.

The Information Commissioner's 'Legal Guidance'[60] also recognizes that the supply of the prescribed information does not guarantee that the processing will be fair saying that 'it is important to note that compliance with the fair processing requirements will not of itself ensure fair processing'. In reaching this conclusion the Information Commissioner was guided by a series of cases heard by the Data Protection Tribunal under the Data Protection Act 1984. These cases were also analysed by Mr Justice Rimer.

Fair obtaining

Paragraph 1(1) of the interpretation is the DPA's extension of the concept of fair processing, as the requirement within paragraph 1(1) is not contained in the Data Protection Directive. Paragraph 1(1) says:

> **In determining for the purposes of the first principle whether personal data are processed fairly, regard is to be had to the method by which they are obtained, including in particular whether any person from whom they are obtained is deceived or misled as to the purpose or purposes for which they are to be processed.**

The methods that data controllers may use to obtain personal data are limited only by the imagination, but whatever method is used it must avoid any possibility of the data subject being deceived or misled. This implies that the method used must impart accurate information about the data controller and the processing activities, which requires the persons collecting the personal data to be transparent about the identity of the data controller and the full range of processing activities. Of course, if the data subject is deceived or misled this will also undermine any consents relied upon for the purposes of Schedule 2 or Schedule 3.

EXAMPLE

There is a bucket on a hotel reception with a sign that reads 'place your business card in the hat to win a bottle of champagne'. If the underlying reason for the offer is to obtain contact information for direct marketing purposes, it can be said that those persons who have entered their business cards might have been deceived or misled.

The nature and extent of the information that needs to be provided to the data subject by the data controller depends upon the circumstances of the particular case, so real care needs to be taken with unusual or non-obvious processing activities. This point is reflected by paragraph 2(3)(d) of the interpretation, which includes a sweeping up provision that requires the data controller to provide the data subject with 'any further information which is necessary, having regard to the specific circumstances in which the data are or are to be processed, to enable processing in respect of the data subject to be fair'. This sweeping up provision is part of the prescribed information.

Statutory obtaining

Paragraph 1(2) of the interpretation makes special provision for cases where the person supplying personal data to the data controller is acting under an enactment or in accordance with an international obligation binding upon the UK. In these cases the interpretation says that the obtaining of the personal data by the data controller is to be treated as being fair. However, the data controller must also supply the prescribed information and the processing must be generally fair in the sense required by Article 6.1.(a) of the Data Protection Directive.

Paragraph 1(2) says:

> **(2) Subject to paragraph 2, for the purposes of the first principle data are to be treated as obtained fairly if they consist of information obtained from a person who –**
> **(a) is authorised by or under any enactment to supply it, or**
> **(b) is required to supply it by or under any enactment or by any convention or other instrument imposing an international obligation on the United Kingdom.**

Transparency and the supply of prescribed information

Paragraph 2(1) of the interpretation says that personal data are not to be treated as processed fairly unless the data controller ensures that the data subject has, is provided with, or has made readily available to them the information prescribed in paragraph 2(3) of the interpretation. The prescribed information in paragraph 2(3) is:

- the identity of the data controller;
- the identity of the data controller's nominated representative, if it has one. Data controllers must nominate representatives if they are not established in the EEA but are using processing equipment in the UK (section 5(2) DPA);
- the purpose or purposes for which the data are intended to be processed;
- any further information that in light of the specific circumstances is necessary to enable the processing to be fair.

The fourth requirement, 'any further information that in light of the specific circumstances is necessary to enable processing to be fair' is clearly very wide in scope, being a sweeping up provision that prevents the giving of definitive advice on the ambit of the prescribed information. Data controllers are required to consider their obligations on a case-by-case basis.

The supply of further information to enable processing to be fair, including the Johnson case

The background to *Johnson v. Medical Defence Union*[61] is discussed in Chapter 1, in the context of the analysis of the meaning of processing, but, in summary, this was a claim for compensation under section 13 of the DPA; Mr Johnson alleged that the defendant had failed to process his personal data fairly, in breach of the first data protection principal. A key component of his case was that the defendant failed to obtain his comments on information contained in 17 files, summaries of which were considered during the defendant's risk assessment procedures that led to the termination of Mr Johnson's insurance cover. The claimant said that the defendant's failure to seek his comments constituted a breach of paragraph 2(3)(d) of the interpretation, which requires the data controller to supply the data subject with any 'further information that in light of the specific circumstances is necessary to enable the processing to be fair.' Mr Justice Rimer summarized the claimant's argument in the following terms:

> The other issue arising under paragraph 2(3) of Part II of Schedule I is whether the MDU provided Mr Johnson with any further information which it was necessary for him to have in satisfaction of paragraph 2(3)(d). Mr Johnson's case on this is that, once Dr Roberts had concluded her preparation of the RAR form, the score sheet and the RAG sheet, the MDU should have submitted them to him for his comments, together with the underlying files from which the information in the RAR form was derived. Mr Johnson would then have had the opportunity to make his input into the risk review exercise that the MDU was undertaking, which would then have been before the RAG.

In determining the claim the court was required to consider the ambit of paragraph 2(3)(d) of the interpretation and whether the requirement to supply 'any further information that in light of the specific circumstances is necessary to enable processing to be fair' extended to consultation with the claimant. Mr Justice Rimer was sure that paragraph 2(3)(d) does not extend that far:

> Coming now to the point based on paragraph 2(3)(d), I consider, first, that in so far as article 10 may be viewed as casting light on the type of 'further information' that paragraph 2(3)(d) has in mind, it provides no support for the proposition that compliance with the fair processing requirements of the first data protection principle required Dr Roberts's processing exercise to be followed by a consultation with Mr Johnson. Nor, in my judgment, does the more succinct language of paragraph 2(3)(d) support the proposition. That sub-paragraph is not concerned with explaining the 'purposes' of the processing, a matter which is covered by paragraph 2(3)(c). Nor is it about consulting with the data subject. It is about providing him with certain 'further information' having regard to 'the specific circumstances in which the data are or are to be processed'. That is not naturally to be interpreted as requiring the data controller to engage in a consultation exercise after the completion of the processing. Article 10 suggests that it might (inter alia) require the data subject to be told of his right of access to, and to rectify, his personal data, but in this case Mr Johnson had already been told of those rights in the processing

> agreement. In a case in which the data was, for example, being, or was to be, processed by a 'data processor' as defined in section 1(1) of the DPA, it might also require notice of that to be given to the data subject. But I do not accept that the paragraph 2(3)(d) extends to the lengths of requiring the MDU to have consulted with Mr Johnson as part of the processing exercise.

Thus, paragraph 2(3)(d) does not require a two-way conversation between the data controller and the data subject. All it requires is the supply of information to the data subject; under paragraph 2(3)(d) information flows in only one direction.

Does the interpretation actually require the supply of prescribed information in every case?

There are some exemptions from the obligation to supply the prescribed information, which are discussed later. Leaving these aside, an important question is whether the interpretation actually requires the data controller to supply the prescribed information in every case? In order to answer this question the full wording of paragraph 2(1) is required:

> 2. – (1) Subject to paragraph 3, for the purposes of the first principle personal data are not to be treated as processed fairly unless –
> (a) in the case of data obtained from the data subject, the data controller ensures so far as practicable that the data subject has, is provided with, or has made readily available to him, the information specified in sub-paragraph (3), and
> (b) in any other case, the data controller ensures so far as practicable that, before the relevant time or as soon as practicable after that time, the data subject has, is provided with, or has made readily available to him, the information specified in sub-paragraph (3).

As a preliminary point it will be noticed that paragraphs 2(1)(a) and 2(1)(b) both refer to 'the information specified in sub-paragraph 3'. So that there is no confusion, 'sub-paragraph 3' means paragraph 2(3) of the interpretation, which specifies the prescribed information.

The focus now is the phrase appearing in both paragraphs 2(1)(a) and 2(1)(b), 'the data controller ensures so far as practicable that the data subject has, is provided with, or has made readily available to him'. This splits down into three concepts:

(1) The data subject 'has'.
(2) The data subject 'is provided with'.
(3) The data subject 'has made readily available to him'.

If these concepts are taken at face value, it must be concluded that the interpretation does not actually require the data controller to supply the prescribed information in each and every case. The phrases 'is provided with' and 'has made readily available to him' are synonymous with supply of information to the data subject by the data controller, but the phrase 'the data subject has' is not.

Where 'the data subject has' the prescribed information the data controller does not have to supply it to them, because they already have it. Thus, the interpretation does not actually require the data controller to supply the prescribed information in every case.

This raises the question in what circumstances will the data subject already have the prescribed information prior to the collection of data so that the obligation on the data controller to supply it is not engaged? The answer is in routine transactions with which the data subject is fully familiar.

EXAMPLE

A data subject makes their regular six monthly visit to the dentist, for a check-up. In this example the data subject knows the data controller's identity and they know the purposes for which personal data are collected, namely for the purposes of providing dental treatment and for organizing the next visit. There are no unusual circumstances so there is no further information to give. It can therefore be said that 'the data subject has' the prescribed information prior to personal data being collected.

Prescribed information where personal data are collected from the data subject – timing of supply of information

The DPA does not identify the time for supplying the prescribed information for cases where the personal data are collected directly from the data subject, but for the obligation to make any sense it must follow that the information should be supplied prior to the commencement of processing, which means before any personal data are collected.

Prescribed information where personal data are collected from a third party – timing of supply of information

Where personal data are collected from a third party, rather than directly from the data subject, the time for supplying the prescribed information is called 'the relevant time'. The relevant time depends upon whether the data controller envisages disclosing the personal data to a third party.

If a data controller does not envisage disclosing personal data to a third party within a 'reasonable period' of the time it first starts to process it, the prescribed information must be supplied to the data subject at the time when the data controller first processes the data.

If a data controller does envisage disclosing the personal data to a third party within a reasonable period of the time when it first starts to process it, the relevant time depends upon whether the personal data are actually disclosed. If they are disclosed to a third party within the reasonable period, the relevant time is the time of disclosure. However, if the data controller realizes before the expiry of the reasonable period that the data will not be disclosed, the relevant time is the time when the data controller first realizes this fact. In any case, the longstop for supplying the prescribed information where the personal data are not disclosed to the third party is the end of the reasonable period.

Exemptions from the requirement to supply the prescribed information – where personal data are collected from a third party

There are two important exemptions from the obligation to supply the prescribed information where the personal data are collected from a third party. The first exemption is for cases where the supply of the prescribed information would involve a 'disproportionate effort'. The second exemption is for cases where the recording or disclosure of the personal data is necessary for compliance with a non-contractual legal obligation, such as where the data controller is a public authority and the processing is necessary for the performance of public functions.

The disproportionate effort exemption

Unfortunately, the DPA does not define 'disproportionate effort' so it is necessary to look elsewhere for help. The Information Commissioner's 'Legal Guidance'[62] provides the following assistance:

> In assessing what does or does not amount to disproportionate effort the starting point must be that data controllers are not generally exempt from providing the fair processing information because they have not obtained data directly from the data subject.
>
> What does or does not amount to disproportionate effort is a question of fact to be determined in each and every case.
>
> In deciding this the Commissioner will take into account a number of factors, including the nature of the data, the length of time and the cost involved to the data controller in providing the information. The fact that the data controller has had to expend a substantial amount of effort and/or cost in providing the information does not necessarily mean that the Commissioner will reach the decision that the data controller can legitimately rely upon the disproportionate effort ground. In certain circumstances, the Commissioner would consider that a quite considerable effort could reasonably be expected. The above factors will always be balanced against the prejudicial or effectively prejudicial effect to the data subject and in this respect a relevant consideration would be the extent to which the data subject already knows about the processing of his personal data by the data controller.

In cases where the disproportionate effort exemption is relied upon, an order[63] made under the DPA will also apply. This order concerns situations where an individual has served a written notice on the data controller asking the data controller to supply the prescribed information before the relevant time or as soon as practicable after that time. If such a notice is received, the data controller may only rely upon the disproportionate effort exemption if it 'does not have sufficient information about the individual in order readily to determine whether he is processing personal data about that individual'. However, in such a case the data controller must 'send to the individual a written notice stating that he cannot provide the [prescribed information] because of his inability to make that determination, and explaining the reasons for that inability'.

In addition, the order says that the data controller must record the reasons for its view that the disproportionate effort exemption applies.

The exemption for processing that is necessary for compliance with a non-contractual legal obligation

The order[64] will also apply in the case of the second exemption provided that the non-contractual legal obligation arises under an enactment or under a court order. The same rules apply as for the disproportionate effort exemption except that the data controller is not required to record the reasons for its view that the second exemption applies.

Cases on fairness, including the Johnson case

Johnson v. Medical Defence Union is currently the leading case on the meaning of fair processing and it has certainly helped to clarify the law. The judge, Mr Justice Rimer, examined first the claimant's allegation that the defendant had failed to supply all of the prescribed information required by paragraph 2 of the interpretation within Schedule 1, Part II of the DPA and he found that there was unfair processing in this regard. However, no separate issues arose in respect of unfair obtaining.

As regards the fairness of the processing purpose, the processing manner and the processing operation, that is, the issues within Article 6.1.(a) of the Data Protection Directive, the judge found that these were all fair, although, as noted earlier, he actually posed himself the questions 'was the processing anyway unfair?' and 'was there any unfairness in Dr Roberts' summaries of the four computerised files?'

The processing purpose identified in *Johnson* was the assessment of risk for insurance purposes. The manner of processing was partly automated and partly manual and the processing operations included creating an electronic summary of information contained in other files, with the decision to refuse continuation of insurance cover being based on printed copies of the summary. However, Mr Johnson was not asked for his views on the information within the files or within the summary, which was his principal complaint. As regards the overall fairness of these activities, Mr Justice Rimer delivered the following judgment:

Approaching the question of fairness head on, I have come to the conclusion that there is in principle nothing relevantly unfair about the MDU's risk assessment policy or about the way in which it processed information in applying that policy. Mr Johnson's big point is that he has a long and, from a claims viewpoint, blameless record. He says other doctors, in particular those specialising in orthopaedics, have had large claims brought against them yet remain MDU members. He has had no claims and yet his membership was terminated. He says that the scoring process applied by the policy is arbitrary and irrational and so capable of producing a like result. He says that the MDU fails to make proper distinctions between minor and major complaints, and that, at least in his case, it had regard to matters which, so he says, cannot rationally be regarded as genuinely predictive of future risk.

It is easy to see how he regards the decision in his case as unfair but it has to be remembered that the policy is directed at risk management – at preserving the MDU funds against a risk of claims, and the incurring of costs, in the future. The MDU experience is that a risk of that nature cannot be measured simply by awaiting the happening of a statistically significant number of occurrences that do in fact cause a drain on its funds. It is also that the risk of complaints is not a matter that is necessarily geared to the clinical competence of a doctor. The likelihood of complaints may well be based just as much on the way in which the doctor gets on with his colleagues and patients. A complaint, when made, may well be unfounded, but may also be expensive to defend. The objective of the risk management policy is to minimise the exposure of MDU funds to such expense. The policy that the MDU has developed is to assess risk by reference to whether the particular doctor attracts complaints. It is not assessed by an attempted investigation of whether there is anything in such complaints, an investigation which in practice could anyway not be carried out in any conclusive way. It would be possible to obtain the member's view of the complaint, but it is not part of the policy to do so because (a) it would only provide part of the picture and (b) it is a part which the policy does not regard as material to the assessment which the risk review is making. A wider investigation would usually be impracticable. In defending the MDU's risk assessment policy as fair, Mr Spearman emphasised that it has to be viewed against the background in which there is a contractual relationship between the MDU and its members and in which the MDU has a positive duty, in the interests of all its members, to adopt a responsible risk assessment policy directed at preserving its assets. The fairness of the processing of a member's personal data has to be considered in that contractual context.

As regards the second question he posed himself, the issue was whether there was any unfairness in the actual creation of the summary:

I have concluded that [apart from the failure to supply the prescribed information] there is in principle no basis for any challenge to the fairness of the MDU's approach to, and execution of, the risk assessment review in relation to Mr Johnson. That does not exclude the possibility that there might have been an element of unfairness in the way that Dr Roberts actually processed

> the data in the files. If she had, for example, materially misstated the nature of an allegation or complaint against Mr Johnson, that might go to the fairness of the processing in which she was engaged; and a consequential question might arise as to whether, but for such misstatement, the [committee making the decision on continuation of insurance cover] would or might have made a different recommendation.

On this question the judge again dismissed Mr Johnson's complaint.

There are other cases on the meaning of fair processing, but these are all decisions of the Data Protection Tribunal under the Data Protection Act 1984 (note that the Data Protection Tribunal was renamed the Information Tribunal by the Freedom of Information Act 2000). These cases are not binding on the Information Tribunal or the courts, but they do help with understanding the meaning of fair processing.

CNN Credit Systems Ltd v. The Data Protection Registrar,[65] a 1991 decision of the Data Protection Tribunal, is one of a series of appeals heard by the Tribunal following the service of enforcement notices on credit reference agencies. These enforcement notices were served under the Data Protection Act 1984 for breach of the first data protection principle within that Act. The first data protection principle said 'the information to be contained in personal data shall be obtained, and personal data shall be processed, fairly and lawfully'. The basic scenario at the heart of the case was presented in the following terms:

> In 1985 Mr Simon Jones, a chartered accountant, sold his house to a Mr J. Watson. In 1988 Mr Jones applied to a building society for a cheque guarantee card. He was refused a card and informed that a credit reference had been sought from CCN. Mr Jones applied to CCN under section 158 of the Consumer Credit Act 1974 for a copy of his file. Among the information supplied was an entry showing a judgment awarded in 1987 against Mr Watson. The only link between Mr Jones and Mr Watson was that they were respectively vendor and purchaser of a house a few years earlier. Put in another way, the only link between them was that they had at different times lived at the same address. Mr Jones was distressed by this incident.

The allegation of unfairness made by the Data Protection Registrar concerned the automatic extraction from a database of all information connected to an address that was provided by an applicant for credit. It was considered that this resulted in material that was irrelevant to the applicant being considered within the credit assessment process, particularly information relating to other individuals with whom the applicant had no other connection bar a connected address. The Data Protection Tribunal agreed that this was unfair processing:

> Having taken due account of the evidence we have heard and the considerations urged upon us we have come to the clear conclusion that it is unfair for a credit reference agency, requested by its customers to supply information by reference to a named individual, so to program the extraction of information as to search for information about all persons associated with a given address or addresses notwithstanding that those persons may have no links with the individual the subject of the enquiry or may have no financial relationship with that individual. We believe this to be so even if the customer has requested address-based information and notwithstanding what is said to be its predictive value. We reject the notion that an organisation like CCN, with its wide specialist knowledge of and experience in credit reference and credit scoring, is a mere 'conduit pipe'. We believe the sort of processing carried out in this case is the very sort of activity at which the Act is aimed. We think it right to say that we accept that CCN did not intend to process data unfairly, and did not believe itself to be acting unfairly. But it is necessary to determine the question of fairness objectively, and in our view the case of unfairness has been made out.

However, the Tribunal did not consider that the first data protection principle in the 1984 Act prevented all extraction of third-party information:

> Would it be unfair to extract information about persons, clearly not the subject, who share the same surname as the subject and who might be members of the same family living with the applicant as members of a single household? Here we recognise that it is possible to hold different views. It would often be accepted, we think, that enquiry into the credit status of members of the subject's immediate family might yield information that was relevant in the Registrar's sense. It would not necessarily be the case, but it would not be possible to form any sort of judgment on this without having the information available. On balance, therefore, our finding is that the extraction of such information would not be unfair, though whether it is possible to program a search with the necessary precision we do not know.

Similar decisions were reached in *Infolink Ltd v. The Data Protection Registrar*[66] and in *Credit and Data Marketing Services Ltd v. The Data Protection Registrar.*[67]

Innovations (Mail Order) Ltd v. The Data Protection Registrar[68] is a 1993 decision of the Information Tribunal. The practice that offended the Data Protection Registrar was non-consensual list broking, whereby Innovations sold customer information to third parties to be used by them for direct marketing purposes. The Registrar considered that this was an act of processing that was not revealed prior to the obtaining of customer information, which made the processing unfair. However, Innovations pointed out that after receiving an order it would send an acknowledgement that also included the following message:

> For your information. As a service to our customers we occasionally make our customer lists available to carefully screened companies whose products or services we feel may interest you. If you do not wish to receive such mailings please send an exact copy of your address label to [address].

The Registrar considered that the notice was insufficient to make the processing fair, because it was provided after the customer information was obtained and because it shifted the obligation to the data subject to opt-out. The Data Protection Tribunal agreed:

> We conclude that a later notice may be a commendable way of providing a further warning, but whether it does so or not, we conclude that the law requires in the circumstance we have here that when possible the warning must be before the obtaining. This can best be done by including the warning in the advertisement itself. Where it may not be possible (e.g. the use of existing names for a new purpose) we consider that the obligation to obtain the data subject's positive consent for the non-obvious use of their data falls upon the data user.

The Tribunal therefore concluded that Innovations' processing was unfair and it upheld the enforcement notice served by the Registrar.

Linguaphone Institute Ltd v. The Data Protection Registrar,[69] a 1995 decision of the Data Protection Tribunal, also concerned an appeal from an enforcement notice served by the Data Protection Registrar under the Data Protection Act 1984, for unfair processing. The Registrar said that Linguaphone's practice of list broking was unfair processing in breach of the first data protection principle in the 1984 Act, because this purpose was not disclosed to Linguaphone's customers and enquirers at the point of collection of their data.

Linguaphone accepted that all names acquired before 1 January 1992 should be deleted from its list, but it disagreed that names acquired after that date should be deleted, because it said that it was making use of 'opt-out' boxes on order forms sent to potential customers. The Data Protection Tribunal was unimpressed, holding Linguaphone's method to be unfair, because it sought to transfer to the data subject the burden of communicating their wish not to have their data transferred to third parties for marketing purposes. Instead, the 1984 Act's fair processing requirement placed the responsibility on Linguaphone to 'obtain the data subject's positive prior consent'. The Data Protection Tribunal was also unimpressed by the fact that the opt-outs were 'in minute print at the bottom of the order form'. In the Tribunal's view 'the position, size of print and wording of the opt-out box does not amount to a sufficient explanation to an enquirer that the company intends or may wish to hold, use or disclose that personal data provided at the time of enquiry for the purpose of trading in personal information'.

British Gas Trading Ltd v. Data Protection Registrar,[70] a 1998 decision of the Data Protection Tribunal, again an appeal from the service of an enforcement notice under the Data Protection Act 1984, also reviewed the fairness of processing for direct marketing purposes. After reviewing the evidence the Tribunal found that there was unfair processing in breach of the first data protection principle in the 1984 Act.

By way of background, British Gas Trading Ltd maintained two databases. The main database, called the 'tariff gas bill database' contained the records of 19 million gas customers and was used to prepare gas bills. The second database was a smaller marketing database that included information gathered from a number of sources, including the tariff gas bill database. The aim of the marketing database was to facilitate effective, targeted direct marketing of related and unrelated products and services provided by British Gas Trading Ltd and by third parties. Furthermore, information on the marketing database would also be disclosed to third parties, so that they too could process for direct marketing purposes. Related to this, between March and June 1997, British Gas Trading Ltd billed all of its customers and included with each bill was a notice entitled 'Your Data Protection Rights – the right to choose the information you need'. This notice said:

> ...we would like to write to you from time to time about our current range of products and services, as well as those we will be developing in the future. Also, we would like to send you information about products and services offered by other reputable organisations. In addition, we would like to pass on information about you to the other companies within our group in order that you may receive information about their products and services directly from those companies.

In respect of fairness, the issues in the appeal can be summarized as follows:
- Would customers expect their personal data to be used for direct marketing purposes? This included the transfer of data from the main database to the marketing database as well as the direct marketing itself.
- Was there a distinction between the direct marketing of related products and services and the direct marketing of unrelated products and services?
- Was there a distinction between direct marketing done by British Gas Trading Ltd and direct marketing done by a third party?
- Assuming that all of the notices served between March and June 1997 were received, what could British Gas Trading Ltd do in the case of persons who did not respond?

The Tribunal found that reasonable customers would expect British Gas Trading Ltd to process their personal data for direct marketing purposes, so that the transfer from the main database to the marketing database was not automatically unfair. However, the direct marketing itself could only be for 'gas related products and services', although it did not matter if British Gas Trading Ltd sent information about their own gas-related products and services or information about the products and services provided by a third party. As regards direct marketing done by a third party, this amounted to a disclosure of personal data and was unfair if done without the data subject's consent. Therefore, only British Gas Trading Ltd could carry out the direct marketing processing in the absence of a consent for the transfer to a third party for direct marketing purposes. The Tribunal said:

> We consider that there is a distinction to be made between the use by BGTL and disclosure by BGTL to third parties, albeit to co-subsidiaries . . . the fact that disclosure is inhibited will not prevent BGTL processing personal data itself (without disclosure) so as to send out, for example, the advertising material of a third party provided that it is not for marketing or promoting suppliers or services of a type which otherwise renders processing unfair.

In respect of the final issue, the Data Protection Tribunal said that:

> we do not consider that it is sufficient merely to send to the customer a leaflet providing them with an opportunity to object to their personal data being processed for purposes beyond those gas related purposes to which we have referred. It would, we consider, be sufficient to prevent processing being unfair if individual customers are informed of the type or types of marketing or promotions BGTL would wish to carry out by processing their personal data, provided that they are given the choice to agree or not and either consent then and there, or do not object to such use. Alternatively thereafter, and before such processing takes place, the customer returns a document to BGTL, or by other means of communication received by BGTL indicates consent to, or by not filling in an opt-out box, or other means, indicates no objection to processing for such type or types of marketing or promotion. One such returned document could be, for example, a direct debit mandate form; others could be a part of a bill, or purpose designed leaflet.

The critical point within the Tribunal's analysis of the final issue is that British Gas Trading Ltd could not infer consent from the data subject's failure to respond. This was the effect of the Data Protection Registrar's argument, which the Tribunal paraphrased in the following manner:

> The Registrar holds the view that any intended use must be clear to the data subject at the time at which the information is collected by the data user, unless it can be shown that there has been subsequent consent and that consent cannot be inferred from a lack of response to a circular offering an opt-out. It can be said that a data subject who receives an unwanted leaflet merely has to ignore it or throw it away.

Another interesting case is *Midlands Electricity Plc v. The Data Protection Registrar,*[71] a decision of the Information Tribunal in 1999. This case also concerned unfair processing under the Data Protection Act 1984 and was an appeal from an enforcement notice served by the Data Protection Registrar. The facts are straightforward. Midlands Electricity sent domestic customers a magazine, *Homebright,* with their quarterly bills. The magazine contained information and advice relating to the supply of electricity, such as information about energy conservation and advertisements for unrelated products and services from third-party suppliers, such as holiday promotions. The Tribunal held that this was unfair processing, because there had been an addition to the processing purpose without consent, namely personal data supplied by customers for the purposes of energy supply was being used for direct marketing purposes. This was despite the fact that no personal data was supplied to third parties and despite the fact that the magazine was unlikely to cause offence.

Although this case was decided under the 1984 Act, it is of continuing assistance, as the structure of the first and second data protection principles in the 1984 Act, which deal with fair and lawful processing and the processing purposes respectively, are very similar to the first and second data protection principles in the DPA. Furthermore, although it concerns postal direct marketing communications, the decision reflects the underlying reasoning in the Directive on Privacy and Electronic Communications (DPEC),[72] which allows data controllers to send direct marketing emails on an opt-out basis only if they are about their own related goods and services. Midland Electricity's problem was the sending of information about unrelated goods and services of third parties.

PROCESSING FOR SPECIFIED PURPOSES (THE SECOND DATA PROTECTION PRINCIPLE)

The second data protection principle says that:

> **Personal data shall be obtained only for one or more specified and lawful purposes, and shall not be further processed in any manner incompatible with that purpose or those purposes.**

The second data protection principle is clearly aiming at transparency in that it requires the data controller to inform the data subject prior to the commencement of processing of the specific purpose for the processing. Paragraph 5 of the interpretation identifies two methods for the giving of the information needed to satisfy the second data protection principle:

> **5. The purpose or purposes for which personal data are obtained may in particular be specified –**

> (a) in a notice given for the purposes of paragraph 2 by the data controller to the data subject, or
> (b) in a notification given to the Commissioner under Part III of this Act.

The first method is to specify the processing purpose in the 'notice' given by the data controller for the purpose of supplying the data subject with the prescribed information required by paragraph 2(3) of the interpretation. This method is appropriate because the prescribed information includes 'the purpose or purposes for which the data are intended to be processed'. However, as has already been explained, the obligation to supply the prescribed information does not arise where the data subject already has it, or where one of the exemptions applies.

If the data controller is not obliged to supply the prescribed information (because the data subject already has it or because of an exemption) then it may choose to specify the processing purpose in a notification to the Information Commissioner. The data controller could, if it wished, choose to serve a notice on the data subject despite the fact that none is required for compliance with the fairness part of the first data protection principle. This is because of the use of the word 'may' in the wording of paragraph 5 of the interpretation; the methods set out in 5(a) and (b) are possible methods for specifying the processing purpose, but they are not the only methods.

NOTIFICATION

Notification is the process by which information about data controllers and their data processing operations comes to be included in a publicly accessible register maintained by the Information Commissioner. The obligation to notify arises under section 17 of the DPA, which says that 'personal data must not be processed unless an entry in respect of the data controller is included in the register maintained by the Commissioner'. However, there are some exemptions to the obligation to notify.

The purpose of notification is threefold. By far and away the most important purpose is to foster transparency in data processing activities. Second, notification assists the Information Commissioner in the discharge of their regulatory functions (the register contains an important source of contact information for the Information Commissioner as well as information to enable the development of targeted regulatory strategies). Third, notification indirectly provides a source of funds for the running of the Information Commissioner's office.

Once they have notified, data controllers are obliged to keep their notifications up to date (section 20 of the DPA). Furthermore, they have to renew their notifications on an annual basis (sections 19(4) and 19(5) of the DPA).

Offences

Where the obligation to notify exists it is a criminal offence to process personal data without having first notified (section 21(1) of the DPA) and it is also an offence to continue processing after failing to renew. Additionally, it is a criminal offence to fail to keep notifications up to date (section 21(2) DPA), but a due diligence defence exists for this offence (section 21(3) DPA).

The DPA pierces the corporate veil in the sense that where offences are committed by a corporate body its owners and managers can be personally prosecuted. Section 61(1) of the DPA says:

> Where an offence under this Act has been committed by a body corporate and is proved to have been committed with the consent or connivance of or to be attributable to any neglect on the part of any director, manager, secretary or similar officer of the body corporate or any person who was purporting to act in any such capacity, he as well as the body corporate shall be guilty of that offence and be liable to be proceeded against and punished accordingly.

How to notify

Notification is given under section 19 of the DPA, which requires the data controller to supply the Information Commissioner with 'registrable particulars', a 'general description of the measure to be taken for the purpose of complying with the seventh data protection principle' and the fee. The Data Protection (Notification and Notification Fees) Regulations 2000[73] give the Information Commissioner the power to determine the form in which this information is to be provided.

Registrable particulars

The registrable particulars are identified in section 16(1) of the DPA. They consist of the following pieces of information:

- the data controller's name and address;
- the name and address of the data controller's nominated representative, if there is one;
- a description of the personal data being processed, or to be processed, by or on behalf of the data controller and the category or categories of data subject to which they relate;
- a description of the purpose or purposes for which the data are being, or are to be, processed;
- a description of any recipient or recipients to whom the data controller intends, or may wish, to disclose the data;
- the names, or a description of, any countries or territories outside the EEA to which the data controller directly or indirectly transfers data, or intends or may wish directly or indirectly to transfer data;

- where the data controller is a public authority, a statement of that fact;
- where any personal data are excluded from the obligation to notify due to the exemption for manual data, or the exemption for processing that is unlikely to prejudice the rights and freedoms of data subject, a statement of that fact.

The seventh data protection principle

The seventh data protection principle requires data controllers and data processors to take 'appropriate technical and organisational measures against unauthorised or unlawful processing of personal data and against accidental loss or destruction of, or damage to, personal data'.

The fee

Section 19(4) of the DPA requires the payment of a fee before an entry can be made on the register. The fee is currently £35, set by the Data Protection (Notification and Notification Fees) Regulations 2000. A fee is also charged for annual renewals, again £35.

Additional information in the register

The Information Commissioner is entitled to include the following additional information in the register:
- the registration number issued to the data controller;
- the date of entry in the register;
- the date when the entry will be removed;
- additional information to assist data subjects communicate with the data controller.

The Information Commissioner's approach

The Information Commissioner is given the power to determine the form in which the registrable particulars and the security statement are provided. The current scheme revolves around an application process devised by the Information Commissioner. This scheme is helpful but it is not as efficient as it should be.

Under the Information Commissioner's system data controllers have three choices:
- They can complete the application form contained on the Information Commissioner's website.
- They can telephone the Information Commissioner's office to ask for the forms to be sent to them.
- They can complete the application form over the telephone.

The Information Commissioner's system needs exchange of correspondence by post, for provision of signatures and payment of the fee, which lessens its efficiency. Whichever method is used it is clear that the Information Commissioner is not expecting the data controller to go into significant detail, as the following passage taken from the online process reveals:

> Your notification must include a general description of the processing of personal data being carried out. We ask data controllers to bear in mind when providing information for notification not to go into unnecessary detail. The aim is to keep the content at a general level with sufficient detail to give an overall picture of the processing.

The Information Commissioner's system is based around a series of templates. The current templates fall into the following categories:

- general;
- education;
- finance;
- health;
- legal;
- leisure;
- local and central government ;
- public bodies;
- religious/political/charitable;
- services.

The templates identify in very general terms the particular aspects of processing falling within the scope of notification, such as the classes of data subjects and category of records. Data controllers can amend the templates or, if no template is suitable they can select from options to build a bespoke notification.

The Information Commissioner's system deals with the requirement for a security statement through a series of questions that require the data controller to select either yes or no answers. The full questions as they are currently appearing on the Information Commissioner's website (www.ico.gov.uk) are as follows:

> Have you taken any measures to guard against unauthorised or unlawful processing of personal data and against accidental loss, destruction or damage? If yes do the methods include:
>
> - Adopting an information security policy? (i.e. providing clear management direction on responsibilities and procedures in order to safeguard personal data)
>
> - Taking steps to control physical security? (for example, locking doors of the office or building where computer equipment is held)
>
> - Putting in place controls on access to information? (for example, introduction of password protection on files containing personal data and encryption)

- Establishing a business continuity plan? (for example, holding a backup file in the event of personal data being lost through flood, fire or other catastrophe)

- Training your staff on security systems and procedures?

- Detecting and investigating breaches of security when they occur?

- Adopting the British Standard on Information Security Management BS7799? (This standard is not a statutory requirement but a business led approach to best practice on information security management.)

The online process explains these questions in this fashion:

Data controllers must give a general description of the measures to be taken for the purpose of protecting against unauthorised or unlawful processing of personal data and against accidental loss or destruction of or damage to personal data. The description does not appear in the public register. Answering the questions provided satisfies the requirement to provide that description. The questions are at a very general level but cover some of the key requirements of effective information security management.

If the data controller uses the online process, it must print a copy of the completed form, sign it and then send it to the Information Commissioner with the fee.

The Data Protection (Notification and Notification Fees) Regulations 2000 identify the Information Commissioner's obligations as they arise following receipt of a notification. The order requires the Information Commissioner to give the data controller a notice confirming the making of an entry in the register 'as soon as practicable and in any event within a period of 28 days after making an entry in the register'. The date when the entry is deemed to have been made in the register is calculated by reference to the postal method used by the data controller for the sending of its signed form. If registered post or recorded delivery is used, the date of entry in the register is the day after the day on which it is received for dispatch at the post office. If ordinary post is used, the date of entry in the register is the date when the notification is received by the Information Commissioner.

Information Commissioner's guidance on notification

The Information Commissioner's 'Legal Guidance' contains very helpful information on notification. In addition, the Information Commissioner has published a comprehensive 45-page 'Notification Handbook'[74] and a 'Self Assessment Guide'[75] explaining how the notification exemptions work in practice.

Obtaining copies of register entries

Section 19(6) of the DPA requires the Information Commissioner to provide facilities 'for making the information contained in the entries in the register available for inspection (in visible and legible form) by members of the public at all reasonable hours and free of charge'. The current facilities consist of the searchable online register, which is accessible from the Information Commissioner's website.

The Information Commissioner is also obliged to 'supply any member of the public with a duly certified copy in writing of the particulars contained in any entry made in the register'. A £2 fee is currently charged for this service.[76]

Keeping notifications up to date

Section 20 of the DPA permits the making of regulations in order to ensure that notifications are kept up to date. Again, the Data Protection (Notification and Notification Fees) Regulations 2000 apply. The obligation placed on the data controller is to notify the Information Commissioner of any respect in which an entry on the register becomes inaccurate or incomplete and to set out the changes that are recorded to make the entry accurate or complete. The notification of the inaccuracy must be given as soon as is practicable but never later than 28 days after the date that the entry in the register became inaccurate or incomplete.

The exemptions

There are a number of very important exemptions to the obligation to notify. These are:
- for safeguarding national security;
- for manual data;
- processing for the purpose of maintaining a public record;
- processing that is unlikely to prejudice the rights and freedoms of data subjects.

National security exemption

Section 28(1) of the DPA says that processing is exempt from the requirement to notify if the exemption is required for the purpose of safeguarding national security.

Manual data exemption

Section 17(2) of the DPA contains the exemption for manual data. It says that except where the processing is 'assessable processing', the prohibition on processing without having first notified does not apply 'in relation to personal data consisting of information which falls neither within paragraph (a) of the definition of "data" in section 1(1) nor within paragraph (b) of that definition'. The categories of data were discussed in Chapter 1 and it will be recalled that the first category concerns data being processed, or to be processed, by equipment operating automatically, while the second category concerns data recorded with the intention that it will be processed by equipment operating automatically.

The manual data exemption does not apply in respect of assessable processing. Section 22 of the DPA describes assessable processing as 'processing which is of a description specified in an order made by the Secretary of State as appearing to him to be particularly likely to cause substantial damage or substantial distress to data subjects, or otherwise significantly to prejudice the rights and freedoms of data subjects'. At the date of publication of this book the Secretary of State has not made any orders under section 22.

Public record exemption

This exemption is contained in section 17(4) of the DPA. It says in very succinct terms that the prohibition on processing without having first notified does not apply in relation to 'any processing whose sole purpose is the maintenance of a public register'.

Processing unlikely to prejudice rights and freedoms of data subjects

The Data Protection (Notification and Notification Fees) Regulations 2000[77] contain a series of exemptions for processing that the Secretary of State considers is unlikely to prejudice the rights and freedoms of data subjects. The power given to the Secretary of State to exempt processing of this nature is contained in section 17(3) of the DPA. If the data controller is processing personal data falling within this section it must state so in its registrable particulars (section 16(g) of the DPA).

This series of exemptions is for:

- processing for the purposes of staff administration;
- processing for the purposes of advertising, marketing and public relations;
- processing for the purposes of accounts and records;
- processing by non-profit-making organizations.

Each of the exemptions in this series identifies the exempt processing purposes, the kinds of data subjects falling within the exemption, the categories of personal data that may be processed within the exemption, the circumstances in which the personal data may be disclosed to a third party and the period for which the personal data may be retained.

The staff administration exemption is set out in paragraph 2 of the Schedule to the Regulations and it applies only to a limited category of processing purposes, all related to staff administration. These exempt purposes are 'appointments or removals, pay, discipline, superannuation, work management or other personnel matters in relation to the staff of the data controller' (paragraph 2(a)).

The personal data falling within this exemption must relate to a data subject falling within one of the categories in the Regulations, namely a past, existing or prospective member of staff of the data controller or 'any person the processing of whose personal data is necessary for the exempt purposes' (paragraph 2(b)). Furthermore, the personal data falling within the exemption is of a limited type, namely 'personal data consisting of the name, address and other identifiers of the data subject or information as to qualifications, work experience or pay or other matters the processing of which is necessary for the exempt purposes' (paragraph 2(c)).

The exemption tolerates only limited disclosures to third parties, namely disclosure with the consent of the data subject or disclosure that is necessary for the exempt purpose (paragraph 2(d)). Finally, the exemption requires destruction or deletion of the personal data after the relationship between the data controller and the staff member ends, unless retention is necessary for the exempt purpose (paragraph 2(d)).

The advertising, marketing and public relations exemption falls within paragraph 3 of the Schedule to the Regulations. The exempt purposes are processing 'for the purposes of advertising or marketing the data controller's business, activity, goods or services and promoting public relations in connection with that business or activity, or those goods or services'. The data subjects falling within the exemption are past, existing or prospective customers or suppliers, or any person the processing of whose personal data is necessary for the exempt purposes. The personal data that may be processed are 'personal data consisting of the name, address and other identifiers of the data subject or information as to other matters the processing of which is necessary for the exempt purposes'. The rules on disclosures to third parties and retention periods are the same as those contained in the staff administration exemption.

The accounts and records exemption falls within paragraph 4 of the Schedule to the Regulations. The exempt processing purposes are processing:

- for the purposes of keeping accounts relating to any business or other activity carried on by the data controller;
- deciding whether to accept any person as a customer or supplier;
- keeping records of purchases, sales or other transactions for the purpose of ensuring that the requisite payments and deliveries are made or services provided by or to the data controller in respect of those transactions;
- for the purpose of making financial or management forecasts to assist the data controller in the conduct of any such business or activity.

The data subjects falling within the exemption are the same as for the advertising, marketing and public relations exemption. The personal data falling within the exemption is name, address and other identifiers of the data subject, or information as to financial standing, or other matters the processing of which is necessary for the exempt purposes. The rules on disclosures to third parties and retention periods are the same as those contained in the staff administration exemption and the advertising, marketing and public relations exemption. This exemption does not apply to personal data processed by, or obtained from, a credit reference agency.

The non-profit-making organizations' exemption falls within paragraph 5 of the Schedule to the Regulations and it applies only where the processing is 'carried out by a data controller which is a body or association which is not established or conducted for profit'. The exempt purposes are processing 'for the purposes of establishing or maintaining membership of or support for the body or association, or providing or administering activities for individuals who are either members of the body or association or have regular contact with it'. The data subjects are past, existing or prospective members of the body or organization, any person who has regular contact with the body or organization in connection with the exempt purposes, or any person the processing of whose personal data is necessary for the exempt purposes. The personal data falling within the exemption are personal data consisting of the name, address and other identifiers of the data subject, or information as to eligibility for membership of the body or association, or other matters the processing of which is necessary for the exempt purposes. The rules on disclosures to third parties and data retention are the same as before.

Notification and processing for domestic purposes

Processing done for purely domestic purposes is completely exempt from the DPA, under section 36.

Exempt processing and supplying relevant particulars

Where the manual data and the processing that is unlikely to prejudice the rights and freedoms of data subjects exemptions apply, data controllers will still be obliged to supply 'relevant particulars' (section 24 DPA). This obligation arises when the data controller receives a written request from any person. Where such a request is received the data controller must supply the relevant particulars within 21 days, free of charge.

Failure to comply with a written request for relevant particulars is a criminal offence, although it is a defence for a data controller to show that it exercised all due diligence to comply.

The relevant particulars are:

- the data controller's name and address;
- the name and address of the data controller's nominated representative, if there is one;
- a description of the personal data being processed or to be processed by, or on behalf of, the data controller and the category or categories of data subject to which they relate;
- a description of the purpose or purposes for which the data are being, or are to be, processed;

- a description of any recipient or recipients to whom the data controller intends, or may wish, to disclose the data;
- the names, or a description of, any countries or territories outside the EEA to which the data controller directly or indirectly transfers, or intends, or may wish, directly or indirectly to transfer, the data.

Notification by partnerships and schools

Special rules apply for notification by partnerships and schools.[78] These state that partnerships can register in the name of the firm, giving the principal place of business as the address. Processing done on behalf of schools by school governors and head teachers may be notified in the name of the school.

It is worth noting that no special rules apply for groups of companies. Each individual company within a group must notify, unless an exemption applies.

Voluntary notification

Data controllers who can claim an exemption from notification may choose to notify on a voluntary basis, although this option is not available where the national security exemption applies or where personal data is processed for personal, domestic or recreational purposes. A data controller who elects to notify on a voluntary basis will not be able to undo its election at a later date and will therefore be bound by the full provisions of the notification regime until it stops processing.

THE RIGHT OF ACCESS TO PERSONAL DATA

The right of access to personal data is probably the most important and controversial of the transparency provisions. Unlike the others, the right of access is within the control of data subjects, the people most incentivized to protect their own personal data.

In brief, the right of access gives the data subject the right to information about the data controller and its data processing activities, information that has to be provided within a short timeframe and for a nominal fee. In theory, the right of access gives the data subject a route to the very heart of government, public sector and business activity. However, there are many important exemptions to the right of access.

According to the Data Protection Directive the right of access exists to enable the data subject to verify the accuracy of the data and the lawfulness of the processing (Recital 41). In the case of *Durant v. Financial Services Authority*,[79] Lord Justice Auld described the purpose of the right of access in the following terms:

> In conformity with the 1981 Convention and the Directive, the purpose of [the right of access], in entitling an individual to have access to information

in the form of his 'personal data' is to enable him to check whether the data controller's processing of it unlawfully infringes his privacy and, if so, to take such steps as the Act provides, for example in sections 10 to 14, to protect it. It is not an automatic key to any information, readily accessible or not, of matters in which he may be named or involved. Nor is to assist him, for example, to obtain discovery of documents that may assist him in litigation or complaints against third parties.

The right of access within the DPA and the sixth data protection principle

The right of access is contained section 7 of the DPA. Section 7 is supplemented by section 8. Section 9 applies the right of access to situations where the data controller is a credit reference agency. Section 9A deals with the right of access where it concerns unstructured personal data held by public authorities.

Compliance with the right of access is elevated in importance by the sixth data protection principle, which says that 'personal data shall be processed in accordance with the rights of data subjects under this Act'. The interpretation within Schedule 1, Part II of the DPA says that the sixth data protection principle will be contravened if the data controller 'contravenes section 7 by failing to supply information in accordance with that section'.

The core entitlements

The right of access actually consists of a series of rights, identified in section 7(1) of the DPA. The first right, set out in section 7(1)(a), entitles the data subject 'to be informed by any data controller whether personal data of which that individual is the data subject are being processed by or on behalf of that data controller'. This initial entitlement may be regarded as a duty to confirm or deny the fact of data processing, which means that a data controller receiving an access request should always reply, even if it is only to deny that it is processing the data subject's personal data.

If the data controller confirms that it is processing the data subject's personal data then the other rights are engaged, which may be said to fall within two categories. In broad terms, these may be described as (1) a right to various descriptions and (2) a right to have information communicated.

The descriptions

If the data controller is processing the data subject's personal data, then it must describe those data, the purposes for which they are being processed and the recipients, or classes of recipients, to whom they are or may be disclosed. These rights are contained in section 7(1)(b)(i)–(iii) of the DPA. The DPA does not provide any assistance with the level of detail that is required in the descriptions.

A useful exercise might be to return to the topic of notification, as it will be seen that the descriptions mirror closely some of the key requirements within the registrable particulars. This close connection in subject matter suggests an equally close connection in terms of the detail to be provided and it has already been explained that during the notification process the Information Commissioner seeks only a 'general description of the processing of personal data being carried out';[80] indeed, he positively discourages the data controller from going into too much detail.

The best answer, which may not be a satisfactory answer, must be that the detail that is required will be determined by the circumstances of the particular case. Unusual or non-obvious processing purposes or recipients are likely to require more description than the more ordinary or routine.

The communication of information

The information to be communicated, if the data controller is processing the data subject's personal data, is identified in section 7(c)(i)–(ii) of the DPA. The information identified is:

- the information constituting the data subject's personal data (section 7(1)(c)(i) DPA);
- any information available to the data controller as to the source of the information (section 7(1)(c)(ii) DPA).

Both pieces of information must be communicated to the data subject 'in an intelligible form'. The data subject's right to receive the personal data in an intelligible form involves two elements, set out in section 8(2) of the DPA. The first is that a copy of the information must be provided in permanent form, unless that is not possible or would involve disproportionate effort, or unless the data subject agrees not to receive a permanent copy. Second, if the copy of the information contains terms that are not intelligible, it must be accompanied by an explanation of the terms, also in permanent form.

Concerning 'disproportionate effort' the Information Commissioner provides the following assistance:[81]

> 'Disproportionate effort' is not defined in the Act. Accordingly, it will be a question of fact in each case as to whether the supply of information in permanent form amounts to disproportionate effort. Matters to be taken into account by the Commissioner may be the cost of provision of the information, the length of time it may take to provide the information, how difficult or otherwise it may be for the data controller to provide the information and also the size of the organisation of which the request has been made. Such matters will always be balanced against the effect on the data subject.

The data subject's right to a copy of the information in permanent form does not oblige the data controller to provide a print out of the electronic file, or photocopies of the documents within a relevant filing system. Instead, the data controller may create a new document, electronic or manual, and may send that to the data subject. Provided that the new document contains an accurate copy of the personal data in the documents existing at the date of receipt of the access request, this approach is valid. The key to under-standing why this is the case turns on understanding the difference between information and a carrier of information.

> **EXAMPLE**
>
> A relevant filing system houses an important manual document that contains information about the data subject that seriously affects their privacy. The data subject makes a request for access to their personal data under section 7. When preparing its response the data controller creates an electronic file on a PC in which it accurately summarizes the information contained in the manual document. The data controller then prints out the electronic summary and sends it to the data subject within the 40-day prescribed period. In this scenario the data controller's actions are perfectly consistent with the DPA, because the right of access is a right of access to information, not documents. The manual document in the relevant filing system is merely a carrier for the information within it.

This distinction between information and documents was touched upon in *Durant v. Financial Services Authority*.[82] Lord Justice Auld explained:

> In September and October 2001, Mr Durant made two requests to the FSA under section 7 of the Act, seeking disclosure of personal data held by it, both electronically and in manual files. In October 2001 the FSA provided Mr Durant with copies of documents relating to him that it held in computerised form, disclosure that went beyond his entitlement under the Act, which is to have communicated to him in an intelligible form 'information constituting any personal data' of which he was the subject.

The communication of the logic of automated decisions

Section 7(1)(d) contains an additional right to information in certain cases where a data controller uses automated equipment to take decisions about the data subject. These decisions must be completely automated and they must be ones that significantly affect the data subject. The decisions falling within this section must be for the purpose of evaluating matters relating to the data subject and some examples are given in the section, namely the evaluation of the data subject's performance at work, their creditworthiness, their reliability or their conduct.

In these cases section 7(1)(d) requires the data controller to communicate to the data subject the 'logic involved' in the decision taking. However, section 8(5) of the DPA sets out an exemption from this obligation, which applies if the logic involved in any decision taking is a trade secret. This exemption is commonly used by data controllers who provide credit to their customers, to avoid giving information about their credit scoring systems.

The information to be provided

The general rule set out in section 8(6) of the DPA is that the information to be provided in response to an access request is the information in existence at the date of receipt of the request. This was examined in the first trial in *Smith v. Lloyds TSB Bank Plc*,[83] where the claimant sought to enforce his rights under section 7 through an application made under section 7(9).

In *Smith* one of the biggest problems faced by the claimant was the fact that by the time he made his access request the defendant no longer possessed any electronic files, only manual files. According to the claimant's barrister, if these manual files were printed from electronic files the 'once processed always processed' argument would cause the manual files to be treated as part of the original automated processing so that the information contained within them would be discloseable under section 7, despite the fact that the manual files were not part of a relevant filing system. The judge, Mr Justice Laddie, rejected this argument, pointing to section 8(6) of the DPA, which restricts the data subject's right of access to the information being processed at the date of receipt of the access request.

Of course, the reality in many cases is that the data subject's personal data might be subject to continual processing with the result that amendment or deletions may occur after receipt of the access request. In these situations the DPA does not require the data controller to stop processing. Instead it may take account of the amendment or deletion and provide the information in existence at the date of the response, not the information in existence at the date of receipt of the access request.

Conversely, the data controller may not amend or delete personal data following receipt of an access request if the amendment or deletion is merely a response to the access request, perhaps to avoid supplying information. To do so would amount to a breach of the access regime.

The formalities of a valid access request

The DPA prescribes a number of formal requirements for the making of a valid request for personal data. These are:

- The request must be made in writing. A request made electronically, such as by email, will count as a written request.
- The written request must be accompanied by the fee, if one is charged.
- The data subject must supply any further information that is reasonably required by the data controller to enable it to be satisfied of the data subject's identity and to enable it to locate the information sought. Of course, the data controller must notify the data subject that it requires this additional information.

Extent of the request

In summary the rights granted to data subjects under section 7 of the DPA are as follows:

- a right to be told whether or not their personal data are being processed by or on behalf of the data controller (section 7(1)(a));
- if their data are being processed, a right to a description of the personal data being processed, a right to a description of the processing purposes and a right to a description of the recipients, or classes of recipient, to whom the data are, or may be, disclosed (sections 7(1)(b)(i)–(iii));
- if their data are being processed, a right to have the personal data communicated in an intelligible form and a right to have communicated any information available to the data controller about the source of the data (section 7(1)(c));
- where the processing is by automatic means for the purpose evaluating matters relating to the data subject and it has constituted or is likely to constitute the sole basis of any decision significantly affecting the data subject, a right to be informed of the logic involved in the decision taking (section 7(1)(d)).

Data subjects may choose to limit their requests to specific information that is described in the request (section 7(7) of the DPA), but if they wish to do this they must make this clear and the fact that a data subject may have merely referred to only one of the rights in section 7 does not entitle the data controller to limit the response.[84] The current Regulations[85] say that a request for information under any provision of sections 7(1)(a),(b) or (c) of the DPA is to be treated as extending also to all other provisions of sections 7(1)(a), (b) and (c).

Conversely, a request under any provision of section 7(1) of the DPA is to be treated as extending to information under section 7(1)(d) only where the request shows an express intention to that effect and a request under section 7(1)(d) is to be treated as extending also to information under any other provision of section 7(1) only where the request shows an express intention to that effect.

Repeated requests

The DPA contains a very important rule against the making of repeated requests. Section 8(3) says that where a data controller has previously complied with a request it is not obliged to comply with a subsequent identical or similar request unless a reasonable period has elapsed between compliance with the previous request and the making of the current request. Section 8(4) identifies the relevant considerations for determining whether a reasonable period has elapsed between requests. It says that 'regard shall be had to the nature of the data, the purpose for which the data are processed and the frequency with which the data are altered'.

Fees

The data controller is not obliged to charge a fee for responding to requests for access to personal data, but where a fee is charged the data controller must make this fact known. The maximum fee that can be charged is currently £10, unless the request is made to a credit reference agency or where the request is for an educational record. For requests made to credit reference agencies the maximum fee is currently £2 and for educational records the maximum fee is currently £50.[86]

The time for responding

The DPA requires data controllers to comply with requests promptly and, in any event, 'before the end of the prescribed period beginning with the relevant day' (section 7(8) DPA).

The prescribed period

The prescribed period for responding to an access request is 40 days (section 7(10) DPA), unless the data controller is a credit reference agency, or unless the request is for an educational record. Where the data controller is a credit reference agency the prescribed period is seven working days and where the request is for an educational record the prescribed period is 15 school days.[87]

There is a modification for the period for responding where the request concerns examination marks and the request is received before the announcement of the examination results.

The relevant day

For the purpose of calculating the time for responding, the relevant day is a vital component. The relevant day is described in section 7(9) as:

> **the day on which the data controller receives the request or, if later, the first day on which the data controller has both the required fee and the information referred to in subsection (3).**

The reference to subsection (3) is a reference to the data controller's right to request any further information that is reasonably required to enable it to be satisfied of the data subject's identity and to enable it to locate the information sought.

Requests involving third-party data

The DPA makes provision for the situation where an access request, if complied with, would involve the disclosure of information relating to a third party. The starting position, contained in section 7(4) of the DPA, is that the data controller does not have to comply with an access request if compliance would require it to disclose information relating to another identified or identifiable individual. Indeed, in the case of *Durant v. Financial Services*

Authority[88] the Court of Appeal said that section 7(4) creates a presumption against the disclosure of information relating to an identified or identifiable third party. The reason for this exemption is to ensure protection of the third party's privacy.

The presumption against disclosure is a rebuttable one, however, meaning that there are circumstances where disclosure of third-party information is allowed.

References merely identifying third party as the source

The third-party information protected by the exemption includes information that merely identifies the third party as the source of the information sought by the data subject, in distinction to information that has the third party as its focus. In these cases the data controller will not be excused from complying with the access request if the information sought can be communicated without identifying the third party, perhaps by editing out the information identifying the third party (section 7(5) DPA).

> **EXAMPLE**
>
> A data subject delivers a written access request to their employer asking for disclosure of the information within their personnel file. The personnel file includes a letter of complaint about the data subject written by a co-worker who signed it at the bottom. Apart from the co-worker's signature the letter of complaint contains no other information relating to the co-worker. In this example the exemption protecting third-party information extends to the co-worker's signature, as this identifies the co-worker as the source of the complaint. However, as the employer can easily remove any evidence of the co-worker's name, the prohibition in section 7(4) DPA does not excuse the data controller from complying with the access request.

Cases where the exemption does not apply

The exemption within section 7(4) does not apply in three cases. These are:

- The third party has consented to the disclosure to the data subject of information that identifies the third party (section 7(4)(a) DPA).
- It is reasonable in all the circumstances to comply with the access request without the consent of the third party (section 7(4)(b) DPA).
- The third-party information is contained in a health record and the third party is a health professional who has compiled, or contributed to, a health record relating to the data subject, or who has been involved in the care of the data subject in their capacity as a health professional (section 7(4)(c) DPA).

As regards the second case, disclosure of the information relating to the third party without consent, the data controller is required to balance the interests of the data subject against the interests of the third party. In performing this balancing exercise section 7(6) of the DPA identifies a series of factors that are to be considered by the data controller. These are:

- any duty of confidence owed to the third party;
- the steps taken by the data controller with a view to seeking the consent of the third party;
- whether the third party is capable of giving consent;
- any express refusal of consent by the third party.

In *Durant v. Financial Services Authority* the Court of Appeal was cautious to emphasize that on an examination of the data controller's decision it is not the Court's role to 'second-guess' the data controller. In addition, the Court of Appeal declined the opportunity to lay down any general principles for the performance of the balancing exercise, although it was willing to identify the process that data controllers must adopt when considering whether it is reasonable in all the circumstances to disclose without consent the information relating to a third party.

The first step for the data controller is to consider whether the information relating to the third party forms part of the data subject's personal data. If it does not, no question arises under section 7(4) and the data controller does not need to disclose the information. If the information relating to the third party does form part of the data subject's personal data, the second step is the carrying out of the balancing exercise itself. The Court of Appeal said that when carrying out the balancing exercise much will depend upon the criticality of the third-party information to the protection of the data subject's privacy, which is then balanced against any obligations of confidence owed to the third party and the sensitivity of the third-party information.

Access requests where the data controller is a credit reference agency

Section 9 of the DPA modified section 7 to address the situation where the data controller is a credit reference agency. The starting position is that the data subject is taken to have limited their access requests to personal data relevant to their financial standing, unless the access request shows a contrary intention. Section 7 is also modified to require the data controller to provide the data subject with a statement in a prescribed format of their rights under section 159 of the Consumer Credit Act 1974. In summary, section 159 of the Consumer Credit Act requires the individual to be informed of their rights to make objections to inaccurate information within their credit files. The prescribed format for the giving of this statement is contained in Schedule 1 to the Consumer Credit (Credit Reference Agency) Regulations 2000.[89]

The credit reference agency must provide its file within seven working days. The maximum fee that may be charged for provision of the file is currently £2.

Access requests for unstructured manual data held by public authorities

It will be recalled that the fifth category of data is recorded information held by a public authority that is manual data. There are two kinds of data within this category: data that is structured to a lesser extent than a relevant filing system and data that is unstructured. Section 9A modifies the right of access in respect of unstructured data. This section was inserted into the DPA by section 69(2) of the Freedom of Information Act 2000.

The starting point is that a public authority is not obliged to comply with an access request relating to unstructured personal data unless the request contains a description of the data. If the request does contain a description of the data, the public authority is still not obliged to comply with the duty to confirm or deny within section 7(1)(a) if the cost of complying with that duty would exceed 'the appropriate limit'. The appropriate limit is defined in Regulations.[90] In the case of government departments, the Houses of Parliament, the Northern Ireland and Welsh Assemblies and most of the armed forces, the appropriate limit is currently £600. For all other public authorities the appropriate limit is currently £450.

Court applications to order compliance

The data subject may enforce the right of access in court by making an application under section 7(9) of the DPA. The court will only make an order if the data subject satisfies it that the data controller has failed to comply in contravention of section 7.

In many cases the court may need to see the information that is processed by the data controller before it can determine whether or not there has been a contravention of section 7. Therefore, section 15(2) gives the court the power to order the data controller to deliver the data to it, so that it may examine it. However, pending determination of the matter in the data subject's favour the court may not allow the data subject to have access to the data.

The case of *Durant v. Financial Services Authority* was brought under section 7(9). In determination of the dispute the court used its powers under section 15(2) to view the disputed data. Of course, Mr Durant was not allowed to see the data.

The right of access and the relationship with litigation disclosure

Parties involved in civil litigation are obliged to give disclosure of documents that are relevant to the issues in the case, including documents that will assist the opponent. In England and Wales litigation disclosure is governed by the Civil Procedure Rules 1999.

Although subject access is about access to information, not documents, there is clearly an overlap between this area and litigation disclosure, but it should not be thought that the focus is the same. Indeed, in *Durant v. Financial Services Authority* Lord Justice Auld pointed out that the right of access 'is not an automatic key to any information, readily accessible or not, of matters in which he may be named or involved. Nor is it to assist him, for example, to obtain discovery of documents that may assist him in litigation or complaints against third parties.'

The relationship between subject access and litigation disclosure was explored further in *Johnson v. Medical Defence Union*,[91] at the second preliminary trial. On this occasion Mr Johnson sought disclosure under the Civil Procedure Rules of the very same documents that he failed to secure access to at the first preliminary trial. The defendant again resisted Mr Johnson's application, arguing that the DPA prevented access to the documents sought. This time Mr Justice Laddie was against the defendant:

> It follows that Mr Johnson's application for disclosure in relation to his claims for breaches by the MDU of the data protection principles is not disposed of by the fact that he failed on his claim under s 7(9). The fact that, in determining the latter application, I looked at documents which, because of s 15(2), Mr Johnson and his lawyers were not allowed to see, does not mean that if some of those documents are relevant to his claims under ss 10, 13 and 14, Mr Johnson cannot seek disclosure of them.

Exemptions in Part IV of the DPA

There are many exemptions to the right of access. These are discussed in the section 'Part IV exemptions', below.

INFORMATION NOTICES

Part V of the DPA is titled 'Enforcement' and it describes a number of very important powers that vest in the Information Commissioner. In the widest sense of the word all enforcement powers aid transparency, but in this section it is only the Information Commissioner's power to serve information notices and special information notices that are considered, as they have the closest direct link with transparency.

The essence of both kinds of information notice is that they require the data controller to supply the Information Commissioner with information to enable the Information Commissioner to properly discharge their statutory functions. This immediately demonstrates the importance of information notices within the legal regime and data controllers will not be surprised to learn that the failure to comply with an information notice is a criminal offence. If the data controller believes that the notice should not have been served, or if it objects to providing some of the information sought, it must appeal to the Information Tribunal.

Information notices

Section 43 of the DPA empowers the Information Commissioner to serve an information notice on a data controller in two circumstances. The first is where the Information Commissioner has received a request for an assessment under section 42 of the DPA. The second is where the Information Commissioner reasonably requires any information 'for the purpose of determining whether the data controller has complied or is complying with the data protection principles'.

The information notice will require the data controller to supply the Information Commissioner with the information specified in the notice in the form specified, within the time specified. The notice may ask the data controller to provide specific information about how it has complied with the data protection principles.

The notice must identify whether the Information Commissioner has received a request for an assessment or whether the Information Commissioner regards the specified information as being relevant for the purpose of their determination of whether the data controller has complied, or is complying, with the data protection principles. If the latter case applies, the Information Commissioner must also state their reasons for regarding the information as being relevant to the determination of the question of compliance with the principles. Finally, the information notice must specify the data controller's rights of appeal.

Requests for assessments

Section 42 of the DPA provides that a person who believes that they have been directly affected by the processing of any personal data may make a request to the Information Commissioner for an assessment as to whether it is likely or unlikely that the processing has been carried out in accordance with the DPA.

The Information Commissioner has discretion as to the manner of their assessment, but it would seem to be the case that they can only to refuse to carry out an assessment if they consider that they do not have enough information to enable them to be satisfied of the identity of the person making the request and to enable them to identify the processing in question. The Information Commissioner may ask the applicant to supply them with additional information to prove the applicant's identity and the identity of the processing in question (section 42(2)).

Section 42(3) identifies factors that the Information Commissioner may have regard to in determining the manner of his assessment. These include:

- the extent to which the request raises a matter of substance;
- any undue delay in making the request;
- whether the applicant could make an access request under section 7.

Special information notices

Section 44 of the DPA says that the Information Commissioner may serve a special information notice in two circumstances. The first is where a request for an assessment has been received under section 42 of the DPA. The second is much more complicated, applying where court proceedings have been stayed under section 32 of the DPA.

Section 32(4) of the DPA says that the court may stay legal proceedings brought under sections 7(9), 10(4), 12(8) or 14 of the DPA where it appears to the court that any personal data to which the proceedings relate are being processed only for the special purposes and with a view to the publication by any person of any previously unpublished journalistic, literary or artistic material. In such a case the proceedings will remain stayed until they are either withdrawn or until the Information Commissioner makes a determination under section 45 of the DPA. Section 45 gives the Information Commissioner the power to 'determine' that personal data are not being processed for the special purposes or are not being processed with a view to the publication.

Where proceedings have been stayed under section 32, the Information Commissioner may serve a special information notice on the data controller, but only where they have reasonable grounds for suspecting that personal data to which the proceedings relate are not being processed only for the special purposes or are not being processed with a view to the publication by any person of any previously unpublished journalistic, literary or artistic material.

Thus, the purpose of special information notices is twofold:

- to ascertain whether personal data are being processed only for the special purposes;
- to ascertain whether the personal data are being processed with a view to the publication by any person of any previously unpublished journalistic, literary or artistic material.

If the special information notice is served as a result of a request for an assessment, the notice must state this fact. If it is served because the Information Commissioner suspects that the personal data are not being processed only for the special purposes or are not being processed with a view to the publication by any person of any previously unpublished journalistic, literary or artistic material, it must state this fact and state the Information Commissioner's grounds for their suspicion. As with information notices, the right of appeal must be stated.

Time for compliance

The service of information notices and special information notices can both be appealed by the data controller. In order to cater for the making of an appeal, the DPA says that the time for providing the information sought shall not expire before the end of the period in which an appeal can be brought (section 43(3) and section 44(5)).

The time for bringing an appeal is specified in Rules made under the DPA[92] and is currently 28 days calculated from the date on which the notice was served on, or given to, the data controller. If an appeal is brought within time, the information does not need to be supplied pending the determination of the appeal, or its withdrawal.

This rule is subject to an important exception, however. In cases where the Information Commissioner considers that the information is required as a matter of urgency they may require its supply before the expiry of the time for appealing, although this is subject to a minimum time for compliance of seven days. This commences with the day on which the notice is served. If the Information Commissioner wishes to rely upon this exception, they must state the reasons for their conclusion that the information is required as a matter of urgency.

Legal professional privilege and the privilege from self-incrimination

The data controller is not required to supply the information if it is protected by legal professional privilege or the privilege against self-incrimination.

Appeals and offences

These matters are discussed in Chapter 7.

PART IV EXEMPTIONS

Part IV of the DPA is titled 'Exemptions'. These exemptions cover more than the exemptions from transparency provisions considered here, namely exemptions from the fair processing requirements, from the requirement to process for specified purposes (the second data protection principle) and from the right of access. These exemptions are additional to those already mentioned.

Section 36 of the DPA contains a complete exemption for processing done for domestic purposes, which is processing 'by an individual only for the purposes of that individual's personal family or household affairs (including recreational purposes)'. This is the DPA's only complete exemption. However, section 28 of the DPA creates the possibility of an equally comprehensive exemption covering processing that is 'required for the purposes of safeguarding national security'.

The remaining exemptions within Part IV are only partial exemptions, meaning that some of the DPA's requirements will survive the exemptions.

The partial exemptions fall into two categories:

- **Class-based exemptions**: If the processing of personal data is of the class described in the exemption, the exemption will apply.
- **Prejudice-based exemptions**: These exemptions require proof or likelihood of prejudice to certain specified interests.

The subject information provisions

Section 27 of the DPA, the first section in Part IV, contains preliminary provisions. This section introduces two important concepts, namely 'the subject information provisions' and 'the non-disclosure provisions'. The subject information provisions are paragraph 2 of Schedule 1, Part II of the Act in combination with section 7. To recap, paragraph 2 of Schedule 1, Part II forms part of the interpretation to the data protection principles and says that personal data are not to be treated as obtained fairly unless the prescribed information in paragraph 2(3) of the interpretation is provided.

Crime and taxation

Among other things section 29(1) contains a partial exemption from the first data protection principle and from section 7, meaning that the data controller does not have to comply with the fair processing requirements. Even if this exemption applies, the data controller will still be obliged to satisfy a Schedule 2 condition (and a Schedule 3 condition if sensitive personal data are processed) and will have to comply with the right of access. This exemption applies where the personal data are processed for:

- the prevention or detection of crime;
- the apprehension or prosecution of offenders; or
- the assessment or collection of any tax or duty,

but only if the provision of that information would be likely to prejudice one of these interests.

If the personal data falling within the section 29(1) exemption are disclosed to another data controller for the purposes of discharging a statutory function, section 29(2) will provide an exemption from the subject information provisions in order to prevent prejudice to the discharge of the statutory function.

Health, education and social work

Section 30(1) gives the Secretary of State the power to exempt from the subject information provisions, or modify those provisions, processing of personal data where the purpose is health, education or social work. In pursuance of these powers a series of three orders have been passed:

- The Data Protection (Subject Access Modification) (Health) Order 2000;[93]
- The Data Protection (Subject Access Modification) (Education) Order 2000;[94]
- The Data Protection (Subject Access Modification) (Social Work) Order 2000.[95]

The Data Protection (Subject Access Modification) (Health) Order 2000

This order applies to personal data consisting of information as to the physical or mental health or condition of the data subject. The focus of this order is:

- The processing of health data by courts: Where personal data consisting of health data are processed by the courts as a result of reports supplied by, or evidence given by, certain public authorities, the subject information provisions will not apply.

- The right of access in section 7 is exempted if its application would 'be likely to cause serious harm to the physical or mental health or condition of the data subject or any other person'. Data controllers who are not health professionals must consult an appropriate health professional, either before or after the receipt of an access request, before they can withhold health data on the grounds that disclosure would be likely to cause the serious harm described. Data controllers who are not health professionals cannot rely on opinions received from appropriate health professionals more than six months before receipt of the access request.
- Likewise, data controllers who are not health professionals must not communicate health data in response to an access request without first consulting an appropriate health professional on whether disclosure would be likely to cause the serious harm described. However, this modification to section 7 does not apply if the data subject has already seen, or has, the information.

The Data Protection (Subject Access Modification) (Education) Order 2000

This order applies to personal data consisting of information constituting an educational record. Educational records are defined in Schedule 11 of the DPA, which needs to be referred to for the full meaning. Within England and Wales an educational record has the following features:

- It is a record of information processed by a school governing body, or by a teacher. This excludes records processed by a teacher for their sole use.
- The information relates to a pupil of the school, or former pupil.
- The information originated from a teacher, the pupil concerned or the pupil's parent.

The order does not apply to educational records that include information about the physical or mental health or condition of the pupil, nor does it apply to any data exempted from the right of access by an order made under section 38 of the DPA.

The main focus of this order is as follows:

- The processing of educational records by the courts: As with the previous order, there is an exemption from the subject information provisions where personal data within educational records are supplied in a report to the court or are given in evidence. The court proceedings affected are criminal proceedings against children.
- The right of access within section 7 is exempted if its application would 'be likely to cause serious harm to the physical or mental health or condition of the data subject or any other person'.
- Child abuse in England, Wales and Northern Ireland: In cases where a person with parental responsibility or powers under a court order

has exercised a statutory right to make a request on behalf of a data subject and the personal data includes information about whether the data subject is or is not at risk of child abuse, the right of access is also exempted if its application would not be in the best interests of the data subject.

The Data Protection (Subject Access Modification) (Social Work) Order 2000

This order applies to personal data falling within either paragraph 1 or paragraph 2 of the schedule to the order. The schedule contains a very long list of personal data to which the order applies. Those in paragraph 1 relate to social work functions, such as the provision of education services, the provision of probation services and the provision of social services. Those within paragraph 2 relate to reports and evidence received by the court. The order does not apply to personal data falling within the other orders and it does not apply to any data that are exempted by an order made under section 38 of the DPA.

The main focus of the order is:

- Personal data of the kind identified in the Schedule are exempt from the subject information provisions.
- Prejudice to social work: There is an exemption from all parts of the rights of access apart from the duty to confirm or deny the processing for personal data and applies if the right of access would be likely to prejudice social work or if serious harm to the physical or mental health or condition of the data subject, or any other person, would be likely to be caused.
- Where a person with parental responsibility or responsibility pursuant to a court order exercises a legal right of access on behalf of a data subject there is an exemption from section 7 if the personal data consists of information that the data subject expected would not be disclosed.

Regulatory activity

Section 31 of the DPA contains an exemption from the subject information provisions if their application would be likely to prejudice the proper discharge of regulatory functions. The regulatory functions falling within the exemption are those concerned with protecting the public, protecting charities and protecting workers. Key regulatory functions specified within the exemption include:

- The regulation of financial services including banks, the insurance industry and investment services. Thus, work done by the Financial Services Authority falls within the exemption.
- The regulation of corporate bodies.

- The regulation of charities. Work done by the Charity Commission falls within the exemption.
- The regulation of health and safety at work.
- The regulation of competition. Thus, work done by the Office of Fair Trading falls within the exemption.

Journalism, literature and art (the special purposes)

Section 32 of the DPA provides many exemptions for processing done for 'the special purposes', which means for the purposes of journalism, or for artistic purposes or for literary purposes (section 4 DPA). These exemptions include exemptions from the subject information provisions and from the second data protection principle. These exemptions are justified on the grounds of freedom of expression, which, like the right to privacy, is a human right.

The exemption will apply if the data controller can show all of the following:

- The processing must be done exclusively for one or more of the special purposes.
- The processing must be undertaken with a view to publication by any person.
- The data controller must reasonably believe that the publication would be in the public interest having regard to 'the special importance of the public interest in freedom of expression'.
- The data controller reasonably believes that compliance with the provision of the DPA in issue (for the purposes of this analysis, the subject information provisions) is incompatible with the special purposes.

When considering the reasonableness of the data controller's belief described in the third bullet point above, regard must be had to compliance with any relevant designated Code of Practice. This includes the Code of Practices designated by the Data Protection (Designated Codes of Practice) (No 2) Order 2000.[96]

During court proceedings under the DPA, a question about the special purposes may arise. In these cases the court is required to stay the proceedings in order to allow the Information Commissioner to carry out a determination under section 45 of the DPA.

Research, history and statistics

Section 33 of the DPA is concerned with processing for research purposes, which includes statistical and historical purposes. This important exemption allows personal data captured for one or more specified purposes to be processed for research purposes where the relevant conditions are met. This therefore acts as an exemption from the second data protection principle. The relevant conditions are:

- The further processing shall not support measures or decisions to be taken in respect to particular individuals.
- The data shall not be processed in a way to cause substantial damage or distress to any data subject.

Where these relevant conditions are met an exemption from the right of access will apply provided that the research results are not made available in a form that identifies any data subjects.

Manual data held by public authorities

The five categories of data were identified in Chapter 1. The fifth category of data, recorded information held by a public authority, is the subject of exemptions within section 33A of the DPA. Section 33A was introduced into the DPA by the Freedom of Information Act 2000.

Among other things section 33A provides an exemption from the first and second data protection principles, meaning that the prescribed information need not be supplied (the first data protection principle) and the processing purpose need not be specified (the second data protection principle).

Information available to the public under an enactment

Section 34 of the DPA contains an exemption from the subject information provisions for information that the data controller is obliged to make available to the public under an Act of Parliament.

Parliamentary privilege

Section 35A of the DPA, again inserted by the Freedom of Information Act, contains a constitutionally significant exemption if an exemption is required for the purposes of avoiding an infringement of the privileges of the Houses of Parliament. This includes an exemption from all of the transparency provisions, apart from notification and the information notice provisions.

Miscellaneous exemptions

Section 37 refers to miscellaneous exemptions contained in Schedule 7 of the DPA. The exemptions in Schedule 7 are in respect of either the subject information provisions or just the right of access within section 7.

Confidential references given by the data controller

Paragraph 1 of Schedule 7 provides that confidential references given by, or to be given by, the data controller are exempt from the right of access within section 7 if they are for the purposes of:

- the education, training, employment (or the prospective education, training or employment) of the data subject;
- the appointment (or prospective appointment) of the data subject to any office;
- the provision (or prospective provision) by the data subject of any service.

It must be emphasized that this exemption does not apply to confidential references received by the data controller. Such references will be governed by the subject access rules contained within section 7(4) of the DPA if they identify the giver of the reference.

On 16 November 2005 the Information Commissioner published guidance entitled 'Data protection good practice note – Subject access and employment references'.[97] This provides a helpful explanation of the distinction between references given by the data controller and references received by the data controller.

Armed forces

Paragraph 2 of Schedule 7 says that personal data are exempt from the subject information provisions if the application of those provisions would be likely to prejudice the combat effectiveness of any of the armed forces.

Judicial appointments and honours

Paragraph 3 of Schedule 7 says that personal data processed for the purposes of assessing a person's suitability for judicial office, or for the office of Queen's Counsel or for the conferring of any honour or dignity by the Crown are all exempt from the subject information provisions.

Crown employment and Crown or Ministerial appointments

Paragraph 4 of Schedule 7 says that the Secretary of State may order the exemption from the subject information provisions for personal data processed for the purposes of assessing any person's suitability for employment by or under the Crown, or to any office to which appointments are made by Her Majesty, by a Minister of the Crown or by a Northern Ireland department.

Management forecasts and management planning

Paragraph 5 of Schedule 7 says that personal data processed for the purposes of management forecasting or for management planning to assist the data controller in the conduct of any business or other activity are exempt from the subject information provisions, if their application would be likely to prejudice the conduct of those activities.

Corporate finance

Paragraph 6 of Schedule 7 contains exemptions from the subject information provisions for 'corporate finance services' provided by a 'relevant person' as defined in the Schedule (including a person authorized to provide a corporate finance service under the Financial Services and Markets Act 2000). The corporate finance services in issue are:

- services consisting of the underwriting or placing of issues of any instrument;
- services consisting of the giving of advice to undertakings on capital structure, industrial strategy and related matters;
- services consisting of advice or other services relating to mergers and the purchase of undertakings.

The exemptions are for two situations. The first is for cases where the application of the subject information provisions could affect the price of any instrument that is already in existence or may come into existence (such as share prices), or for cases where the data controller reasonably believes that there could be such an effect. The second is for cases where the exemption is required for the purposes of safeguarding an important economic or financial interest of the UK.

Negotiations

Paragraph 7 of Schedule 7 provides an exemption from the subject information provisions for personal data consisting of records of the intentions of the data controller in relation to any negotiations with the data subject. Again, for this exemption to apply there would otherwise be prejudice, in this case to the negotiations.

Examination marks

Paragraph 8 of Schedule 7 modifies the right of access within section 7 where the request concerns personal data consisting of examination marks processed by the data controller in two circumstances. The first is for the purposes of determining the results, or enabling the determination of the results, of an academic, professional or other examination. The second is for processing done in consequence of the determination of results. The modifications are as follows:

- If the access request is received before the day on which the examination results are announced, the time for responding is extended until the end of five months commencing from the date of receipt or the end of 40 days commencing from the date of the announcement of the results, whichever is the earlier.
- If the response to the access request is given more than 40 days after the receipt of it, the information that is to be supplied is that in existence at the date of receipt of the request as well as that in existence at the date of response, if different.

Examination scripts

Paragraph 9 of Schedule 7 contains an exemption from the right of access within section 7 for personal data consisting of information recorded by candidates during an examination falling within the scope of paragraph 8, namely an academic, professional or other examination.

On 2 August 2005 the Information Commissioner issued a press release announcing new guidance on students' rights to examination information. The guidance is contained in a document entitled 'Data protection good practice note: Individuals' rights of access to examination records', dated 29 July 2005.[98]

Legal professional privilege

Paragraph 10 of Schedule 7 contains an exemption from the subject information provisions for personal data protected by legal professional privilege, or a claim of confidentiality of communications in Scotland.

Self-incrimination

Paragraph 11 of Schedule 7 contains an exemption from the right of access if compliance with an access request or an order made under section 7(9) would reveal evidence that would expose the data controller to proceedings for an offence. If a data controller complies with a request or order and in so doing reveals evidence of the commission of an offence, that evidence is not admissible in proceedings against the data controller for that offence.

Exemptions made by order

Section 38 of the DPA gives the Secretary of State the power to order, among other things, further exemptions from the subject information provisions. This power may be used in respect of personal data the disclosure of which is prohibited or restricted by an enactment, but only if the Secretary of State considers that the exemption is necessary for safeguarding the interests of the data subject or the rights and freedoms of any other person.

The current order is the Data Protection (Miscellaneous Subject Access Exemptions) Order 2000.[99] This order contains an exemption from section 7 only, not from the full subject information provisions, for the enactments and instruments specified in the Schedule to the order. These include:

- The Human Fertilisation and Embryology Act 1990 concerning information kept in a register by the Human Fertilisation and Embryology Authority about the provision of treatment services, the keeping of gametes and embryos and whether identifiable individuals were born as a result of such treatment.
- The Adoption Act 1976 and related legislation concerning the information within adoption reports and records and parental order records and reports.
- The Education (Special Educational Needs) Regulations 1994 concerning the information within statements of a child's special educational needs.

3 General Rules on Lawfulness

INTRODUCTION

The processing of personal data, like any other activity, must be lawful in the sense that it must comply with the laws of the land in which the processing is carried out. In addition, the processing of personal data must comply with the rules within the DPA.

Chapter II of the Data Protection Directive is titled 'general rules on the lawfulness of the processing of personal data' and it provides the substance of the title of this chapter. The topics covered by Chapter II of the Directive are:

- the principles relating to data quality;
- the criteria for making data processing legitimate;
- the special categories of processing;
- the information to be given to the data subject;
- the right of access;
- exemptions and restrictions;
- the right to object;
- confidentiality and security of processing;
- notification.

The information to be given to the data subject, the right of access and notification were examined in Chapter 2, together with relevant exemptions, as they collectively form the DPA's transparency provisions. However, it must be understood that the transparency provisions also form part of the general rules on lawfulness. The right to object is examined in Chapter 4.

The data protection principles and the interpretation

As mentioned earlier, the DPA contains eight data protection principles, which are found in Schedule 1, Part I to the Act. The principles are accompanied by the interpretation, contained in Schedule 1, Part II. Section 4 of the DPA places the obligation to comply with the data protection principles on the data controller. However, Part IV of the DPA contains many powerful exemptions, which have already been introduced in the context of the transparency provisions.

To recap, the eight data protection principles are as follows:

(1) Personal data shall be processed fairly and lawfully and, in particular, shall not be processed unless –

   (a) at least one of the conditions in Schedule 2 is met, and

   (b) in the case of sensitive personal data, at least one of the conditions in Schedule 3 is also met.

(2) Personal data shall be obtained only for one or more specified and lawful purposes, and shall not be further processed in any manner incompatible with that purpose or those purposes.

(3) Personal data shall be adequate, relevant and not excessive in relation to the purpose or purposes for which they are processed.

(4) Personal data shall be accurate and, where necessary, kept up to date.

(5) Personal data processed for any purpose or purposes shall not be kept for longer than is necessary for that purpose or those purposes.

(6) Personal data shall be processed in accordance with the rights of data subjects under this Act.

(7) Appropriate technical and organisational measures shall be taken against unauthorised or unlawful processing of personal data and against accidental loss or destruction of, or damage to, personal data.

(8) Personal data shall not be transferred to a country or territory outside the European Economic Area unless that country or territory ensures an adequate level of protection for the rights and freedoms of data subjects in relation to the processing of personal data.

The eighth data protection principle does not form part of the general rules on the lawfulness of the processing of personal data contained in Chapter II of the Data Protection Directive. It is therefore discussed separately at Chapter 5 of this book.

THE FIRST DATA PROTECTION PRINCIPLE

The construction of the first data protection principle places three obligations on the data controller. The first is to process personal data fairly. The second is to process personal data lawfully. The third is to meet one of the conditions in Schedule 2 if personal data are processed and, if sensitive personal data are processed, to meet also one of the conditions in Schedule 3.

The requirement for fair and lawful processing is contained in the Data Protection Directive within the 'principles relating to data quality' (Article 6). The equivalent requirement to a Schedule 2 condition appears in the Directive under the 'criteria for making data processing legitimate' (Article

7). The equivalent requirement to a Schedule 3 condition appears in the Directive under 'special categories of data' (Article 8).

Fair processing

Dealing with the requirement for fair processing, this has been examined in depth in Chapter 2. To recap, fair processing consists of a series of distinct elements:

- The processing purpose must be fair.
- The processing manner must be fair.
- The processing operation must be fair.
- Information must be fairly obtained.
- The data subject must be supplied with the prescribed information.

Lawful processing

It might be fair to question why the Data Protection Directive feels that there is a need to impose a separate requirement of lawful processing, when the failure to comply with the fair processing component renders the processing unlawful as does a failure to comply with any of the other specific provisions within the DPA. It might be suggested quite fairly that the lawfulness requirement serves no practical purpose. Furthermore, it is noteworthy that the interpretation in Schedule 1, Part II does not make any comment about lawfulness.

The best possible justification for the inclusion of the lawfulness component is that it causes the data controller to reflect upon the overall legal framework within which data processing sits, rather than just the framework within the DPA. The key point at the very heart of this observation is that compliance with the DPA will not render data processing lawful within the widest meaning of the word if the data controller has failed to comply with another rule of law that is relevant to the act of data processing.

EXAMPLE

An independent financial advisor (IFA) is required to be registered with the FSA. The IFA obtains their clients' consent to process their personal data and does so fairly and in accordance with the data protection principles and after having notified. However, the IFA has failed to register with the FSA. This renders their activities, including their data processing activities, unlawful.

The Information Commissioner's 'Legal Guidance'[100] provides the following assistance with the requirement for lawful processing:

> The Act does not provide any guidance on the meaning of 'lawful'. The natural meaning of unlawful has been broadly described by the Courts as 'something

which is contrary to some law or enactment or is done without lawful justification or excuse' ...The term applies equally to the public and private sector
and to breaches of both statute and common law, whether criminal or civil.
An example of information unlawfully obtained might be information which
is obtained as a result of a breach of confidence or in breach of an enforceable contractual agreement. Since 2 October 2000 it applies to a breach of the
Human Rights Act 1998 by a data controller bound by that Act.
This means that a data controller must comply with all relevant rules of law
whether derived from statute or common law, relating to the purpose and
ways in which the data controller processes personal data.

Schedule 2 and 3 conditions

These are discussed below, following the analysis of the seventh data protection principle.

THE SECOND DATA PROTECTION PRINCIPLE

The second data protection principle says:

2. Personal data shall be obtained only for one or more specified and lawful
purposes, and shall not be further processed in any manner incompatible
with that purpose or those purposes.

As with the first data protection principle, the construction of the second
data protection principle places three obligations on the data controller.
First, the purpose of the processing must be specified. Second, the purpose
of the processing must be lawful. Third, any further processing subsequent to
the specified, lawful purpose must not be 'incompatible' with the specified,
lawful purpose.

The first obligation has been discussed in Chapter 2, as part of the transparency provisions. To recap, the interpretation to the second data principle
envisages the data controller giving the data subject some form of 'notice'
in which the processing purpose is specified. The interpretation says that
this notice may be given within the prescribed information required by the
interpretation to the first data protection principle, or in the data controller's
notification. However, the inclusion of the word 'may' shows that the data
controller may use another method to specify the purpose. An alternative
method might be in the relevant particulars supplied by the data controller
following a request made by a data subject under section 24 of the DPA.

The second obligation, the lawfulness of the specified purpose, essentially
covers the same ground as the requirement for lawfulness within the first data
protection principle. It is also noticeable that, as for the first data protection
principle, the interpretation to the second data protection principle says
nothing about lawfulness.

The interpretation does, however, provide some assistance with the third obligation, which prevents any further processing that is incompatible with the specified purpose for which the personal data were originally collected. The interpretation says:

> **In determining whether any disclosure of personal data is compatible with the purpose or purposes for which the data were obtained, regard is to be had to the purpose or purposes for which the personal data are intended to be processed by any person to whom they are disclosed.**

The assistance provided by the interpretation is of limited value, however, as it deals only with the situation where personal data are intended to be disclosed to a third party. Indeed, it might also be suggested that the requirement to consider the intentions of the third party when examining compatibility is somewhat obvious. There is, however, a very important point lying within the requirement to consider the intentions of the third party, because if the third party processes the personal data in a manner that is incompatible with the purpose originally specified on collection of the data, this could leave the data controller vulnerable to enforcement action if the data controller failed to enquire into the third party's intentions prior to disclosure.

The meaning of incompatibility is unclear and will remain so until examined by the courts. However, it is possibly the case that the incompatibility test presents data controllers with major opportunities to further process data. Much depends upon whether a narrow meaning of the word is justified, or a wide meaning. If a wide meaning is the correct meaning then it is suggested that the subsequent processing will need to be antagonistic to the original purpose to fall foul of the compatibility test.

EXAMPLE

CCTV cameras are installed outside an office building to monitor the staff car park, because of a recent spate of thefts from parked vehicles. The cameras were installed with the full approval of the workers who understood that the cameras would also capture incidental footage of their comings and goings. This incidental footage reveals that a worker habitually arrives late for work and leaves early, so it is used to support disciplinary proceedings against them. The use of the footage within the disciplinary proceedings is a purpose that is secondary to the original purpose, namely security, but it is not incompatible with the original purpose.

THE THIRD DATA PROTECTION PRINCIPLE

The third data protection principle says:

> **3. Personal data shall be adequate, relevant and not excessive in relation to the purpose or purposes for which they are processed.**

The third data protection principle imposes three identifiable requirements on the data controller. First, the personal data must be adequate. Second, the personal data must be relevant. Third, the personal data must not be excessive.

Unfortunately, Schedule 1, Part II of the DPA does not contain any interpretation for the third data protection principle, but it is clear from its wording that the third data protection principle requires the data controller to process the correct amount of information of the correct type, judged by reference to the specified, lawful purpose. In effect, the third data protection principle imposes both minimum and maximum requirements on the data controller. The data controller must process enough data, but not too much.

The adequacy requirement points at a requirement to process a sufficient amount of personal data of sufficient quality. Thus, a surgeon performing a complicated operation will need to know that they have been properly apprised of the patient's medical condition. This is likely to include information about the patient's medical history, perhaps information about the medical history of the patient's family members and information from relevant test results. The relevancy requirement points to a requirement for congruency. Thus, an employer performing a disciplinary function within an office environment is highly unlikely to require information about the employee's shopping habits. The final requirement, not excessive, speaks for itself; data will be excessive if they are not required for the processing purpose. To a great extent excessive data is synonymous with irrelevant data.

EXAMPLE

Individuals wish to receive an email newsletter from a UK-based travel company. The online registration process requires the individuals to give their name, their email address and to identify their holiday preferences, so that a relevant newsletter can be sent. The information that the individuals supply to the website is adequate, relevant and not excessive judged by reference to the processing purpose, which is to deliver an email newsletter about holidays. The situation would be very different if the individuals were also asked to provide their postal address, telephone number, age, occupation and salary details, as none of this information is required for the delivery of an email newsletter about holidays.

The Information Commissioner's 'Legal Guidance' provides the following assistance with the third data protection principle:

In complying with this Principle, data controllers should seek to identify the minimum amount of information that is required in order properly to fulfil their purpose and this will be a question of fact in each case. If it is necessary to hold additional information about certain individuals, such information should only be collected and recorded in those cases.

This guidance has been endorsed by the Data Protection Tribunal in the context of the 1984 Act in the case of Runnymede Borough Council CCRO and Others v The Data Protection Registrar (November 1990). Where a data controller holds an item of information on all individuals which will be used or useful only in relation to some of them, the information is likely to be excessive and irrelevant in relation to those individuals in respect of whom it will not be used or useful and should not be held in those cases.

It is not acceptable to hold information on the basis that it might possibly be useful in the future without a view of how it will be used. This is to be distinguished from holding information in the case of a particular foreseeable contingency which may never occur, for example, where an employer holds details of blood groups of employees engaged in hazardous occupations.

Cases on the third data protection principle

In the case of *Community Charge Registration Officer Of Rhondda Borough Council v. Data Protection Registrar*,[101] a decision of the Data Protection Tribunal under the Data Protection Act 1984, it was held that the Community Charge Registration Officer's request for the supply of dates of births from people in his area would be likely to contravene the fourth data protection principle in the 1984 Act, which said that 'personal data held for any purpose or purposes shall be adequate, relevant and not excessive in relation to that purpose or those purposes' (the fourth data protection principle in the 1984 Act is the equivalent of the third data principle in the DPA). The Tribunal reasoned as follows:

There was evidence before us that nationally less than 1% of households contained persons with the same surname and same first name. There was no evidence before us as to percentages applying within the area of Rhondda Borough Council, although it was probable that they were greater than the national figure. We approached the question of whether the information was irrelevant and excessive without taking too restrictive a view of the discretion that a particular C.C.R.O [Community Charge Registration Office] might exercise as to the amount of information he considered would assist him to carry out his statutory duties. We found that it was established that the Appellant held and wished to continue holding dates of birth information on as many as possible. The information was to be obtained from answers voluntarily given on canvas forms. We found that the Appellant did not seek to limit the information to be held on his database to those who would shortly attain the age to become charge payers or to identify persons living at the same address with identical names. The information as to dates of birth was personal data and was to cover persons generally at least insofar as the information had been

> voluntarily provided. We find that the information the Appellant wishes to hold on database concerning individuals exceeds substantially the minimum amount of information which is required in order for him to fulfil the purposes for which he has sought registration namely to fulfil his duty to compile and maintain the Community Charges Register.
>
> We find it established that the Registrar was satisfied that the Appellant was likely to contravene the 4th Data Protection Principle in relation to dates of birth information. We are satisfied by the evidence before us that the wide and general extent of the information about dates of birth is irrelevant and excessive.

In three combined cases under the Data Protection Act 1984, *Community Charge Registration Officer of Runnymede Borough Council v. Data Protection Registrar, Community Charge Registration Officer of South Northamptonshire District Council v. Data Protection Registrar* and *Community Charge Registration Officer of Harrow Borough Council v. Data Protection Registrar,*[102] the Data Protection Tribunal also held that the holding of property type information on the Community Charges Register also contravened the fourth data protection principle in the 1984 Act.

See also the discussion below in the section 'The fifth data protection principle', for the case *The Chief Constables of West Yorkshire, South Yorkshire and North Wales Police v. The Information Commissioner.*[103]

THE FOURTH DATA PROTECTION PRINCIPLE

The fourth data protection principle says:

> 4. Personal data shall be accurate and, where necessary, kept up to date.

The meaning of the fourth data protection principle is assisted by the interpretation and by the definition of inaccuracy contained in section 70(2) of the DPA, which is:

> For the purposes of this Act data are inaccurate if they are incorrect or misleading as to any matter of fact.

There are two obligations within the fourth data protection principle. The first is that personal data shall be accurate. This is a mandatory requirement that seems to permit no exceptions. The second obligation, that personal data shall be kept up to date, only arises where that is necessary. This suggests that where personal data are subject to multiple acts of processing, as opposed to a single act of processing, the data controller must consider at sufficient intervals whether the information is up to date. Of course, the steps that the data controller needs to take to ensure that personal data are accurate and kept up to date are fact sensitive, depending on the circumstances of the case. Where sensitive personal data are subject to repeated use over a prolonged period of time the data controller will carry a heavier burden of review than where non-sensitive personal data are subject to single use.

The interpretation within Schedule 1, Part II of the DPA deals with cases where, although the data controller has accurately recorded the information it has received from the data subject or from a third party, there are inaccuracies in the personal data nonetheless. In such cases the fourth data protection principle will not be regarded as being contravened if the data controller has taken 'reasonable steps', measured by reference to the processing purpose, to ensure the accuracy of the data. However, if the data subject notifies the data controller of their view that the data are inaccurate, the data controller must ensure that the data subject's views are recorded with the data.

EXAMPLE

Following a consultation, the data subject's GP records information about the data subject's drinking habits in the data subject's medical records, which are held electronically. The data subject later realizes that they have grossly overestimated the weekly units of alcohol they consume and inform their GP of this fact at their next visit to the surgery. The GP is required to make a new entry in the medical records correcting the first entry. Failure to do so will put the GP in breach of the fourth data protection principle.

In situations like those described in the interpretation the data controller cannot automatically assume that it can record information received from the data subject or from a third party without checking for accuracy. As already explained, the data controller's duty is to take reasonable steps to ensure accuracy, which means, of course, that the data controller will need to identify whether any checks are necessary. If checks are necessary, the data controller will need to implement a system for carrying out those checks.

The construction of the interpretation, which deals with the accurate recording of inaccurate personal data collected from the data subject and third parties, means that it is implicit that the DPA sees a third scenario, namely where the data controller inaccurately records accurate information. In this scenario the data controller will be in automatic breach of the fourth data protection principle.

THE FIFTH DATA PROTECTION PRINCIPLE

The fifth data protection principle says:

> **5. Personal data processed for any purpose or purposes shall not be kept for longer than is necessary for that purpose or those purposes.**

Like the third data protection principle the fifth data protection principle is not supported by any interpretation, but this should not cause too many difficulties as it is self-evident that it requires the data controller to delete, destroy or 'anonymize' personal data at the completion of the processing purpose. The correlation of this is that all information that is held by the data controller must be justified against a particular purpose, either one that has been specified pursuant to the second data protection principle or a subsequent purpose that is not incompatible with the one specified.

The deletion of personal data can be effected by merely deleting the personal identifiers, a process known as 'anonymization'. This is because once all personal identifiers are removed the information ceases to identify an individual and therefore it ceases to be personal data. Anonymization is recognized by the Data Protection Directive as a valid response to the prohibition against keeping data for longer than is necessary.

Data controllers who process electronic data need to ensure that the data are properly deleted when the processing purpose is complete, because very often all a delete function does to active electronic data is to remove the reference to it in the tables that the computer searches against. To properly delete an active electronic file a process colloquially known as 'electronic shredding' needs to be followed, which involves the repeated overwriting of the file to be shredded with new binary code. An equally problematic issue for electronic data is the deletion of backup data. The data controller who successfully manages to delete active data may still find itself in breach of the fifth data protection principle for neglecting to put in place procedures for the deletion of backup data. Finally, there is the issue of electronic data proliferation, where the same piece of electronic data comes to be stored in various places at the same time. In addition to official backups, electronic data may be copied from central servers to remote PCs, to portable storage media and to mobile devices, such as PDAs (personal digital assistants), mobile telephones and music players. The data controller's compliance strategy needs to bear this in mind.

Cases on the fifth data protection principle

The most significant case on the fifth data protection principle also addresses the third data protection principle: *The Chief Constables of West Yorkshire, South Yorkshire and North Wales Police v. The Information Commissioner,*[104] a consolidated appeal from the service of three enforcement notices by the Information Commissioner. These enforcement notices all concerned the disclosure of very old conviction data held by the police on the UK Police National Computer, which the Information Commissioner considered should be deleted. In summary, the Information Tribunal considered that the long-term retention of conviction data by the police does not contravene the third or fifth data protection principles, although it does engage Article 8 of the ECHR. However, there is a distinction between police use of retained data and disclosure to third parties and in each of the cases under appeal the Tribunal directed that the data could be retained, but for police access only. It is worth noting that none of the convictions under review were for indecency, or mistreatment of the vulnerable or for serious violence. Apart from one conviction for assault occasioning actual bodily harm, all of the offences were to do with petty theft or were motoring offences.

THE SIXTH DATA PROTECTION PRINCIPLE

The sixth data protection principle says:

> **6. Personal data shall be processed in accordance with the rights of data subjects under this Act.**

The data subject's rights fall into two broad categories, namely the right to information and the right to object. The data subject's rights to information form part of the DPA's transparency provisions, arising under the first and second principles under section 7 (the right of access), under section 24 (the right to relevant particulars) and under section 42 (the right to an assessment). The rights to object are contained in section 10 (the right to prevent processing likely to cause damage or distress), section 11 (the right to prevent processing for the purposes of direct marketing), section 12 (the right to prevent automated decision taking), section 12A (rights in relation to exempt manual data) and section 14 (the right to rectification, blocking, erasure and destruction of data).

The interpretation within Schedule 1, Part II makes it clear that the sixth data protection principle is concerned only with the rights in sections 7, 10, 11 and 12, however. The interpretation says:

> **A person is to be regarded as contravening the sixth principle if, but only if –**
>
> **(a) he contravenes section 7 by failing to supply information in accordance with that section,**
>
> **(b) he contravenes section 10 by failing to comply with a notice given under subsection (1) of that section to the extent that the notice is justified or by failing to give a notice under subsection (3) of that section,**
>
> **(c) he contravenes section 11 by failing to comply with a notice given under subsection (1) of that section, or**
>
> **(d) he contravenes section 12 by failing to comply with a notice given under subsection (1) or (2)(b) of that section or by failing to give a notification**

> under subsection (2)(a) of that section or a notice under subsection (3) of that section.

The right of access within section 7 is examined in Chapter 2. The rights in sections 10, 11 and 12 are examined in Chapter 4.

THE SEVENTH DATA PROTECTION PRINCIPLE

The seventh data protection principle exists to ensure the security of personal data undergoing processing. It says:

> **7. Appropriate technical and organisational measures shall be taken against unauthorised or unlawful processing of personal data and against accidental loss or destruction of, or damage to, personal data.**

Appropriate technical measures

The interpretation says the following about appropriate technical measures:

> Having regard to the state of technological development and the cost of implementing any measures, the measures must ensure a level of security appropriate to –
>
> (a) the harm that might result from such unauthorised or unlawful processing or accidental loss, destruction or damage as are mentioned in the seventh principle, and
>
> (b) the nature of the data to be protected.

There are four issues at the heart of the interpretation on the meaning of appropriate technological measures, namely:
- the state of technological development;
- the cost of implementing technological security measures;
- the harm that might result from unauthorized or unlawful processing and so on;
- the nature of the data to be protected.

Keeping abreast of technological developments

The data controller's obligation to have regard to the state of technological development effectively requires the data controller to keep up to date with the development of security technologies. This reflects the fact that the threats to electronic data, particularly malicious threats, are constantly developing. It also reflects the fact that flaws in the security features of technology are regularly uncovered. Finally, it reflects the fact that what might now be considered to be new, exciting technology will soon fall in price and become either a standard security requirement or a major security threat.

Thus, the requirement to have regard to the state of technological development has a dual focus:

- The data controller needs to keep abreast of developments in technological security measures.
- The data controller needs to keep abreast of technological threats to personal data.

Keeping abreast of developments in technological security measures

If the example of purely domestic processing is considered, which is actually exempt from the DPA (see section 36), it will soon be appreciated that most new PCs intended for home use come supplied with firewall and anti-virus software as standard. If not, this software can be purchased from reputable vendors at very little cost. The use of email encryption technology and digital signatures are also becoming widely used in the home. Strong passwords can be added to electronic files and changed as a matter of routine. Against this background it must be fair to say that the seventh data protection principle now requires all data controllers to have a firewall and anti-virus software installed, to use passwords and to consider encryption and digital signatures for email. These features serve a definite technological purpose and they are relatively inexpensive.

Although these security features might be adequate for individuals and small-scale computer users, they are unlikely to be sufficient in a networked environment or for public authorities and large organizations, particularly those used to dealing with large volumes of sensitive or confidential information. Advance technological measures that are already on the market include biometric security equipment, such as fingerprint and iris readers. Many large organizations are moving their electronic data into 'digital safes'.

Keeping abreast of technological threats to personal data

Obvious examples of technological threats to personal data include viruses, worms, Trojan horses, cookies, adware and spyware. A good quality firewall and regularly updated anti-virus software should keep many of these threats at bay, but the data controller needs to keep abreast of new entry points for malicious code and software. Many data controllers will already focus their attentions on the use of email and the internet, while over looking the threats posed by instant messaging, for example.

Hardware and computer peripherals also pose a significant threat to data security. Many different types of portable storage devices are brought into the workplace, such as PDAs, mobile telephones, USB drives and MP3 players, all of which can be used to transport data out of the workplace. Data controllers must implement policies to address the use of these items.

Another major threat to the security of electronic data is the phenomenon of data proliferation, where the same piece of data comes to be stored in many different places and in many different formats. Factors that result in proliferation include the use of portable storage media, teleworking, lack of discipline over file structures and the use of backup tapes and disks. The key problem caused by proliferation is the loss of control over the data, so that data exists outside the parameters of the data controller's security system.

The use of magnetic backup tapes is now being recognized as posing a threat to electronic data. These tapes degrade over a period of time, which threatens the electronic data contained within them. If degraded data are called into service, perhaps as part of a disaster recovery plan, the data controller risks a charge of non-compliance with the seventh data protection principle and other principles.

Wi-Fi and Bluetooth technologies also pose their own threats. Nowadays it is easy to obtain free wireless internet access in high-street coffee shops, hotels, restaurants, supermarkets and on public transport. Data controllers who allow their workers to take advantage of these new facilities must also pay consideration to the security implications.

The phenomenon of teleworking, where the worker works part or all of their time from their own home, is a major security concern for data controllers, due to the loss of direct control over the worker, the working environment and the data. In addition to causing potential data proliferation problems, mentioned above, the data controller is exposed to risks of unauthorized access to its data, perhaps by family members of the teleworker who are also users of the teleworker's PC.

Determining what technological measures are appropriate

The second, third and fourth issues at the heart of the interpretation of the meaning of appropriate technological measures effectively oblige the data controller to carry out some form of risk assessment to identify the threats to their personal data and to determine the nature and extent of the harm that might result from unauthorized or unlawful processing, or accidental loss or destruction of, or damage to, personal data.

If the threat of proliferation is considered, one solution might be an IT system that keeps information safe and secure in one place only, the digital safe. While the initial costs of such a system might be many thousands of pounds, the outlay may seem modest when measured against the cost of a security breach, particularly when significant security breaches are likely to result in major reputational damage for the data controller in addition to the settling of fines, damages claims and loss of trade. For data controllers dealing with large volumes of sensitive data, for example public authorities, banks, health care providers, insurance companies, trade unions, political organizations, recruitment consultants and retailers, it is highly likely that compliance with the seventh data protection principle will require significant financial outlay on solutions.

Appropriate organizational measures

Data controllers' organizational measures will include their technical measures and the measures they put in place to deal with workers and any data processors used. Naturally, all of these measures may be categorized as management measures in the sense that they are within the sphere of management responsibility. The interpretation deals with employees and data processors in a similar fashion, essentially requiring the data controller to be sure of the reliability of these persons.

Organizational measures concerning employees

The interpretation says that a data controller must take 'reasonable steps to ensure the reliability of any employees of his who have access to personal data'. As with the appropriateness of the technical measures taken, the reasonableness of the steps taken to ensure employee reliability is a fact-sensitive issue that depends upon the nature of the data processed and the processing purpose. Of course, the purpose of the measures is to prevent 'unauthorised or unlawful processing of personal data and accidental loss or destruction of, or damage to, personal data'.

The interpretation does not provide any assistance with the meaning of the word 'reliability' but a common sense approach would suggest that the data controller should do the following:

- Carry out appropriate background checks before hiring the employee. This will often include the taking-up of references. In certain sensitive circumstances, such as the hiring of teachers and persons working with children, the carrying out of background checks with the Criminal Records Bureau will be required. It is worth remembering that confidential references given to the data controller for employment purposes are exempt from the right of access within section 7 of the DPA (section 37 and Schedule 7).
- Insert appropriate data protection clauses in the contract of employment and the company handbook.
- Provide appropriate training for the employee, as part of induction procedures and periodically thereafter.
- Implement a system of monitoring in appropriate cases. This may extend to the interception of electronic communications in defined circumstances.
- Implement a disciplinary procedure for employee breaches of data protection. Such a procedure will be defined in the company handbook and will specify any particular breaches that could lead to dismissal.

The Information Commissioner has introduced a code of practice under section 51 of the DPA, which deals with these issues (and more). The Employment Practices Code[105] is divided into four parts: (1) recruitment and selection; (2) employment records; (3) monitoring at work; and (4) information about workers' health. Data controllers should consult the Code and its supplementary guidance for a detailed analysis of the Information Commissioner's position on the processing of employee data. For the purposes of this discussion, ensuring the reliability of employees, the following points should be noted:

- **Pre-employment vetting**: The Information Commissioner recognizes the importance of pre-employment vetting, but cautions that such activities must be proportionate. It is vital for data controllers to take account of the laws that limit or curtail pre-employment vetting and those that support it. For example, section 55 of the DPA creates offences of unlawful obtaining and unlawful disclosure of personal data, offences that could be committed by an over-zealous data controller performing pre-employment enquiries. In addition, section 56 of the DPA creates an offence commonly known as enforced subject access, which is committed where an employer (or potential employer) wanting more background information about an employee's (or prospective employee's) character requires an employee (or prospective employee) to exercise their rights under section 7 of the DPA to obtain records about their convictions and cautions. Similarly, the Rehabilitation of Offenders Act 1974 provides that spent convictions do not have to be declared in response to questions about criminal records. This rule is subject to exceptions contained in the Rehabilitation of Offenders Act 1974 (Exceptions) Order 1975, which in limited circumstances allows prospective employers to obtain disclosures directly from the Criminal Records Bureau (or Disclosure Scotland) about spent and unspent convictions, cautions and non-conviction information held by the police. Circumstances covered by this order include the employment of persons working with children and other vulnerable persons.

- **Employee monitoring**: The Information Commissioner cautions that employees are entitled to respect for their privacy while at work. Thus, data controllers carrying out monitoring should make it clear to workers that they are doing so, how it is being done and why.

- **Covert monitoring**: The Information Commissioner is very discouraging of covert monitoring for obvious reasons, but does acknowledge that it has its role. In the Supplementary Guidance to the Employment Practices Code[106] the Information Commissioner says:

> covert monitoring will only be justified in a particular case if openness would be likely to prejudice the prevention or detection of crime or equivalent malpractice or the apprehension or prosecution of offenders. There may be cases where one of the other exemptions in the Act could apply, but these are unlikely to arise in the employment context. It is therefore essential that the employer makes a considered and realistic assessment of whether such prejudice is likely. A reliable test of whether covert monitoring is justified is to consider whether the

> activity being monitored is of sufficient seriousness that it would be reasonable for the police to be involved. This does not mean, though, that the employer need necessarily involve the police. However, the implications of covert monitoring are such that senior management authorisation ought to be a prerequisite.

- **Interception of communications:** Within the workplace this is covered by the Telecommunications (Lawful Business Practice) (Interception of Communications) Regulations 2000,[107] made under the Regulation of Investigatory Powers Act 2000. These regulations permit the monitoring of certain business-related electronic communications (telephone calls, emails, internet access and fax transmissions) provided that the data controller has taken all reasonable steps to notify their employees that interception will take place. Workplace interception that does not comply with the Regulations is an offence.

Organizational measures concerning data processors

A data processor is a person or organization that processes personal data on behalf of a data controller. A data processor cannot be an employee of the data controller. The essence of a data controller–data processor relationship is that the data controller continues to control the purpose and manner of the processing done by the data processor. Of course, it is also the essence of the relationship that the data processor gains access to, or takes possession of, the personal data processed by the data controller. The implications for personal privacy in these relationships are clearly very serious indeed. However, if the data processor starts to determine the purpose or manner of the processing, they will become a data controller in their own right.

The interpretation says the following about data controllers' use of data processors:

> 11. Where processing of personal data is carried out by a data processor on behalf of a data controller, the data controller must in order to comply with the seventh principle –
>
> (a) choose a data processor providing sufficient guarantees in respect of the technical and organisational security measures governing the processing to be carried out, and
>
> (b) take reasonable steps to ensure compliance with those measures.
>
> 12. Where processing of personal data is carried out by a data processor on behalf of a data controller, the data controller is not to be regarded as complying with the seventh principle unless –
>
> (a) the processing is carried out under a contract –

> (i)   which is made or evidenced in writing, and
>
> (ii) under which the data processor is to act only on instructions from the data controller, and
>
> (b) the contract requires the data processor to comply with obligations equivalent to those imposed on a data controller by the seventh principle.

These obligations are designed to protect the data subject's personal data when they are undergoing processing by the data processor. When this interpretation is distilled down to its key ingredients it becomes apparent that relationships between data controllers and data processors must be governed by contracts. Although these contracts may be 'evidenced in writing', the prudent data controller will ensure that they are made in writing. These written contracts will contain provisions dealing with the following:

- The data processor will guarantee that appropriate technical and organizational measures have been taken and/or will be taken.
- The data processor will provide facilities to the data controller to enable the data controller to be sure that the data processor has implemented appropriate technical and organizational measures and to enable periodic verification of continuing compliance.
- The data processor will promise to act only on the data controller's instructions.

Of course, the interpretation effectively requires the data controller to carry out necessary due diligence on the data processor, hence the phrase 'choose a data processor providing sufficient guarantees'. This form of words points directly to the need for a pre-contractual process that will enable the data controller to make an informed decision about the data processor's operations. In respect of this process in many cases it will be sufficient for the data controller to rely upon the data processor's representations about its technical and organizational measures, but there are also many cases where the data controller will need to carry out a detailed process of review, including auditing and inspection of the data processor's site, the testing of apparatus and interviews with the data processor's workers.

EXAMPLES

(1) The data controller is a small company with an online presence. It collects personal data through its website for the purposes of administering an email newsletter. The data controller's website is hosted on a shared server by a reputable ISP. In this example the data controller will be justified in relying upon the ISP's standard terms and conditions and will not need to attend the ISP's data warehouse or conduct any other pre-contractual due diligence.

(2) The data controller is a famous clearing bank with many millions of customers. It plans to outsource its call centre facilities to a company

> in India. As part of its pre-contractual due diligence process the bank
> is probably required to visit the company in India and audit its security
> features.

The interpretation also requires data controllers to take reasonable steps
to ensure that the data processor is complying with the required technical
and organizational measures. This implies a continual process of review
throughout the lifecycle of the relationship between the data controller and
the data processor. If the pre-contractual due diligence process required site
visits, audits, interviews of the processor's staff and similar it is only fair to
assume that these processes should be repeated at sufficient intervals.

The content of data controller–data processor contracts

Apart from what is said in the interpretation, the DPA is silent on the necessary
content of a data controller–data processor contract. However, the EC has
approved model contractual clauses to cover the transfer of personal data to
data processors situated outside the EEA.[108] These model clauses, approved
also by the Information Commissioner on 18 March 2003,[109] provide a useful
template for the creation of general data controller–data processor contracts.
In respect of the data processor's guarantee to process only on the data
controller's instructions these model clauses provide:

> The data importer agrees and warrants:
> (a) to process the personal data only on behalf of the data exporter and in com-
> pliance with his instructions and the clauses; if he cannot provide such com-
> pliance for whatever reasons, he agrees to inform promptly the data exporter
> of his inability to comply, in which case the data exporter is entitled to suspend
> the transfer of data and/or terminate the contract.

If this clause is to be used, it must be adapted so that 'data importer' refers
to data processor and 'data exporter' refers to data controller.

The time for taking the technical and organizational measures

Recital 46 of the Data Protection Directive identifies the time at which the data
controller should take the technical and organizational measures required
by the seventh data protection principle. Recital 46 provides:

> the protection of the rights and freedoms of data subjects with regard to the
> processing of personal data requires that appropriate technical and organiz-
> ational measures be taken, both at the time of the design of the processing
> system and at the time of the processing itself.

This identifies that the data controller must incorporate security features
during the design stage of its processing systems and that the measures must

be implemented during the processing operations, supporting the view that periodical verification of the measures is required.

The Information Commissioner's 'Legal Guidance'

The Information Commissioner's 'Legal Guidance' provides a very helpful checklist of illustrative issues for data controllers to consider.[110] These are listed under five headings, (1) security management, (2) controlling access to information, (3) ensuring business continuity, (4) staff selection and training and (5) detecting and dealing with breaches of security. The checklist is as follows:

Security management

- Does the data controller have a security policy setting out management commitment to information security within the organisation?

- Is responsibility for the organisation's security policy clearly placed on a particular person or department?

- Are sufficient resources and facilities made available to enable that responsibility to be fulfilled?

Controlling access to information

- Is access to the building or room controlled or can anybody walk in?

- Can casual passers-by read information off screens or documents?

- Are passwords known only to authorised people and are the passwords changed regularly?

- Do passwords give access to all levels of the system or only to those personal data with which that employee should be concerned?

- Is there a procedure for cleaning media (such as tapes and disks) before they are reused or are new data merely written over old? In the latter case is there a possibility of the old data reaching somebody who is not authorised to receive it? (e.g. as a result of the disposal of redundant equipment).

- Is printed material disposed of securely, for example, by shredding?

- Is there a procedure for authenticating the identity of a person to whom personal data may be disclosed over the telephone prior to the disclosure of the personal data?

- Is there a procedure covering the temporary removal of personal data from the data controller's premises, for example, for staff to work on at home?

What security measures are individual members of staff required to take in such circumstances?

- Are responsibilities for security clearly defined between a data processor and its customers?

Ensuring business continuity

- Are the precautions against burglary, fire or natural disaster adequate?

- Is the system capable of checking that the data are valid and initiating the production of backup copies? If so, is full use made of these facilities?

- Are backup copies of all the data stored separately from the live files?

- Is there protection against corruption by viruses or other forms of intrusion?

Staff selection and training

- Is proper weight given to the discretion and integrity of staff when they are being considered for employment or promotion or for a move to an area where they will have access to personal data?

- Are the staff aware of their responsibilities? Have they been given adequate training and is their knowledge kept up to date?

- Do disciplinary rules and procedures take account of the requirements of the Act? Are these rules enforced?

- Does an employee found to be unreliable have his or her access to personal data withdrawn immediately?

- Are staff made aware that data should only be accessed for business purposes and not for their own private purposes?

Detecting and dealing with breaches of security

- Do systems keep audit trails so that access to personal data is logged and can be attributed to a particular person?

- Are breaches of security properly investigated and remedied, particularly when damage or distress could be caused to an individual?

SCHEDULE 2 CONDITIONS (FOR PERSONAL DATA AND SENSITIVE PERSONAL DATA)

The conditions in Schedule 2 to the DPA apply to both personal data and sensitive personal data, whereas the Schedule 3 conditions apply only to sensitive personal data. This is because sensitive personal data can only be processed if a Schedule 3 condition is met in addition to a Schedule 2 condition.

The necessity test

In five of the six conditions contained in Schedule 2 there is a requirement to show that the processing is 'necessary', which will referred to as the 'necessity test'. It is only the first condition, the data subject's consent, that does not contain the necessity test.

The ordinary meaning of the word necessity indicates that something more than desirable is required to justify processing for contractual purposes. At its highest it means that the processing is essential or indispensable to the performance of the contract or to the creation of the contract. The Information Commissioner's 'Legal Guidance'[111] on the meaning of necessity points to there being a high burden to overcome to reliance upon contractual necessity:

> The Commissioner takes the view that data controllers will need to consider objectively whether:
>
> • the purposes for which the data are being processed are valid,
>
> • such purposes can only be achieved by the processing of personal data, and
>
> • the processing is proportionate to the aim pursued.

The data subject has given consent

The first condition says:

> 1. The data subject has given his consent to the processing.

The data subject's consent was discussed in Chapter 2, but to recap the Data Protection Directive describes consent as meaning 'any freely given specific and informed indication of [the data subject's] wishes by which the data subject signifies his agreement to personal data relating to him being processed'. This is expanded upon by Article 7(b) of the Data Protection Directive, which says that consent for these purposes must be given unambiguously. The essential components of this definition are:

- The consent must be freely given. Consent that is obtained through coercion or duress is not freely given.
- The consent must be specific. This means that the data controller cannot rely upon consent given for one purpose to justify another distinct processing purpose. Of course, due to the construction of the second data protection principle a data controller may process personal data for a second, compatible purpose.
- The consent must be informed. This requires the data controller to furnish the data subject with information about the processing purposes, unless the purposes are obvious, prior to the data subject making their decision whether or not to give consent.
- The data subject must communicate their agreement to the data controller. This means that the data controller cannot rely upon the data subject's silence.
- The consent must be unambiguous. This suggests that if there is any ambiguity the consent will not of sufficient quality, hence unreliable.

Contractual necessity

The second condition says:

> 2. The processing is necessary –
> (a) for the performance of a contract to which the data subject is a party, or
> (b) for the taking of steps at the request of the data subject with a view to entering into a contract.

Two scenarios are envisaged within this condition. The first scenario applies where the data subject has entered into a contract, although it is not a requirement of this condition that the contract is with the data controller. The second scenario applies prior to the creation of a contract between the data subject and some other person.

Non-contractual legal necessity

The third condition says:

> 3. The processing is necessary for compliance with any legal obligation to which the data controller is subject, other than an obligation imposed by contract.

This condition covers the situation where the data controller is required by law to process personal data. This obligation can arise under many circumstances, for example under an Act of Parliament or pursuant to a court order.

Vital interests necessity

The fourth condition says:

> **4. The processing is necessary in order to protect the vital interests of the data subject.**

It is easy to think of scenarios where the data subject's vital interests are at stake, with an obvious example being the emergency medical situation where the data subject's physical or mental condition prevents them from giving consent, perhaps within the context of a serious accident or a sudden collapse. However, the meaning and implications of this condition are not absolutely clear. On the one hand the vital interests condition might be said to be referring to life or death situations, such as serious road traffic accidents, which is the restrictive meaning. On the other hand it could be referring to matters significantly less serious than life or death situations, but which are vital to life itself nonetheless, such as the need for food, or the need for water or the need for good health.

Many commentators point to Recital 31 within the Data Protection Directive to support the restrictive construction. This says:

> **Whereas the processing of personal data must equally be regarded as lawful where it is carried out in order to protect an interest which is essential for the data subject's life.**

It is moot whether this recital takes matters much further, but for now the consensus would seem to be that a restrictive interpretation is required. The Information Commissioner's 'Legal Guidance' says:

> **The Commissioner considers that reliance on this condition may only be claimed where the processing is necessary for matters of life and death, for example, the disclosure of a data subject's medical history to a hospital casualty department treating the data subject after a serious road accident.**

Of course, even with the restrictive meaning there is still the question of at what point does the data subject's vital interests become engaged? Are they engaged in truly emergency situations, where the data subject's life could be in the balance with death an imminent likelihood? Or, alternatively, are they engaged when a chain of events could lead ultimately to death albeit after a much longer period of time than in the true emergency situation? These questions are unresolved.

Public functions necessity

The fifth condition says:

> 5. The processing is necessary –
> (a) for the administration of justice,
> (aa) for the exercise of any functions of either House of Parliament,
> (b) for the exercise of any functions conferred on any person by or under any enactment,
> (c) for the exercise of any functions of the Crown, a Minister of the Crown or a government department, or
> (d) for the exercise of any other functions of a public nature exercised in the public interest by any person.

There is obviously a very close connection with the public functions covered by this condition and the obligations covered by the non-contractual legal necessity condition. However, they are not dealing with the same things.

First, the non-contractual legal necessity condition is relevant to both the private and public sectors, whereas this condition is concerned with public functions only. Of course, public functions can be performed by private sector entities, meaning that this condition is applicable to the private sector also, but the non-contractual legal necessity condition is not limited by a public function criterion.

Second, the non-contractual legal necessity condition is concerned with processing done pursuant to an obligation, whereas this condition is not so limited. The distinction, if there is one, is that this condition refers to processing done under a power, rather than processing done under an obligation.

Legitimate interests necessity

The first part of the sixth condition says:

> 6. – (1) The processing is necessary for the purposes of legitimate interests pursued by the data controller or by the third party or parties to whom the data are disclosed, except where the processing is unwarranted in any particular case by reason of prejudice to the rights and freedoms or legitimate interests of the data subject.

This condition contains two tests, which require the data controller to perform a balancing exercise:

- Is the processing for the purpose of the data controller's legitimate interests? If the answer is yes, the processing must be necessary, raising the same issues as discussed under the second condition.
- Is the processing unwarranted by reason of prejudice to the rights and freedoms or legitimate interests of the data subject?

The DPA does not provide any assistance with the meaning of the phrase 'legitimate interests', but it is obvious that it requires the interests to be lawful. The balancing exercise also implies that the data controller's legitimate interests are reasonable ones, as measured against the data subject's interests.

This condition is a powerful condition for data controllers, particularly those in the private sector engaged in commercial activity. However, private sector data controllers choosing to rely on this condition must be warned that it is highly vulnerable to challenge, due to the specific reference to the competing interests of the data subject. In the most basic of terms this condition identifies the real challenge at the heart of data protection laws, namely the need to find balance between competing legitimate interests.

EXAMPLE

A business is considering launching a new product and as part of its due diligence procedures it wishes to use the services of a market analysis company with expertise in discerning future buying trends of potential customers. Therefore, it discloses details of its customers and their purchasing history to the market analysis company. In this example the data controller is clearly pursuing a legitimate interest, but its actions are susceptible to challenge as they may be in breach of the data subjects' rights under the second data protection principle.

Secretary of State powers

The second part of the sixth condition says:

> 6. – (2) The Secretary of State may by order specify particular circumstances in which this condition is, or is not, to be taken to be satisfied.

At the date of publication of this book the Secretary of State has not made any order under the second part of the sixth condition.

SCHEDULE 3 CONDITIONS (FOR SENSITIVE PERSONAL DATA)

The conditions in Schedule 3 apply to sensitive personal data. To recap, sensitive personal data is defined in section 4 of the DPA and it means personal data consisting of information as to:

> (a) the racial or ethnic origin of the data subject,
> (b) his political opinions,
> (c) his religious beliefs or other beliefs of a similar nature,
> (d) whether he is a member of a trade union (within the meaning of the Trade Union and Labour Relations (Consolidation) Act 1992),
> (e) his physical or mental health or condition,
> (f) his sexual life,

(g) the commission or alleged commission by him of any offence, or

(h) any proceedings for any offence committed or alleged to have been committed by him, the disposal of such proceedings or the sentence of any court in such proceedings.

In order to ensure compliance with the first data protection principle, it is also necessary for data controllers processing sensitive personal data to satisfy a Schedule 2 condition.

The necessity test

The requirement of necessity appears in six of the nine conditions contained in Schedule 3. The tenth condition, which allows the Secretary of State to make orders describing circumstances in which sensitive personal data may be processed, has introduced further situations in which the necessity test must be satisfied.

Explicit consent

The first condition says:

1. The data subject has given his explicit consent to the processing of the personal data.

Clearly, there is a distinction between the explicit consent required by the first condition in Schedule 3 and the consent required by the first condition in Schedule 2. Although the distinction has not been defined in the DPA, it seems obvious that explicit consent leaves no room for inferring consent from a course of dealing. The essence of explicit consent would seem to be that the data subject has to positively indicate their consent, for example by ticking an 'opt-in' box on a website form that is preceded with a detailed description of the processing purposes that includes all of the information required by the first and second data protection principles. Of course, this does not mean that explicit consent always requires written consent (explicit consent can be obtained during a conversation), but written consent will always provide the data controller with significantly more evidential protection and comfort.

As for the requirement to show both a Schedule 2 condition and a Schedule 3 condition, this is done by obtaining explicit consent.

Employment necessity

The second condition says:

2.–(1) The processing is necessary for the purposes of exercising or performing any right or obligation which is conferred or imposed by law on the data controller in connection with employment.

(2) The Secretary of State may by order –

> (a) exclude the application of sub-paragraph (1) in such cases as may be specified, or
> (b) provide that, in such cases as may be specified, the condition in sub-paragraph (1) is not to be regarded as satisfied unless such further conditions as may be specified in the order are also satisfied.

The first point to note is that the second condition is not limited to relationships between employees and employees. The words 'in connection with employment' indicates that data controllers may rely upon this condition to process personal data where the data subjects are not their employees.

The second substantial point is actually a question, namely what is meant by the phrase 'any right or obligation which is conferred or imposed by law'? Does this mean that the second condition may apply to processing that is covered by a contract of employment, or does it mean that the second condition is restricted to statutory rights or obligations? At the date of publication of this book there have been no court cases to provide assistance, but it is submitted that the correct interpretation is that the second condition is referring only to statutory rights and obligations, not to contractual rights and obligations. If contractual rights and obligations were intended to be included the words 'which is conferred or imposed by law on the data controller' would have been omitted. Alternatively, the condition could easily have referred to contractual rights obligations.

There are many circumstances that give rise to a right or obligation to process personal information in connection with employment. For example, employers are required by health and safety legislation to maintain accident books in which details of injuries sustained at work are recorded. Records will also be created in relation to redundancies, the transfer of undertakings, the payment of taxes and the employment of disabled workers to prevent disability discrimination, and the employment of gay and lesbian workers to prevent sexual orientation discrimination.

As regards the requirement to show a Schedule 2 condition, data controllers relying upon this condition could also rely upon the third and fifth conditions and, possibly, the second and sixth conditions within Schedule 2.

Finally, at the date of publication of this book no orders have been made by the Secretary of State under the second part of this condition.

Vital interests necessity

The third condition says:

> 3. The processing is necessary –
> (a) in order to protect the vital interests of the data subject or another person, in a case where –
> (i) consent cannot be given by or on behalf of the data subject, or
> (ii) the data controller cannot reasonably be expected to obtain the consent of the data subject, or

> (b) in order to protect the vital interests of another person, in a case where consent by or on behalf of the data subject has been unreasonably withheld.

There is a considerable overlap between this condition and the fourth condition in Schedule 2, which says that 'the processing is necessary in order to protect the vital interests of the data subject'. The distinctions between these two conditions are:

- This condition concerns the vital interests of data subjects and other persons.
- This condition makes consent a relevant factor.

These distinguishing features create a curious result. In many respects this condition is wider than the fourth condition in Schedule 2 because of the reference to other persons. It also seems to be narrower in the sense that it is dealing with cases where consent is absent. However, the extent to which it can be said that this condition is narrower due to the consent point is moot, because the fourth condition in Schedule 2 is an alternative to the first condition in Schedule 2, implying that the fourth condition in Schedule 2 will only be relied upon in cases where consent has not been obtained, which is exactly the same position with this condition.

The real importance of the consent factor is found in the fact that the other person may not be identified, or may form part of a defined class or group of unspecified individuals, such as people within a particular geographical location, or people within a particular age group. Indeed, it is hard to see why this condition would refer to other persons if those persons were identified, because once identified they would inevitably become data subjects in their own right if their data were processed, meaning that the data controller would have to demonstrate independent Schedule 2 and/or Schedule 3 conditions for their data.

EXAMPLE

The data subject is suffering from a serious, communicable disease. In order to protect the vital interests of people who may come into contact with the data subject, people whose identities are presently unknown, health authorities may process sensitive personal data about the data subject without consent relying upon the third condition in Schedule 3.

Paragraph 3(a)(i) contains a interesting reference to cases where consent cannot be given on behalf of the data subject. This is intended to deal with a limited category of cases where a third party has the power to act on the data subject's behalf, such as in a parent–child situation, or where someone is acting under a power of attorney or under an order of the court. This condition may apply in a very tragic accident, where parents and child are all rendered incapacitated, or where a parent, guardian, next of kin or similar cannot be traced.

In respect of satisfying a Schedule 2 condition, it would seem to be the case that where the processing is done to protect the data subject's vital interests the fourth condition in Schedule 2 will be satisfied. However, where the processing is done to protect the vital interests of another person, it is hard to see how the fourth condition in Schedule 2 will apply. In the example given above, which concerned the protection of the public from communicable diseases, health authorities will probably be able to rely upon the third condition in Schedule 2, namely processing that is necessary for compliance with a non-contractual legal obligation.

Legitimate interests of not-for-profit organizations

The fourth condition says:

> 4. The processing –
> (a) is carried out in the course of its legitimate activities by any body or association which –
> (i) is not established or conducted for profit, and
> (ii) exists for political, philosophical, religious or trade-union purposes,
> (b) is carried out with appropriate safeguards for the rights and freedoms of data subjects,
> (c) relates only to individuals who either are members of the body or association or have regular contact with it in connection with its purposes, and
> (d) does not involve disclosure of the personal data to a third party without the consent of the data subject.

There are many parallels between this condition and the legitimate interests condition in Schedule 2 although, of course, this condition is strictly limited to not-for-profit organizations. These organizations may or may not be registered charities.

In order for this condition to apply the data controller needs to satisfy each and every sub-clause, but the meaning of 'appropriate safeguards for the rights and freedoms of data subjects' is unclear. It might be pointing to security issues, but these are covered by the seventh data protection principle. Alternatively, it might just stand as emphasis, perhaps reminding not-for-profit organizations that relatively meagre resources do not absolve them from the need to meet the requirements of the DPA.

Information made public

The fifth condition says:

> 5. The information contained in the personal data has been made public as a result of steps deliberately taken by the data subject.

The justification for this exemption seems to be obvious; data subjects are entitled to decide for themselves whether they wish to forego protection for their sensitive personal data. The difficulty, if there is one, lies in deciding what amounts to the deliberate taking of steps to make information public. For example, in the *Lindqvist*[112] case one of the grounds of complaint was that Mrs Lindqvist had mentioned on her website that one of her fellow parishioners 'had injured her foot and was on half-time on medical grounds', but it is arguable that the fact of a foot injury, if not concealable, is information that is deliberately made public. The converse argument, of course, is that all because a medical condition is obvious does not mean that it is deliberately made public; it is made public because it is obvious and despite the intentions of the data subject.

Clearly, what amounts to the taking of deliberate steps and what amounts to making public are both questions of fact that need to be decided on a case-by-case basis.

Legal proceedings, legal advice and legal rights necessity

The sixth condition says:

> 6. The processing –
> (a) is necessary for the purpose of, or in connection with, any legal proceedings (including prospective legal proceedings),
> (b) is necessary for the purpose of obtaining legal advice, or
> (c) is otherwise necessary for the purposes of establishing, exercising or defending legal rights.

This condition is designed to allow data controllers to disclose personal data to their legal advisers. In the employment context it will be obvious that the data controller will need to take legal advice on a discrimination case brought by an employee or a former employee, or on an accident at work case. This condition will protect the employer as well as the legal advisers. In addition, if the legal advisers need to obtain expert advice to assist their client, perhaps from a medical expert, this condition will be relied upon.

Public functions necessity

The seventh condition says:

> 7. – (1) The processing is necessary –
> (a) for the administration of justice,
> (aa) for the exercise of any functions of either House of Parliament,
> (b) for the exercise of any functions conferred on any person by or under an enactment, or
> (c) for the exercise of any functions of the Crown, a Minister of the Crown or a government department.
> (2) The Secretary of State may by order –

> (a) exclude the application of sub-paragraph (1) in such cases as may be specified, or
> (b) provide that, in such cases as may be specified, the condition in sub-paragraph (1) is not to be regarded as satisfied unless such further conditions as may be specified in the order are also satisfied.

This condition is a mirror of the fifth condition in Schedule 2, except that it does not include an equivalent to 'the exercise of any other functions of a public nature exercised in the public interest by any person' requirement found within paragraph 5(d) of Schedule 2. Thus, this condition is narrower in scope. Furthermore, the necessity condition will be harder to satisfy than the one in the fifth condition in Schedule 2.

At the date of publication of this book the Secretary of State has not made any orders under the second part of this condition.

Medical purposes necessity

The eighth condition says:

> 8. – (1) The processing is necessary for medical purposes and is undertaken by –
> (a) a health professional, or
> (b) a person who in the circumstances owes a duty of confidentiality which is equivalent to that which would arise if that person were a health professional.
> (2) In this paragraph 'medical purposes' includes the purposes of preventative medicine, medical diagnosis, medical research, the provision of care and treatment and the management of healthcare services.

This condition complements the vital interests conditions discussed earlier, dealing with non life or death situations. The meaning of 'health professional' is contained in section 69 of the DPA. The list of health professionals in section 69 includes GPs, dentists, opticians and pharmacists but because the list is a finite list, paragraph 8(1)(a) extends coverage to persons who are not listed in section 69 but who owe similar duties of confidence, such as acupuncturists and herbalists.

Racial or ethnic monitoring necessity

The ninth condition says:

> 9. – (1) The processing –
> (a) is of sensitive personal data consisting of information as to racial or ethnic origin,
> (b) is necessary for the purpose of identifying or keeping under review the existence or absence of equality of opportunity or treatment between persons of different racial or ethnic origins, with a view to enabling such equality to be promoted or maintained, and

> (c) is carried out with appropriate safeguards for the rights and freedoms of data subjects.
>
> (2) The Secretary of State may by order specify circumstances in which processing falling within sub-paragraph (1)(a) and (b) is, or is not, to be taken for the purposes of sub-paragraph (1)(c) to be carried out with appropriate safeguards for the rights and freedoms of data subjects.

This condition is specifically limited to the processing of information about racial or ethnic monitoring, so it does not cover monitoring for the purposes of ensuring equal treatment between the sexes, or equal treatment for the disabled (but see the next paragraph) or for homosexuals. The condition is not limited to employer–employee relationships, so it can be relied upon by service providers, including public authorities.

The Secretary of State has not made any order under 9(2), although the Data Protection (Processing of Sensitive Personal Data) Order 2000,[113] discussed below, does extend the power of equal opportunities monitoring to cover religious and similar beliefs and physical or mental health or condition.

Processing pursuant to order of the Secretary of State

The tenth condition says:

> 10. The personal data are processed in circumstances specified in an order made by the Secretary of State for the purposes of this paragraph.

The Secretary of State has made two orders under this condition. These are the Data Protection (Processing of Sensitive Personal Data) Order 2000[114] and the Data Protection (Processing of Sensitive Personal Data) (Elected Representatives) Order 2002.[115]

THE DATA PROTECTION (PROCESSING OF SENSITIVE PERSONAL DATA) ORDER 2000

This order is made under paragraph 10 of Schedule 3 to the DPA and describes additional circumstances pursuant to which sensitive personal data may be processed. Ten situations are identified in the schedule to the order, the majority of which also contain the necessity test. Five of the circumstances also require that the processing be carried out 'in the substantial public interest'.

As far as the substantial public interest test is concerned, this involves a test of proportionality, that is, the interference with the data subject's rights must be proportionate judged by reference to the public interest served, which itself must be 'substantial'. The fact that the processing might be beneficial to the public interest will not provide sufficient grounds for the processing.

The prevention or detection of unlawful acts

The first circumstance says:

> **1. – (1) The processing –**
> **(a) is in the substantial public interest;**
> **(b) is necessary for the purposes of the prevention or detection of any unlawful act; and**
> **(c) must necessarily be carried out without the explicit consent of the data subject being sought so as not to prejudice those purposes.**
> **(2) In this paragraph, 'act' includes a failure to act.**

This circumstance is not looking for criminal acts. Rather it is concerned with unlawful acts, which includes not only criminal acts but also civil wrongs including, potentially, contractual breaches and torts, such as negligence and nuisance. Thus, this circumstance is potentially very wide indeed.

In terms of privacy the real peril for data subjects lies in the fact that this circumstance is concerned with situations where their explicit consent will not be sought because of a risk of prejudice to the processing purpose, namely the prevention or detection of unlawful acts. The data subject's privacy will be affected because the data subject has no information to enable them to exercise any control over the processing. For these reasons this potentially very wide circumstance is seriously restricted by the need for the data controller to overcome four distinct hurdles:

- The data controller must satisfy the substantial public interest test.
- The data controller must satisfy the necessity test.
- The data controller must show that the processing must be necessarily carried out without consent.
- The data controller must show that the seeking of consent would cause prejudice to the processing purpose.

These very strict tests erect very high barriers to a data controller's reliance upon this circumstance and they point very clearly to the benefit of doubt always being exercised in the data subject's favour. The likelihood of prejudice being caused to the processing purpose if the data subject's consent were sought must be very real. In the case of *R (on the application of Alan Lord) v. The Secretary of State for the Home Department*[116] the High Court confirmed that the likelihood of prejudice need not be more likely than not, but, conversely, a fanciful risk will not suffice.

Consequently, data controllers wishing to rely upon this circumstance must be clear in their thinking and reasoning. From a compliance perspective this encourages the data controller to record its thinking and reasoning, so that in the event of scrutiny by the data subject, the Information Commissioner, the Information Tribunal or the courts, the data controller's motivations will be indisputable.

EXAMPLE

A person brings a claim for damages for personal injury following a road traffic accident. The claimant says that their injuries prevent them from working and from participating in any sport. The defendant, while admitting that the accident was their fault, seriously disputes what the claimant says about their injuries, relying upon independent medical evidence that casts considerable doubt on the claimant's claims. In order to protect themselves from an exaggerated claim, the defendant engages the services of a firm of private detectives who follow the claimant with a hidden video camera and record footage of their comings and goings. In this example the video footage will record the claimant's sensitive personal data (information about their physical conditions). It is highly likely that the secret videoing will be justified on the grounds of preventing or detecting an unlawful act.

Protecting the public and regulatory activity

The second circumstance says:

2. The processing –
(a) is in the substantial public interest;
(b) is necessary for the discharge of any function which is designed for protecting members of the public against –
(i) dishonesty, malpractice, or other seriously improper conduct by, or the unfitness or incompetence of, any person, or
(ii) mismanagement in the administration of, or failures in services provided by, any body or association; and
(c) must necessarily be carried out without the explicit consent of the data subject being sought so as not to prejudice the discharge of that function.

As with the first circumstance, the data controller has very significant hurdles to overcome before it can rely upon this exemption.

This circumstance can be relied upon by a data controller who is required to discharge a function designed to protect the public from the perils listed. Data controllers who rely on this exemption include regulators such as the FSA, the Office of Communications (Ofcom), the Office of Fair Trading, the Law Society and the General Medical Council.

Special purposes disclosures

The third circumstance says:

3. – (1) The disclosure of personal data –
(a) is in the substantial public interest;
(b) is in connection with –

> (i) the commission by any person of any unlawful act (whether alleged or established),
> (ii) dishonesty, malpractice, or other seriously improper conduct by, or the unfitness or incompetence of, any person (whether alleged or established), or
> (iii) mismanagement in the administration of, or failures in services provided by, any body or association (whether alleged or established);
> (c) is for the special purposes as defined in section 3 of the Act; and
> (d) is made with a view to the publication of those data by any person and the data controller reasonably believes that such publication would be in the public interest.
> (2) In this paragraph, 'act' includes a failure to act.

This circumstance deals with only one aspect of processing, namely disclosures and it concerns only disclosures made for the special purposes, namely journalistic, literary and artistic purposes. The primary effect of this circumstance is to support the media in its reporting of wrongdoing, as part of the protections for freedom of expression.

Counselling, advice and support

The fourth circumstance says:

> 4. The processing –
> (a) is in the substantial public interest;
> (b) is necessary for the discharge of any function which is designed for the provision of confidential counselling, advice, support or any other service; and
> (c) is carried out without the explicit consent of the data subject because the processing –
> (i) is necessary in a case where consent cannot be given by the data subject,
> (ii) is necessary in a case where the data controller cannot reasonably be expected to obtain the explicit consent of the data subject, or
> (iii) must necessarily be carried out without the explicit consent of the data subject being sought so as not to prejudice the provision of that counselling, advice, support or other service.

This circumstance is intended to facilitate counselling and similar services where it is necessary for a counsellor or advisor to learn of personal matters relating to people connected with the person undergoing counselling, for example during marriage guidance counselling where the counsellor speaks to the spouses separately or to only one of them.

Insurance company and pension schemes processing of medical data

The fifth circumstance says:

> 5. – (1) The processing –
> (a) is necessary for the purpose of –
> (i) carrying on insurance business, or
> (ii) making determinations in connection with eligibility for, and benefits payable under, an occupational pension scheme as defined in section 1 of the Pension Schemes Act 1993;
> (b) is of sensitive personal data consisting of information falling within section 2(e) of the Act relating to a data subject who is the parent, grandparent, great grandparent or sibling of –
> (i) in the case of paragraph (a)(i), the insured person, or
> (ii) in the case of paragraph (a)(ii), the member of the scheme;
> (c) is necessary in a case where the data controller cannot reasonably be expected to obtain the explicit consent of that data subject and the data controller is not aware of the data subject withholding his consent; and
> (d) does not support measures or decisions with respect to that data subject.

The effect of this circumstance is that it allows insurance companies and pension schemes to process medical data of the insured's or scheme member's family, provided that the data are not used to support decisions or measures with respect to the family member concerned.

Insurance company and pension scheme established processing

The sixth circumstance says:

> 6. The processing –
> (a) is of sensitive personal data in relation to any particular data subjects that are subject to processing which was already under way immediately before the coming into force of this order;
> (b) is necessary for the purpose of –
> (i) carrying on insurance business, as defined in section 95 of the Insurance Companies Act 1982, falling within Classes I, III or IV of Schedule 1 to that Act; or
> (ii) establishing or administering an occupational pension scheme as defined in section 1 of the Pension Schemes Act 1993; and
> (c) either –
> (i) is necessary in a case where the data controller cannot reasonably be expected to obtain the explicit consent of the data subject and that data subject has not informed the data controller that he does not so consent, or
> (ii) must necessarily be carried out even without the explicit consent of the data subject so as not to prejudice those purposes.

The sixth circumstance concerns sensitive personal data that was being processed by insurance companies and pension schemes prior to the coming into force of the Data Protection (Processing of Sensitive Personal Data) Order 2000[117] on 1 March 2000. Unlike the fifth circumstance, this circumstance concerns any type of sensitive personal data, not just medical data relating to family members of the insured or pension scheme member. It is designed to ensure that insurance companies and pension schemes are not unduly hindered by the coming into effect of the DPA.

Equal opportunities processing

The seventh circumstance says:

> 7. – (1) Subject to the provisions of sub-paragraph (2), the processing –
> (a) is of sensitive personal data consisting of information falling within section 2(c) or (e) of the Act;
> (b) is necessary for the purpose of identifying or keeping under review the existence or absence of equality of opportunity or treatment between persons
> (i) holding different beliefs as described in section 2(c) of the Act, or
> (ii) of different states of physical or mental health or different physical or mental conditions as described in section 2(e) of the Act,
> with a view to enabling such equality to be promoted or maintained;
> (c) does not support measures or decisions with respect to any particular data subject otherwise than with the explicit consent of that data subject; and
> (d) does not cause, nor is likely to cause, substantial damage or substantial distress to the data subject or any other person.
> (2) Where any individual has given notice in writing to any data controller who is processing personal data under the provisions of sub-paragraph (1) requiring that data controller to cease processing personal data in respect of which that individual is the data subject at the end of such period as is reasonable in the circumstances, that data controller must have ceased processing those personal data at the end of that period.

This circumstance effectively expands the ninth condition in Schedule 3 to the DPA, concerning equal opportunities monitoring. The expansion thereby allows data controllers to process sensitive personal data about data subjects' religious or similar beliefs or their physical or mental health or condition. The key limitations on the use of this circumstance are:

- The processing must be necessary for equal opportunities monitoring.
- The processing cannot justify measures or decisions relating to the data subject. Explicit consent is needed for such measures or decisions.
- The processing cannot be allowed to cause substantial damage or distress to the data subject or to other persons.
- The processing must cease following a request from the data subject.

Political parties processing

The eighth circumstance says:

8. – (1) Subject to the provisions of sub-paragraph (2), the processing –
(a) is of sensitive personal data consisting of information falling within section 2(b) of the Act;
(b) is carried out by any person or organisation included in the register maintained pursuant to section 1 of the Registration of Political Parties Act 1998 in the course of his or its legitimate political activities; and
(c) does not cause, nor is likely to cause, substantial damage or substantial distress to the data subject or any other person.
(2) Where any individual has given notice in writing to any data controller who is processing personal data under the provisions of sub-paragraph (1) requiring that data controller to cease processing personal data in respect of which that individual is the data subject at the end of such period as is reasonable in the circumstances, that data controller must have ceased processing those personal data at the end of that period.

This circumstance provides registered political parties with a limited right to process information about a person's political opinions without consent, provided that neither substantial damage or distress is caused and provided that the processing stops following a request from the data subject.

Research

The ninth circumstance says:

9. The processing –
(a) is in the substantial public interest;
(b) is necessary for research purposes (which expression shall have the same meaning as in section 33 of the Act);
(c) does not support measures or decisions with respect to any particular data subject otherwise than with the explicit consent of that data subject; and
(d) does not cause, nor is likely to cause, substantial damage or substantial distress to the data subject or any other person.

This is a very limited circumstance that allows processing for research, statistical and historical purposes without explicit consent, provided that neither substantial damage or distress are caused. The other safeguards are the requirement to satisfy the substantial public interest test and the necessity test.

Processing by police constables

The tenth circumstance says:

10. The processing is necessary for the exercise of any functions conferred on a constable by any rule of law.

Again, this is another wide circumstance that allows police constables to process sensitive personal data without the data subject's explicit consent if the processing is necessary.

THE DATA PROTECTION (PROCESSING OF SENSITIVE PERSONAL DATA) (ELECTED REPRESENTATIVES) ORDER 2002

This order allows for the processing of sensitive personal data consisting of processing by elected representatives and disclosures of sensitive personal data by data controllers to elected representatives. Elected representatives are members of the House of Commons, the Welsh Assembly, the Scottish Parliament, the Northern Ireland Assembly, a UK Member of the European Parliament and mayors and councillors of local authorities and similar bodies, such as the London Assembly. This order covers cases where an elected representative is asked by a data subject to take action on their behalf, or on behalf of another person. Basically, it facilitates the performance of the elected representative's functions. If an elected representative contacts a data controller, the data controller can disclose sensitive personal data to the elected representative without fear of breaching the DPA, but if a data controller is contacted by an elected representative, it should consult the order before disclosing sensitive personal data.

THE DATA PROTECTION (PROCESSING OF SENSITIVE PERSONAL DATA) ORDER 2006

This order is also made under paragraph 10 of Schedule 3 to the DPA and it permits the processing of sensitive personal data in respect of convictions or cautions for child pornography offences. This order enables the police to liaise with banks, credit card companies and other financial institutions to prevent the use of bank accounts and payment cards in the connection with child pornography offences, provided that there has been a conviction or caution.

PART IV EXEMPTIONS

Part IV of the DPA contains exemptions from the 'subject information provisions' and the 'non-disclosure provisions'. The exemptions from the subject information provisions, which are essentially exemptions from the transparency provisions of the DPA, were discussed in Chapter 2. This section deals with the exemptions from the non-disclosure provisions.

The non-disclosure provisions

The disclosure of personal data is an act of processing and section 27 identifies the non-disclosure provisions of the DPA to be:

- The first data protection principle's requirement for fair and lawful processing. However, the first data protection principle's requirement for the data controller to satisfy a Schedule 2 or Schedule 3 condition does not form part of the non-disclosure provisions.
- The second, third, fourth and fifth data protection principles.
- Section 10, which contains the data subject's right to object to processing likely to cause substantial and unwarranted damage or distress.
- Section 14(1) to (3), which empowers the court to order the rectification, blocking, erasure or destruction of inaccurate personal data and the notification of the fact of rectification, blocking, erasure or destruction to third-party recipients of the personal data.

Where Part IV contains an exemption from the non-disclosure provisions, these provisions will not apply to the processing in question. As explained in Chapter 2, section 36 of the DPA contains a complete exemption for processing done for domestic purposes and section 28 creates the possibility of an equally comprehensive exemption where such an exemption is required 'for the purposes of safeguarding national security'. It should also be remembered that the exemptions in Part IV fall into two categories: prejudice-based exemptions and class-based exemptions.

Table 3.1 lists the subject information provisions and the non-disclosure provisions.

TABLE 3.1 *The subject information provisions and the non-disclosure provisions*

Subject information provisions	Non-disclosure provisions
The first data protection principle, apart from the prescribed information	The first data protection principle, apart from the requirement to show a Schedule 2 or 3 criterion for legitimacy.
Section 7 – The data subject's right of access	The second data protection principle.
	The third data protection principle.
	The fourth data protection principle.
	The fifth data protection principle.
	Section 10 – the right to prevent processing likely to cause substantial and unwarranted damage or distress.
	Sections 14(1)–(3) – The court's power to order rectification etc. of inaccurate data.

Crime and taxation

Where the processing is for the purposes of the prevention or detection of crime, the apprehension or prosecution of offenders, the assessment or collection of any tax or duty the non-disclosure provisions will not apply if they would be likely to prejudice any of these functions.

Journalism, literature and art (the special purposes)

The non-disclosure provisions do not apply where the processing is for the special purposes. The conditions to be satisfied are the same as those identified in Chapter 2. It should also be noted that the exemption in section 32 extends further than the subject information provisions and the non-disclosure provisions, because the first data protection principle is excluded in its entirety as are the sixth and eighth data protection principles and section 12 (the right to object to automated decision taking).

Manual data held by public authorities

In addition to the exemptions identified in Chapter 2 and in addition to the non-disclosure provisions (the fourth data protection principle excluded) the exemptions for processing by way of recorded information held by public authorities extends to the whole of the first data protection principle, to the seventh data protection principle, to the eighth data protection principle, to section 11 (the right to object to processing for direct marketing purposes), section 12, section 13 (apart from where damage is caused as a result of a breach of section 7, or where distress is caused as a result of a breach of the fourth data protection principle), to Part III (notification) and to section 55 (unlawful obtaining or disclosure of personal data).

Information available to the public under an enactment

In the same circumstances described in Chapter 2, section 34 of the DPA also contains an exemption from the non-disclosure provisions.

Disclosures required by law or made in connection with legal proceedings

Section 35 of the DPA contains an exemption from the non-disclosure provisions in the following circumstances:

- where disclosure is required under an enactment, by any rule of law or by order of a court;
- where the disclosure is required for the purposes of, or in connection with, any legal proceedings, or prospective legal proceedings;
- where the disclosure is necessary for the purpose of obtaining legal advice;
- where the processing is necessary for the purposes of establishing, exercising or defending legal rights.

The subject information provisions are not excluded under section 35.

Parliamentary privilege

In the same circumstances as described in Chapter 2, section 35A also contains an exemption from the non-disclosure provisions in addition to the exemption from section 7.

4 The Right to Object

INTRODUCTION

Another critical control mechanism introduced by the Data Protection Directive is the right to object, which is contained in Chapter II, section VII. The Directive envisages three situations in which the right to object will apply. These are:

- Where the processing is necessary for the performance of public functions or where the processing is necessary for the data controller's legitimate interests. Member States are allowed to extend the right to object to other kinds of processing, but in all cases the data subject may only object on 'compelling legitimate grounds relating to his particular situation' (Article 14(a)). These higher barriers to objection are in place because of the second goal of data protection laws, the maintenance of transborder data flows.
- Where the processing is for the purposes of direct marketing (Article 14(b)). The rules on direct marketing have been added to by the Directive on Privacy and Electronic Communications.[118]
- Where decisions significantly affecting the data subject are based solely on automated processing. These decisions must be intended to evaluate personal aspects relating to the data subject, such as performance at work, creditworthiness, reliability and conduct.

The right to object is exercised by the data subject giving written notice to the data controller asking the data controller to cease, or to not begin, processing. Within the DPA the right to object is contained in sections 10, 11, 12 and 12A. Section 12A, which concerns certain types of manual processing, applies only until 23 October 2007. Each right to object is enforceable before the courts by the data subject.

SUBSTANTIAL AND UNWARRANTED DAMAGE OR DISTRESS

The right to prevent processing that is causing, or that is likely to cause, substantial and unwarranted damage or distress is contained in section 10 of the DPA and is intended to implement Article 14(a) of the Data Protection Directive. To recap, Article 14(a) of the Directive allows the data subject the right to object to data processing that is necessary for public functions or to data processing necessary for legitimate interests, provided that the objection is made on 'compelling legitimate grounds'. These compelling legitimate grounds are for the Member States to define and under section 10 of the

DPA they equate to substantial and unwarranted damage or distress actually being suffered, or likely to be suffered, by the data subject or by another person. The extension of the protection to cover the interests of persons other than the data subject is an important issue for data controllers.

The right to object to processing likely to cause substantial and unwarranted damage or distress does not apply where the Schedule 2 criterion for legitimacy is either the data subject's consent, or where the processing is necessary for the performance of a contract, or where the processing is necessary in the data subject's vital interests. This means that the right to object as implemented by the DPA extends no further than the specific processing operations identified in Article 14(a) of the Directive, namely processing that is necessary in the performance of public functions and processing that is necessary for the data controller's legitimate interests.

Is substantial and unwarranted damage or distress likely?

These cases are the most complex, involving three difficult interrelated issues, which can be put as follows:

- What is meant by substantial?
- What is meant by unwarranted?
- What is meant by likely?

The precise meaning of each of these words will need to be defined by the courts, but in combination they seem to present large obstacles to the data subject. This reflects the powerful scope for processing contained in the public functions and legitimate interests criteria for legitimacy as well as the Data Protection Directive's second aim of maintaining flow of information around the EEA and to adequate third countries. The Information Commissioner's 'Legal Guidance' says:

> It is for a court to decide in each case whether the damage or distress is substantial and unwarranted. The Commissioner takes the view that a data subject notice is, therefore, only likely to be appropriate where the particular processing has caused, or is likely to cause, someone to suffer loss or harm, or upset and anguish of a real nature, over and above annoyance level, and without justification.[119]

The choice of the word 'likely' means that the data subject does not have to prove that the suffering of damage or distress as a consequence of the processing will be certain. Conversely, it is obvious that a mere fanciful chance of damage or distress being suffered will not be sufficient, as the Information Commissioner has pointed out.

The data subject notice: Form and content

The right to object is exercised by the giving of a written notice by the data subject to the data controller. This is known as a 'data subject notice' (section

10(3) DPA). The data subject notice can be given in letter form or in an electronic form, often email, but there is no mandatory or approved format for the notice.

There is some mandatory content, however. First, the data subject needs to include a form of words that enables the data controller to understand that it is being asked not to process the data subject's personal data. The words used and the detail to be provided are matters for the data subject. Second, the data subject must state that the processing is causing, or is likely to cause, substantial and unwarranted damage or distress to them or to another person. Third, the data subject must give reasons for their belief that substantial and unwarranted damage or distress has been caused or is likely to be caused.

The data subject notice does not have to specify a deadline for the cessation of processing, because the DPA grants the data controller a reasonable time to bring processing to a halt, which may be longer than the period envisaged by the data subject. However, a data subject may wish to set a deadline as part of their reasoned argument, for example in cases of urgency.

In cases where the data subject believes that substantial and unwarranted damage or distress is or will be caused to another person, the data subject is not obliged to give the other person's identity. However, the identity of the third party may be relevant to the data controller's reaction.

The data controller's reaction

The data controller has 21 days commencing with the date of receipt of a data subject notice to give the data subject a written notice in response. This notice must state one of the following:

- The data controller has complied with, or intends to comply with, the data subject notice.
- The extent to which the data controller regards the data subject notice as being unjustified and the extent to which it has complied or intends to comply with it. Of course, the data controller may regard the entire data subject notice as being unjustified, meaning that it will not comply with it to any extent.

Court action

If the data controller refuses to comply with a data subject notice, the data subject may bring an action before the court. If the court considers that the notice is justified but the data controller has failed to comply with it, the court may order the data controller to take such steps as it thinks are required to make the data controller comply. The court has unlimited discretion in the steps that it may order, provided they are proportionate.

DIRECT MARKETING

Section 11 of the DPA gives individuals the right to prevent processing for direct marketing purposes. Section 11(3) defines direct marketing as being 'the communication (by whatever means) of any advertising or marketing material which is directed at particular individuals'.

The procedure to be followed under section 11 is very similar to the procedure under section 10 (substantial and unwarranted damage or distress), except that the data controller is not required to serve a notice in response to the individual's notice. As before, the data subject notice must be in writing. As for its contents, it must merely state that the data subject wishes to prevent direct marketing. The data controller then has a reasonable period during which to comply. If the data controller fails to comply, the data subject can enforce their rights in court and if the court agrees with the data subject it may make such order as it sees fit.

The construction of section 11 is very favourable to data controllers in that it allows them to send direct marketing communications to individuals until they formally object, or 'opt-out' as it is often called. So, in an opt-out situation the data subject needs to exercise the right to object to put an end to processing for direct marketing purposes. The opposite of opt-out is opt-in. In an opt-in situation processing for direct marketing purposes is not allowed to start without the data subject's prior consent, which, as with all other consents under the DPA, must be freely given, unambiguous and specific.

Direct marketing using electronic communications services

Section 11 of the DPA must be read in light of the rules contained in the Privacy and Electronic Communications (EC Directive) Regulations 2003,[120] which were introduced in order to give effect to the requirements of the Directive on Privacy and Electronic Communications.[121] The direct marketing rules within the 2003 Regulations concern direct marketing that uses electronic communications services, namely automated calling systems, fax, telephone and email, meaning that only postal communications and other non-electronic equivalents are now covered by the opt-out rule in section 11 DPA.

The beneficiary of the protections contained in the 2003 Regulations are known as 'subscribers'. A subscriber is a natural person (a living individual) or legal person (a company or other organization) who is a 'party to a contract with a provider of public electronic communications services for the supply of such services'. Thus, the 2003 Regulations extend the protection of data protection laws to corporate bodies.

The rules on direct marketing are summarized in Table 4.1.

Table 4.1 shows that as far as direct marketing using electronic communications services is concerned, data protection laws legitimize both the 'opt-out' approach and the 'opt-in' approach, depending upon the form of

TABLE 4.1 *Direct marketing*

	Individual subscribers	Corporate subscribers	Preference registers
Automated calling systems	Individual and corporate subscribers are treated equally. The use of automated calling systems for direct marketing communication is prohibited without the subscriber's consent, which must be given in advance.		
Fax machines	The sending of direct marketing information by fax to individual subscribers is prohibited without their consent, which must be given in advance.	The sending of direct marketing information by fax to corporate subscribers is allowed until the corporate subscriber exercises the right to object.	The sender should consult the Fax Preference Service register, which records telephone numbers to which fax direct marketing information may not be sent.
Telephone	Again, individual and corporate subscribers are treated equally. Cold calling by telephone for direct marketing is allowed until the subscriber exercises the right to object.		The sender should consult the Telephone Preference Service register, which records telephone numbers to which cold calls may not be made.
Email	The sending of direct marketing information by email to individual subscribers is prohibited without their consent, which must be given in advance. However, if there are pre-existing commercial relationships and the email is about similar products or services, these emails can be sent without prior consent. This is often called a 'soft opt-in'. If emails are sent pursuant to the pre-existing relationships exception, the subscriber must be given a simple means to exercise the right to object.	The sending of direct marketing information by email to corporate subscribers is allowed until the corporate subscriber exercises the right to object.	
Spam email	Spam emails, where the sender's identity or email address are concealed, are prohibited.		

the direct marketing communication. As far as individuals are concerned, opt-out is allowed for cold calls and for emails where there is a pre-existing commercial relationship between the sender and the recipient. Opt-in is required for automatic calling equipment, fax and all other emails. Thus, the individual subscriber will need to exercise their right to object to put an end to cold calls and some kinds of emails.

Cases on direct marketing

Four decisions of the Data Protection Tribunal under the Data Protection Act 1984 give assistance on the meaning of consent for the purposes of direct marketing. These cases, *Innovations (Mail Order) Ltd v. The Data Protection Registrar*,[122] *Linguaphone Institute Ltd v. The Data Protection Registrar*,[123] *British Gas Trading Ltd v. Data Protection Registrar*[124] and *Midlands Electricity Plc v. The Data Protection Registrar*[125] are discussed in the section 'Cases on fairness' in Chapter 2.

Information Commissioner's guidance on direct marketing by email

On 2 November 2005 the Information Commissioner published a document titled 'Data Protection Good Practice Note – Electronic mail marketing'.[126] This explains in practical terms the effect of the 'soft opt-in' for direct marketing emails where there is a pre-existing relationship (see Table 4.1). Advice on direct marketing by SMS text messaging is given also.

AUTOMATED DECISION TAKING

Section 12 of the DPA is concerned with automatic processing of personal data that is done for the purposes of evaluating matters relating to the data subject, such as performance at work, creditworthiness, reliability or conduct. The right to object in section 12 does not allow the data subject to prevent this kind of processing operation. Instead, it is concerned with decisions that are based solely on automatic evaluation-processing, if those decisions will significantly affect the data subject. Section 12 gives the data subject the right to prevent these decisions being taken, but it does not give the right to prevent the automatic evaluation-processing itself. If the data subject wishes to prevent the processing itself, recourse could possibly be found in section 10 of the DPA, if substantial and unwarranted damage or distress were caused.

Exercising the right to object

Again, the data subject can only exercise the right to object by giving written notice to the data controller (this will be called the 'first data subject notice'). No special form is required for the first data subject notice, but it must contain words that convey the message that the data controller is being asked to ensure that no decisions significantly affecting the data subject are taken that are based solely on automatic evaluation-processing.

If the data controller fails to comply with the first data subject notice, or if no such notice is served, and it goes on to take a decision, then it must notify the data subject as soon as reasonably practicable after taking the decision that it has been taken and state that it is based solely on automatic evaluation-processing (this will be called the 'first data controller notice'). The data subject may respond by serving another written notice (this will be called the 'second data subject notice') within 21 days asking the data controller to reconsider the decision or to take a new decision that is not based solely on automatic evaluation-processing. The data controller then has a further 21 days to serve a second written notice on the data subject (this will be called the 'second data controller notice') identifying the steps that it intends to take in compliance with the second data subject notice.

The sequence of notices summarized

The sequence of notices is as follows:

(1) The first data subject notice. This is a written notice served under section 12(1) of the DPA. It will ask the data controller to ensure that no decisions significantly affecting the data subject are taken that are based solely on automatic evaluation-processing.

(2) The first data controller notice. If the data controller does not comply with a notice given under section 12(1) of the DPA, or if no such notice is given, the data controller must notify the data subject within a reasonable period of the taking of a decision significantly affecting the data subject that is based solely on automatic evaluation-processing. This notice is served under section 12(2)(a) of the DPA.

(3) The second data subject notice. If the data subject receives a notice from the data controller under section 12(2)(a) of the DPA, it may serve a written notice on the data controller asking it to reconsider its decision or to take another decision not based solely on automatic evaluation-processing. The data subject must serve this notice within 21 days of the date of receipt of the first data controller notice. The second data subject notice is served pursuant to section 12(2)(b) of the DPA.

(4) The second data controller notice. If the data subject serves a second data subject notice, the data controller must serve a notice in response within 21 days of receipt of it, stating the steps that it intends to take in compliance. The second data controller notice is served under section 12(3) of the DPA.

Enforcement before the courts

As with the other rights to object, the right to object under section 12 can be enforced by the data subject before the court. If the court is satisfied that a data subject notice given under either section 12(1) or section 12(2)(b) has not been complied with, it may order the 'responsible person' to reconsider the decision or to take a new decision that is not based solely on automatic evaluation-processing.

Exempt decisions

The right to object does not apply to exempt decisions, of which there are essentially two kinds. The first kind of exempt decision concerns contracts between the data controller and the data subject. The second kind concerns decisions authorized or required by an enactment.

Decisions about contracts

For this exemption to apply the decision must be taken in the course of steps taken for the purpose of considering whether to enter into contract with the data subject, or with a view to entering into such a contract or in the course of performing a contract. Furthermore, the decision must 'grant a request of the data subject'.

The effect of this exemption is that the data subject is not given a right to object where a decision based solely on automatic evaluation-processing is taken for the benefit of a contract with the data subject and if it achieves a result that the data subject requested. Thus, in the financial services field the data subject cannot object if as a result of automatic evaluation-processing they are issued with a credit card that they applied for.

Decisions under an enactment

This exemption benefits public authorities. Public authorities, such as the police or HM Revenue & Customs, may take decisions based solely on automatic evaluation-processing provided that 'steps have been taken to safeguard the legitimate interests of the data subject'. Section 12(7)(b) then goes on to identify as an example a facility under which the data subject may make representations as being a step that safeguards the data subject's legitimate interests.

EXEMPT MANUAL DATA

Section 12A contains two rights which will expire on 23 October 2007. The first is a right to require the data controller to rectify, block, erase or destroy 'exempt manual data'. The second is a right to object to the data controller holding exempt manual data in a way that is incompatible with the data controller's legitimate purposes.

Exempt manual data is manual data that is either a relevant filing system, an accessible record or recorded information held by a public authority. This information will only be exempt manual data if it was processed before 24 October 1998.

THE RIGHT TO OBJECT AND THE SIXTH DATA PROTECTION PRINCIPLE

The sixth data protection principle says that 'personal data shall be processed in accordance with the rights of data subjects under this Act'. In light of the interpretation in Schedule 1, Part II of the DPA, the failure to comply with any of the rights to object, apart from the right to object in respect of exempt manual data, will amount to a breach of the sixth data protection principle. Failure to comply with the sixth data protection principle can justify the Information Commissioner taking enforcement action.

5 Transborder Data Flows

INTRODUCTION

The maintenance of free flows of personal data between countries is the second aim of data protections laws, with the first being the protection of privacy. This is because international sponsors of data protection laws, such as the OECD, the Council of Europe and the EC, consider free flows of personal data to be essential to the economy and to the performance of certain public functions, such as the prevention and detection of crime. Within the EC it is accepted without demur that the internal market cannot properly establish or prosper without transborder data flows.

Of course, there is an inherent tension between the protection of privacy and free flows of personal data, because at its most basic level the protection of privacy, particularly the protection of informational privacy, can prevent flows of personal data. To counter this problem data protection laws need to find a balance between the protection of privacy and data flows between countries. This balance is achieved by making data processing conditional upon compliance with the data protection principles and provided that the data controller meets the minimum standards described in the relevant national law that implements the Data Protection Directive it will be free to transfer personal data to other countries within the EEA.

The correlation of free flows within the EEA is the Directive's prohibition against transfers of personal data to countries outside the EEA that do not provide an adequate level of protection for the privacy of personal data that are undergoing processing. Article 25.1. of the Directive expresses the prohibition in the following fashion:

> The Member States shall provide that the transfer to a third country of personal data which are undergoing processing or are intended for processing after transfer may take place only if, without prejudice to compliance with the national provisions adopted pursuant to the other provisions of this Directive, the third country in question ensures an adequate level of protection.

The prohibition against transfers to non-adequate countries outside the EEA effectively imposes a European-style 'adequacy test' on the rest of the world. The prohibition against transfers of personal data to countries outside the EEA that do not provide an adequate level of protection has massive ramifications for global organizations and for the effective discharge of public functions and it is highly controversial.

However, it is not a complete ban, a vital point that needs to be understood at the very outset. The fact that the ban is not total is proved by Article

26 of the Directive, entitled 'derogations', which is another word for 'exceptions'. This article permits transfers to non-adequate countries in a few select circumstances namely:

- where the data subject has given unambiguous consent;
- where the transfer is necessary for contractual reasons;
- where the transfer is in the public interest;
- where the transfer is necessary for the protection or exercise of legal rights;
- where the transfer is necessary for the protection of the data subject's vital interests;
- where the transfer is of information contained within a public register.

In addition to these exceptions, the Directive allows Member States to authorize transfers to non-adequate countries in cases where the data controller provides evidence of adequate safeguards. Importantly, these safeguards may be contained in contracts between the EU data controller and the data importer situated in the non-adequate country.

The difference between transfers and transit

The prohibition in Article 25 of the Data Protection Directive is concerned with transfers of personal data to non-adequate countries, not the transit of personal data through these countries. The distinction between transfers and transit is therefore a very important one, albeit at times a fine one.

The transit of personal data through a non-adequate country implies the routing of data through that country without any other data processing operations. This is typically the case of data transferred electronically in packets across the internet. The internet is a packet-switched network where an electronic communication is divided into smaller pieces of data, transferred through the best route possible between the sender and the recipient and then reassembled at the recipient's end. In this kind of communication between two European countries personal data can easily be routed through a non-adequate country. In a transfer there is further processing in the non-adequate country, such as where an importer of data acquires data from an exporter of data, or where the importer of data does work on behalf of the data exporter, subject to the data exporter's instructions.

THIRD COUNTRIES AND ADEQUATE PROTECTION

The harmonization of national laws within the EC following the introduction of the Data Protection Directive means that the current state of the law is straightforward; all countries within the EEA provide adequate protection for the rights and freedoms of data subjects whose personal data are processed within their borders. The lawfulness of data transfers to countries outside the EEA depends upon whether the other country offers an adequate level of protection for personal data, that is, whether it satisfies the adequacy test, or whether an exception applies.

The adequacy test

The Data Protection Directive provides very clear guidance on how the adequacy of third countries is to be measured. Article 25.2. says that adequacy 'shall be assessed in the light of all the circumstances surrounding a data transfer operation or a set of data transfer operations' and then goes on to identity particular factors to be considered. These factors are:

- the nature of the data to be transferred;
- the purpose of the processing operation;
- the duration of the processing operation;
- the country of origin of the personal data;
- the country of final destination;
- the rules of law in operation in the country in question;
- the professional rules that are complied with in the country in question;
- the security measures that are complied with in the country in question.

The meaning of the adequacy test has been the subject of detailed examination by the Article 29 Working Party. In a 1998 Working Document[127] the Article 29 Working Party explained that 'data protection rules only contribute to the protection of individuals if they are followed in practice', which means that 'it is therefore necessary to consider not only the content of rules applicable to personal data transferred to a third country, but also the system in place to ensure the effectiveness of such rules'. Therefore the main focus of the adequacy test in practice is:

- the content of the rules that are applicable;
- the means for ensuring their effective compliance.

The Article 29 Working Party includes 'content principles' in its 1998 Working Document, which prescribe the minimum contents of adequate rules. Quoting directly from the Working Document these content principles are:

- **The purpose limitation principle – data should be processed for a specific purpose and subsequently used or further communicated only insofar as this is not incompatible with the purpose of the transfer.**

- **The data quality and proportionality principle – data should be accurate and, where necessary, kept up to date. The data should be adequate, relevant and not excessive in relation to the purposes for which they are transferred or further processed.**

- **The transparency principle – individuals should be provided with information as to the purpose of the processing and the identity of the data** controller in the third country, and other information insofar as this is necessary to ensure fairness.

- The security principle – technical and organisational security measures should be taken by the data controller that are appropriate to the risks presented by the processing. Any person acting under the authority of the data controller, including a processor, must not process data except on instructions from the controller.

- The rights of access, rectification and opposition – the data subject should have a right to obtain a copy of all data relating to him/her that are processed, and a right to rectification of those data where they are shown to be inaccurate. In certain situations he/she should also be able to object to the processing of the data relating to him/her.

- Restrictions on onward transfers – further transfers of the personal data by the recipient of the original data transfer should be permitted only where the second recipient (i.e. the recipient of the onward transfer) is also subject to rules affording an adequate level of protection.

The mechanisms that are required to ensure effective compliance with the content principles are also described by the Article 29 Working Party in the 1988 Working Document. Recognizing that effective mechanisms may take many different forms the Working Document goes on to say that the objectives of these mechanisms are:

- To deliver a good level of compliance with the rules. (No system can guarantee 100% compliance, but some are better than others). A good system is generally characterised by a high degree of awareness among data controllers of their obligations, and among data subjects of their rights and the means of exercising them. The existence of effective and dissuasive sanctions can play an important in ensuring respect for rules, as of course can systems of direct verification by authorities, auditors, or independent data protection officials.

- To provide support and help to individual data subjects in the exercise of their rights. The individual must be able to enforce his/her rights rapidly and effectively, and without prohibitive cost. To do so there must be some sort of institutional mechanism allowing independent investigation of complaints.

- To provide appropriate redress to the injured party where rules are not complied with. This is a key element which must involve a system of independent adjudication or arbitration which allows compensation to be paid and sanctions imposed where appropriate.

The structure and content of the adequacy test as described in Article 25.2. of the Data Protection Directive points clearly to there being a greater likelihood of industrialized Western democracies being considered to be adequate, measured by European standards, than developing countries, but this is not to say that the former can regard the badge of adequacy as being a foregone conclusion. A classic illustration of this point concerns the relationship between the EC and the US.

The adequacy of the US

The EC and the US are both equally committed to the protection of privacy and the maintenance of transborder data flows. Both took a major role in the initial development of data protection laws in the 1970s and the US had formal recognition during the preparatory work undertaken by the Council of Europe that led to the Data Protection Convention. Likewise, there is parity in respect for the rule of law and for democracy. It will therefore come as no surprise to learn that there are many pieces of legislation in the US that concern themselves with the protection of privacy and data protection. Major laws include:

- Fair Credit Reporting Act 1970;
- Health Insurance Portability and Accountability Act 1996 (HIPPA);
- Children's Online Privacy Protection Act 1998 (COPPA);
- Financial Services Modernization Act 1999;
- Telemarketing and Consumer Fraud and Abuse Prevention Act (2003);
- Controlling the Assault of Non Solicited Pornography and Marketing Act 2003 (CAN SPAM).

Against this background it would be fair to expect the EC to treat the US as being adequate for the purposes of transborder data flows, but this is simply not the state of the law. Furthermore, there is a major difference between how the EC treats public sector data transfers to the US and how it treats private sector data transfers.

Dealing first with the transfer of personal data by the EC Member States and their public authorities to a US State and its public authorities, it is clear that these are assisted by the Data Protection Directive to such an extent that the adequacy test very rarely comes in to focus. The justifications for this statement are threefold. First, the Directive does not apply to activities falling outside the scope of community law, such as public security, defence, State security and the State's activities in areas of criminal law. Second, the Directive allows Member States to make wide exemptions from their laws, with particular reference to State and public sector activities. Third, the Directive's position on the prohibition against transfers to non-adequate countries is that derogations are allowed where they are 'necessary or legally required on important public interest grounds'. All of this points to an absence of significant obstacles to the transfer of public sector data between EC Member States and the US.

The position with the transfer of personal data by private sector data controllers is much more complicated and at the moment there is no general presumption that US law is adequate. However, a scheme known as 'Safe Harbor' alleviates many of the problems.

The US Safe Harbor scheme

On 21 July 2000 the US Department of Commerce issued the Safe Harbor Privacy Principles[128] with supporting 'frequently asked questions' (FAQs). These principles and FAQs are intended to satisfy the Data Protection Directive's adequacy test. The US Department of Commerce explains:

> the Department of Commerce is issuing this document and Frequently Asked Questions ('the Principles') under its statutory authority to foster, promote, and develop international commerce. The Principles were developed in consultation with industry and the general public to facilitate trade and commerce between the United States and European Union. They are intended for use solely by U.S. organizations receiving personal data from the European Union for the purpose of qualifying for the safe harbor and the presumption of 'adequacy' it creates.

The essence of the Safe Harbor scheme is that commercial undertakings wishing to import personal data from EC Member States may do so by joining the scheme. By joining the scheme US commercial undertakings will be regarded as providing adequate protection for personal data transferred from the EEA. Participation in the Safe Harbor scheme is entirely voluntary and there are many ways in which a US commercial undertaking may join. For example, an undertaking may join the safe harbor by participating in a self-regulatory group that adheres to the Safe Harbor principles. Alternatively, an undertaking can develop its own self-regulatory privacy policy that is in conformity with the Safe Harbor principles. Another route is by being part of a class of undertakings that is subject to a law or rule requiring privacy protection.

Whatever the route that is taken by the US commercial undertaking, actual participation in the Safe Harbor scheme is conditional upon a self-certification to the US Department of Commerce. The US Department of Commerce explains:

> In all instances, safe harbor benefits are assured from the date on which each organization wishing to qualify for the safe harbor self-certifies to the Department of Commerce (or its designee) its adherence to the Principles in accordance with the guidance set forth in the Frequently Asked Question on Self-Certification.

The FAQs describe how an organisation may self-certify:

> To self-certify for the safe harbor, organizations can provide to the Department of Commerce (or its designee) a letter, signed by a corporate officer on behalf

of the organization that is joining the safe harbor, that contains at least the following information:

(1) name of organization, mailing address, e-mail address, telephone and fax numbers;

(2) description of the activities of the organization with respect to personal information received from the EU; and

(3) description of the organization's privacy policy for such personal information, including: (a) where the privacy policy is available for viewing by the public, (b) its effective date of implementation, (c) a contact office for the handling of complaints, access requests, and any other issues arising under the safe harbor, (d) the specific statutory body that has jurisdiction to hear any claims against the organization regarding possible unfair or deceptive practices and violations of laws or regulations governing privacy (and that is listed in the annex to the Principles), (e) name of any privacy programs in which the organization is a member, (f) method of verification (e.g. in-house, third party) (1), and (g) the independent recourse mechanism that is available to investigate unresolved complaints.

There are seven Safe Harbor principles entitled: notice, choice, onwards transfers, security, data integrity, access and enforcement. In summary the effect of these principles is as follows:

- **Notice**: Echoes the notice requirements of the first and second data protection principles contained in the DPA. US organizations participating in the Safe Harbor scheme are required to provide individuals with contact information, information about the purposes for which data are collected, information about the uses to which the data are put, information about third parties to whom the data are disclosed and information about how the individual can limit the use or disclosure of their data. This information must be provided to the individual 'in clear and conspicuous language' before the individual is first asked to supply their personal information or as soon thereafter as is practicable.

- **Choice**: Individuals must be given a chance to opt-out from disclosure to third parties and from uses that are incompatible with the original purposes for which their data are collected. Where the personal data are sensitive, individuals must be given an opt-in choice, which means that disclosures to third parties and incompatible processing must not occur until the individual has specifically exercised their choice to permit the same.

- **Onwards transfer**: Where the US organization intends to transfer the data to a third party acting as an agent it must first ascertain that the third party also provides adequate protection, whether by being a member of the Safe Harbor scheme or through some other mechanism. If the US organization does carry out the necessary enquiries, it will not be held responsible for any processing operations undertaken by the third party that are contrary to any restrictions or representations applying to the US organization provided also that it did not know, or was not expected to know, of the third party's contravention. A third party is an agent for the purposes of the onwards transfer principle where it 'is acting as an agent to perform task(s) on behalf of and under the instructions of the organization'.

- **Security**: This principle requires organizations 'creating, maintaining, using or disseminating personal information' to take 'reasonable precautions to protect it from loss, misuse and unauthorized access, disclosure, alteration and destruction'.

- **Data integrity**: This principle provides that personal information must be relevant for the purposes for which it is to be used, that organizations may not process personal information in a manner that is incompatible with the purposes for which it was collected and that the organization should take reasonable steps to ensure that the information is reliable, accurate, complete and current.

- **Access**: The access principle requires that individuals be given access to the information held by the organization and an opportunity to correct, amend or delete inaccurate information. However, these rights are excepted where the burden or expense of compliance would be disproportionate or where compliance would violate the rights of other individuals.

- **Enforcement**: The enforcement principle contains three elements. First, there must be mechanisms for assuring compliance with the Safe Harbor principles. Second, there must be readily available and affordable independent recourse mechanisms for individuals affected by non-compliance, including the payment of damages where the law allows. Third, there must be consequences for organizations that fail to comply with the principles, namely sanctions that are 'sufficiently rigorous to ensure compliance'. A significant part of the enforcement mechanisms is the requirement for 'follow up procedures for verifying that the attestations and assertions businesses make about their privacy practices are true and that privacy practices have been implemented as presented'.

EC approval of the US Safe Harbor scheme

On 26 July 2000 the European Commission made a decision[129] about the adequacy of the protection provided by the Safe Harbor principles and their supporting FAQs. This decision was made under Article 25.6. of the Data Protection Directive. Article 1 of this decision confirms that the Safe Harbor principles and the FAQs do provide an adequate level of protection. There are, however, two very important qualifications to this decision, which are contained in Article 1. These are:

- The organization within the safe harbor must have 'unambiguously and publicly disclosed its commitment to comply with the Principles implemented in accordance with the FAQs'.
- The organization within the safe harbor must be subject to the statutory powers of either the US Federal Trade Commission or the US Department of Transportation. Article 1.2.(b) explains why this qualification is so important saying that these US public authorities are 'empowered to investigate complaints and to obtain relief against unfair or deceptive practices as well as redress for individuals, irrespective of their country of residence or nationality, in case of non-compliance with the Principles implemented in accordance with the FAQs'.

Adequacy and Article 25.6. and the 'white list' countries

The EC's decision on the adequacy of the US Safe Harbor scheme was made under Article 25.6. of the Data Protection Directive. This article allows the European Commission to find that a non-EEA country ensures an adequate level of protection 'by reason of its domestic law or of the international commitments it has entered into'. In addition to its safe harbor decision the European Commission has used Article 25.6. to make decisions about the adequacy of Switzerland[130] (2000), Hungary[131] (2000), Canada[132] (2001), Argentina[133] (2003), Guernsey[134] (2003) and the Isle of Man[135] (2004). These countries are commonly known as the 'white list' countries. Of course, Hungary is now a member of the EC and no longer needs to rely upon the European Commission decision in its favour.

The text of the white list decisions and the national laws to which they relate need to be considered by data controllers before they are relied upon. For instance, the decision about the adequacy of Canada does not provide a complete authority for all kinds of data transfers to Canada, but is limited in scope.

Adequacy, Article 25.6. and passenger name records

As part of the response to 9/11 the US government introduced a law[136] requiring all foreign passenger airlines traveling to and from the US to provide the Bureau of Customs and Border Protection (part of the US Department of Homeland Security) with electronic access to passenger name records. Passenger name records are records about each passenger's travel requirements containing all of the information required by airlines to enable reservations to be processed and controlled. Airlines that refused to cooperate were to be forbidden access to US airspace, a threat with massive consequences for international travel, for the global economy and for the beleaguered international airline industry.

The US's requirements for access to this information were – and are – very controversial and, as discussed earlier, there is no rule of law within the EC that regards the US as being generally adequate for the purposes of Article 25.

The apparent solution to the conflict between the US's requirements and the Directive's prohibition against transfers to non-adequate countries was found in Article 25.6., which was used to declare the US Safe Harbor scheme adequate and to create the white list of adequate countries. Thus, on 14 May 2004 the European Commission made a decision[137] stating that 'for the purposes of Article 25(2) of Directive 95/46/EC, the United States' Bureau of Customs and Border Protection (hereinafter referred to as CBP) is considered to ensure an adequate level of protection for passenger name record (PNR) data transferred from the Community concerning flights to or from the United States'. Pursuant to this decision, EC airlines were permitted to transfer 34 separate items of personal data without fear of being in breach of data protection laws.

On 17 May 2004 the EC Council issued a complementary decision,[138] underscoring the importance and sensitivity of the matter. This decision gave the EC's formal approval to the arrangements for the transfer of passenger name records to the Bureau of Customs and Border Protection.

The transfer of passenger name records to the US was only part of the picture, however. Canada and Australia also sought access to this information and in 2004 the Article 29 Working Party issued opinions on the adequacy of the protections in these countries. The opinion on the adequacy of Australia's[139] protections was favourable, the opinion on Canada's[140] less so.

On 30 May 2006 the PNR scheme came to an abrupt end, due to the decisions of the European Court of Justice (ECJ) in the joined cases of *European Data Protection Supervisor v. Council of the European Communities*[141] and *European Data Protection Supervisor v. Commission of the European Communities*.[142] In these cases the ECJ held that the PNR scheme could not be legitimized through the Data Protection Directive, as the scope of the Data Protection Directive does not extend to activities of the State concerning public security and criminal law. The formal end of the PNR scheme was 30 September 2006.

DEROGATIONS AND BINDING CORPORATE RULES

As mentioned earlier, Article 26 of the Data Protection Directive contains derogations from the prohibition within Article 25 against the transfer of personal data from the EEA to a non-adequate country. The full list of derogations is contained in Article 26.1. They are:

> (a) the data subject has given his consent unambiguously to the proposed transfer; or
>
> (b) the transfer is necessary for the performance of a contract between the data subject and the data controller or the implementation of precontractual measures taken in response to the data subject's request; or

(c) the transfer is necessary for the conclusion or performance of a contract concluded in the interest of the data subject between the data controller and a third party; or

(d) the transfer is necessary or legally required on important public interest grounds, or for the establishment, exercise or defence of legal claims; or

(e) the transfer is necessary in order to protect the vital interests of the data subject; or

(f) the transfer is made from a register that according to laws or regulations is intended to provide information to the public and is open to consultation either by the public in general or by any person who can demonstrate legitimate interest, provided that that the conditions laid down in law for consultation of the register are fulfilled in the particular case.

In addition to the list of derogations in Article 25.1., Article 26.2. contains a very important power for Member States to authorize transfers to non-adequate countries. Article 26.2. says:

a Member State may authorize a transfer or a set of transfers of personal data to a third country which does not ensure an adequate level of protection within the meaning of Article 25(2), where the controller adduces adequate safeguards with respect to the protection of the privacy and fundamental rights and freedoms of individuals and as regards the exercise of the corresponding rights; such safeguards may in particular result from appropriate contractual clauses.

The National Supervisory Authorities (NSAs) established pursuant to Article 28 of the Data Protection Directive, coordinated by the Article 29 Working Party, have taken advantage of the powers within Article 26.2. to develop a scheme for multinational groups of companies under which they can obtain fast-track approvals for a self-regulatory scheme allowing inter-group transfers of personal data that involve transfers to non-adequate countries. This scheme is called Binding Corporate Rules.

Binding Corporate Rules

On 3 June 2003 the Article 29 Working Party adopted Working Document 74, entitled 'Applying Article 26(2) of the EU Data Protection Directive to Binding Corporate Rules for International Data Transfer'.[143] Binding Corporate Rules (BCR) provide multinational groups of companies with a solution to the problem of how to overcome the prohibition against the transfer of personal data to non-adequate countries outside the EEA. This solution provides an alternative to the multi-contract approach (discussed below in the section 'Derogations and contractual clauses').

BCR have been introduced to address the very real problems faced by the multinational group of companies whose need to process personal data across jurisdictions is a fundamental part of their legitimate activities. Moreover, the law recognizes that such transfers are a necessary ingredient of successful economic functioning and are vital to the health of the global economy as well as for social enrichment. BCR approach this issue in a very pragmatic fashion, effectively allowing a new kind of self-regulation approved under the cooperation procedure described in Article 26.3. of the Directive, which says:

> The Member State shall inform the Commission and the other Member States of the authorizations it grants pursuant to paragraph 2.
>
> If a Member State or the Commission objects on justified grounds involving the protection of the privacy and fundamental rights and freedoms of individuals, the Commission shall take appropriate measures in accordance with the procedure laid down in Article 31(2).
>
> Member States shall take the necessary measures to comply with the Commission's decision.

Multinational groups of companies are invited by the Working Party, whose members include all the NSAs, to present a case of special interest that essentially provides a fast-track route to pan-European compliance, but before describing the detail and mechanics of BCR it is necessary to understand the disadvantages that BCR are intended to resolve.

The multinational group is required to identify a mechanism that will guarantee the lawfulness of transfers from all of the Member States in which it is established to all of the third countries in which it is established. Prior to the European Commission's approval of BCR the main mechanism was multiple, inter-group contracts supported, if applicable, by reliance upon any relevant European Commission decisions on white list countries and safe harbor. This approach can sometimes be cumbersome, slow, confusing and inelegant, however.

BCR provides an alternative solution, with the added attraction of a fast-track route to officially approved self-regulation. In return for involving the NSAs through a negotiation and approval process, the multinational group gains the seal of approval of the NSAs, is spared the burdens and disadvantages of the current approach and it takes charge of complaints about its behaviour received by the NSAs. There are many powerful advantages in self-regulation and the NSAs are committed to making the scheme work, so it is expected that BCRs will increase in number as the benefits become more widely appreciated. The NSAs are pleased to participate because it boosts their profile and increases their influence, for example, through increased powers of audit.

Applying for BCR approval

In April 2005 the Article 29 Working Party issued a working document[144] on the procedure to be followed for getting NSA approval for a BCR scheme.

(1) The applicant group of companies identifies the 'lead authority' for the cooperation procedure, with priority being given to the place of the group's European headquarters. The NSAs may accept, decline or assert jurisdiction and they reserve for themselves the right to decide the question of jurisdiction between themselves, but ultimately they are supervised by the courts.

(2) The group submits an application to the lead NSA, the contents of which are prescribed in an official checklist. The submission of the application then triggers a process of discussion and negotiation between the lead NSA and the applicant group, which concludes with the creation of a 'consolidated draft'.

(3) The lead NSA distributes the consolidated draft to all concerned NSAs for their comments, which should be provided within one month.

(4) If comments are received, the lead NSA incorporates these into the consolidated draft, which then triggers a second process of discussion and negotiation with the applicant. If at the end of this second process of discussion and negotiation the lead NSA is of the view that the applicant is able to satisfactorily address the comments of the other NSAs it will invite the applicant to submit a 'final draft'.

(5) The lead NSA submits the final draft to the other concerned NSAs inviting them to confirm that they are satisfied with the adequacy safeguards described. If the concerned NSAs confirm that they are satisfied, this constitutes an agreement between them and the applicant to provide the necessary permits or authorizations at national level for transfer of personal data from their jurisdiction to companies within the applicant group established in non-adequate countries. The NSAs' confirmation does not, however, absolve the companies within the group from their obligations to notify in accordance with the national laws of the Member States in which they are established.

The BCR checklist

On 14 April 2005 the Article 29 Working Party adopted Working Document 108,[145] which contains a checklist for prospective applicants for BCR approval. The checklist describes the documentation that must be submitted to the lead NSA and the issues that the documentation needs to address. According to this, the applicant must:

- provide evidence that its BCR are legally binding within the group and externally for the benefit of individuals;
- explain how compliance with its BCR will be verified;
- describe its processing operations and the flows of information;

- describe its data protection safeguards, which must address transparency, the processing purpose, data quality, security, the right of access and the right to object and the restrictions placed on onward transfers out of the group;
- explain its mechanism for reporting and recording changes.

The BCR documentation

The documentation identified by the checklist falls into three categories:

- **Contact information and choice of lead authority**: This is a standalone document that identifies the responsible person within the group to whom the lead NSA may address any queries. Full contact information for this person is required. In addition, this document must explain the applicant's choice of lead NSA. This explanation must contain all relevant information, including information about the group's corporate structure, its processing activities within the EEA, the location of its decision making (implying the location of managers and personnel with the power to determine the nature of the processing operations), the places within the EEA from where transfers to third countries take place and the identity of the third countries to which personal data are transferred.
- **Background paper**: This document summarizes how the applicant will comply with all of the requirements of BCR. To confirm, these requirements are those identified in the section immediately above (e.g. the BCR must be legally binding, there must be a verification mechanism and the data protection safeguards must be met).
- **BCR documents**: These documents form the BCR. They will include group policies, codes, notices, procedures and contracts.

The legally binding nature of BCR

A scheme of self-regulation will only work if it is legally binding, that is, if it can be enforced by the beneficiary against the regulated entity. If the scheme is not legally binding, the scheme will not be able to satisfy the test of adequacy within Article 25 of the Data Protection Directive. There are two elements to this. First, the scheme must be binding within the group. Second, the scheme must be binding for the benefit of external individuals.

The checklist does not extend to providing a 'to do' list which, when completed, will leave the applicant with a legally binding scheme. Instead, it explains that there are a number of routes to a legally binding scheme, which depend upon the structure and size of the group. Also, it cautions that the national laws and any applicable regulatory requirements of each place of establishment must be considered.

The checklist poses four questions for the applicant, which must be answered within the background paper. These questions are:

- How are the rules binding between the component parts of the organisa-tion?

- How are the rules binding on employees?

- How are the rules made binding on subcontractors handling the data?

- How are the rules binding externally for the benefit of individuals?

In respect of the first question, the checklist makes four suggestions for making BCR binding within the component parts of the organization. The first suggestion is that binding corporate or contractual rules can be implemented that the responsible person can enforce against other members of the group. Second, the parent company in the group can make unilateral declarations or undertakings that are binding on others in the group. Third, the group can incorporate regulatory measures into its legal framework. Fourth, the group can incorporate its BCR within its general business principles, supported by appropriate policies, audits and sanctions. Of course, these suggestions must be checked against the national laws in place in each Member State of establishment.

In respect of the second question, how the BCR are binding on employees, the checklist suggests that this might be achieved 'by way of specific obligations contained in a contract of employment and by linking observance of the rules with disciplinary procedures'. The checklist also highlights the requirement for 'adequate training programmes and senior staff commitment'. The sanctions for breach of the BCR by employees must also be explained.

In respect of the third question, how the BCR are binding on subcontractors, the checklist identifies the only solution, contracts between the group and its subcontractors. These contracts will be submitted as part of the BCR documents.

The fourth question, how the BCR are binding externally for the benefit of individuals, requires the applicant to address the following matters:

- The BCR must be enforceable by the NSAs and in the courts.
- The individual must have the choice of commencing claims in the jurisdiction of the group member at the origin of the data transfer, or in the jurisdiction of the group's EU headquarters, if different.
- The practical steps that the data subject needs to take to obtain a remedy must be defined.
- The group's complaint handling procedure must be defined as must the practical steps that the data subject needs to take to use it.
- The group must have sufficient assets within the EU or have made sufficient arrangements to enable payment of compensation for any breaches of its BCR.

- The burden of proof in respect of any breaches of the BCR will rest with the member of the group at the origin of the transfer or the European headquarters, if different.
- The data subject's rights under the Data Protection Directive must be acknowledged.
- The applicant must cooperate with the NSAs with regard to any decisions made by them or advice given.

Verifying compliance with BCR

It is fundamental to the approval process that the applicant provides an explanation as to how its compliance with its BCR will be verified. This requires an audit programme and an audit plan, with the audits being performed by external or internal auditors, or a combination of both. The audit plan must make provision for auditing by the NSAs if they so require. The NSAs' auditing power is of major significance, as currently the Information Commissioner, the NSA for the UK, does not have standalone powers of audit.

The processing and information flows covered by BCR

The applicant must provide a detailed explanation of the processing and information flows covered by the BCR. This is very important because BCR can be limited to particular categories of data and particular categories of information flow; the applicant is not obliged to extend its BCR to all its processing operations or to all of its transborder flows of information. The purposes of all processing and all information flows covered by the BCR must be explained.

The data protection safeguards within BCR

The data protection safeguards essentially require the applicant to explain how it will comply with the key aspects of data protection laws. These key aspects are the transparency safeguards, the general rules on lawfulness (including security), the right to object and onwards transfers. The checklist requires the applicant to 'provide a summary of how this has been addressed in the binding corporate rules adopted by your organisation with supporting documentation e.g., relevant policies'.

Mechanisms for reporting and recording changes to BCR

The applicant needs to provide a description of how changes to its BCR will be communicated to all of the companies within the group. From time to time some of these changes will need to be reported to the concerned NSAs, but the checklist envisages that the lead NSA will provide the applicant with advice on this matter.

DEROGATIONS AND CONTRACTUAL CLAUSES

Article 26.2. of the Data Protection Directive empowers EC Member States to authorize transfers to non-adequate countries where the data controller 'adduces adequate safeguards with respect to the protection of the privacy and fundamental rights and freedoms of individuals'. One of the mechanisms identified by Article 26.2. for securing adequate safeguards is the use of contractual clauses.

Related to this, Article 26.4. gives the European Commission the power to decide that 'certain standard contractual clauses offer sufficient safeguards' and if the European Commission makes a decision to that effect, the same article then goes on to provide that 'Member States shall take the necessary measures to comply with the Commission's decision'.

Using its powers under Article 26.4. the European Commission has made two decisions approving standard contractual clauses. The first decision, dated 15 June 2001,[146] approves standard contractual clauses for exports of data to third countries. This decision was amended by the European Commission through a decision dated 27 December 2004.[147] The second decision approves standard contractual clauses for transfers of personal data to data processors situated in non-adequate countries.

Approved contractual clauses for exports to non-adequate countries

The European Commission's decision made on 15 June 2001, amended by the decision made on 27 December 2004, concerns only data exports to non-adequate countries, not transfers to data processors. The distinction between exports and transfers is an important one, because where data is exported the data controller loses control over the data, but where data are transferred to a data processor the data controller retains control over the processing purposes and the processing manner, as the data processor agrees to process only on the instructions of the data controller.

The idea behind the approved contractual clauses is that the data controller (the exporter) and the data importer in the non-adequate country will incorporate the clauses into their commercial contracts and in so doing they will ensure that personal data are adequately protected in the non-adequate country. Thus, the contract is used satisfy the adequacy test. However, a contractual environment can only mirror the requirements of the Data Protection Directive if the data subject receives all the benefits of the protections. With this proviso in mind, the first set of approved contractual clauses contained in the 2001 decision contain a 'third-party beneficiary' clause (clause 3) that entitles the data subject, or a representative like a trade union, to enforce a number of key clauses.

The contractual clauses are contained in the annex to the decision, entitled 'standard contractual clauses'. In addition to the third-party beneficiary clause these contractual clauses address the following key elements:

- the data exporter's obligations, consisting of agreements and war-ranties;
- the data importer's obligations, also consisting of agreements and warranties;
- joint and several liability;
- dispute resolution;
- jurisdiction and governing law;
- termination of contract;
- relationships with NSAs;
- variation of contract.

The contractual clauses provide that the governing law will be the law of the Member State within which the data exporter is established and that the courts of the data exporter's country of establishment will have jurisdiction. These clauses survive any termination of any other contractual arrangements between the data exporter and the data importer and they cannot be varied.

The data exporter's obligations are satisfied by a series of warranties and agreements dealing with the lawfulness of the data exporter's processing operations, the data subject's rights and cooperation with the NSA. The data exporter warrants that its processing operations are lawful in the country of its establishment, including the transfer itself and that it will notify the importer of any changes of substance to the law. In addition the data exporter warrants that it has notified and will notify the data subject of any transfers, in advance. Finally the exporter warrants to make the contractual clauses available to the data subject upon request and to respond to enquiries from the data subject and the NSA.

The data importer's obligations are also satisfied by a series of warranties and agreements that mirror those provided by the data exporter. The importer warrants that:

- there are no laws preventing performance of the contractual clauses, which is accompanied by an obligation to notify the data exporter of any substantial changes to the law;
- it will process in accordance with the principles contained either in Appendix 2 or Appendix 3 to the model clauses;
- it will promptly and properly deal with reasonable inquiries from the data exporter or the data subject and that it will cooperate with the NSA;
- it will allow an independent audit of its operations upon the request of the data exporter;
- it will make the contractual clauses available to the data subject and will provide information about its office that handles complaints.

Appendix 2 and Appendix 3 to the model clauses provide alternative sets of mandatory data protection principles to be observed by the data importer. Which set is chosen is a matter for the data exporter and the data controller to agree. Appendix 2 consists of nine 'mandatory data protection principles' that mirror very closely the 'content principles' identified by the Article 29 Working Party in a 1998 Working Document.[148] These mandatory data protection principles say:

(1) Purpose limitation: data must be processed and subsequently used or further communicated only for the specific purposes in Appendix I to the Clauses. Data must not be kept longer than necessary for the purposes for which they are transferred.

(2) Data quality and proportionality: data must be accurate and, where necessary, kept up to date. The data must be adequate, relevant and not excessive in relation to the purposes for which they are transferred and further processed.

(3) Transparency: data subjects must be provided with information as to the purposes of the processing and the identity of the data controller in the third country, and other information insofar as this is necessary to ensure fair processing, unless such information has already been given by the data exporter.

(4) Security and confidentiality: technical and organisational security measures must be taken by the data controller that are appropriate to the risks, such as unauthorised access, presented by the processing. Any person acting under the authority of the data controller, including a processor, must not process the data except on instructions from the controller.

(5) Rights of access, rectification, erasure and blocking of data: as provided for in Article 12 of Directive 95/46/EC, the data subject must have a right of access to all data relating to him that are processed and, as appropriate, the right to the rectification, erasure or blocking of data the processing of which does not comply with the principles set out in this Appendix, in particular because the data are incomplete or inaccurate. He should also be able to object to the processing of the data relating to him on compelling legitimate grounds relating to his particular situation.

(6) Restrictions on onwards transfers: further transfers of personal data from the data importer to another controller established in a third country not providing adequate protection or not covered by a decision adopted by the Commission pursuant to Article 25(6) of Directive 95/46/EC (onward transfer) may take place only if either:

    (a) data subjects have, in the case of special categories of data, given their unambiguous consent to the onward transfer or, in other cases, have been given the opportunity to object.

    The minimum information to be provided to data subjects must contain in a language understandable to them:

    ✦ the purposes of the onward transfer,

    ✦ the identification of the data exporter established in the Community,

    ✦ the categories of further recipients of the data and the countries of destination, and

✦ an explanation that, after the onward transfer, the data may be processed by a controller established in a country where there is not an adequate level of protection of the privacy of individuals; or

(b) the data exporter and the data importer agree to the adherence to the Clauses of another controller which thereby becomes a party to the Clauses and assumes the same obligations as the data importer.

(7) Special categories of data: where data revealing racial or ethnic origin, political opinions, religious or philosophical beliefs or trade union memberships and data concerning health or sex life and data relating to offences, criminal convictions or security measures are processed, additional safeguards should be in place within the meaning of Directive 95/46/EC, in particular, appropriate security measures such as strong encryption for transmission or such as keeping a record of access to sensitive data.

(8) Direct marketing: where data are processed for the purposes of direct marketing, effective procedures should exist allowing the data subject at any time to 'opt-out' from having his data used for such purposes.

(9) Automated individual decisions: data subjects are entitled not to be subject to a decision which is based solely on automated processing of data, unless other measures are taken to safeguard the individual's legitimate interests as provided for in Article 15(2) of Directive 95/46/EC. Where the purpose of the transfer is the taking of an automated decision as referred to in Article 15 of Directive 95/46/EC, which produces legal effects concerning the individual or significantly affects him and which is based solely on automated processing of data intended to evaluate certain personal aspects relating to him, such as his performance at work, creditworthiness, reliability, conduct, etc., the individual should have the right to know the reasoning for this decision.

Appendix 3 contains an alternative, truncated set of three mandatory data protection principles, namely the first, fifth and sixth principles in Appendix 2. The Appendix 3 principles may only be used where the parties have explicitly agreed to do so and only if the parties process the data in accordance with the data protection laws of the country of the data exporter's establishment and in accordance with any decisions made by the European Commission about white list countries.

The data exporter and the data importer agree that they will be joint and severally liable for any damage suffered by the data subject as a consequence of violation of any of the clauses, subject to the third-party beneficiary clause, although neither will be liable if neither is responsible for the violation. This means that the data subject will be able to obtain compensation from the data exporter for any breaches by the data importer, and vice versa. There is also an optional indemnity clause which the data exporter and data importer may take advantage of, through which they may recover from the other all or part of any compensation paid to the data subject.

The dispute resolution clause is one of the most important third-party beneficiary rights. Pursuant to this clause the data subject may request independent mediation, which includes an option for mediation by the NSA, and may refer any dispute to the courts. In addition, where the data subject and the data exporter, the data importer, or both, if appropriate, agree, there can be resolution of disputes by arbitration.

The 2004 decision amending the 2001 decision

The 2004 decision amended the 2001 decision by adding a second set of contractual clauses that the data exporter and the data importer may choose to rely upon. This alternative set of conditions was proposed by a coalition of business associations and was analysed in depth by the Article 29 Working Party in Opinion 8/2003 'on the draft standard contractual clauses submitted by a group of business associations ("the alternative model contract")' adopted on 17 December 2003.[149]

The data exporter carries five specific obligations under these alternative clauses, which are satisfied by warranties and undertakings. The data exporter will:

- collect, process and transfer the data in accordance with the national laws of its EC country of establishment;
- make reasonable efforts to determine the data importer's ability to satisfy its own obligations (the data exporter carries the burden of proving that it made reasonable efforts);
- provide the data importer on request with copies of the laws of its EC country of establishment;
- respond to enquiries from data subjects and NSAs about the data importer's processing, unless the parties agree otherwise;
- make the contractual clauses available to the data subject upon request, although it may delete confidential parts (unless the NSA orders otherwise).

The data importer carries nine specific obligations under these clauses, which again are satisfied by warranties and undertakings. The importer will:

- take appropriate technical, organizational and security measures to guard against accidental or unlawful destruction, loss, alteration or access to the personal data;
- implement procedures to ensure that any third parties that it allows to access the personal data will also maintain security and confidentiality and it will require any data processors to process only upon its instructions;
- confirm that it does not have any reason to believe that there are any local laws substantially affecting the guarantees given by the clauses;
- will process only for the purposes defined in the agreement;
- will identify to the data exporter a contact point within its organization and will cooperate in good faith with the data exporter, the data

subject and the NSA, which extends to being responsible for compliance with the data exporter's duty of cooperation in the event of the data exporter's dissolution;

- will provide the data exporter upon request with evidence that it has sufficient financial resources to meet any liability under the clauses;

- upon request from the data exporter, submit to a process of audit, review or certification by the data exporter or by a person nominated by the data exporter;

- process pursuant to the national laws of the data exporter, or in accordance with any decision made by the European Commission in respect of white list countries or pursuant to the data protection principles contained in Annex A to the clauses;

- not disclose data to another data controller situated outside the EEA. This clause is subject to four exemptions: (i) unless the third-party data controller processes in accordance with a European Commission decision on adequacy for white list purposes; or (ii) unless the third-party data controller becomes a signatory to the clauses; or (iii) unless the data subject has declined to object after being given an opportunity to do so; or (iv) unless, where sensitive personal data are transferred, the data subject has given unambiguous consent.

The data protection principles in Annex A to the clauses read as follows:

(1) **Purpose limitation:** Personal data may be processed and subsequently used or further communicated only for purposes described in Annex B or subsequently authorised by the data subject.

(2) **Data quality and proportionality:** Personal data must be accurate and, where necessary, kept up to date. The personal data must be adequate, relevant and not excessive in relation to the purposes for which they are transferred and further processed.

(3) **Transparency:** Data subjects must be provided with information necessary to ensure fair processing (such as information about the purposes of processing and about the transfer), unless such information has already been given by the data exporter.

(4) **Security and confidentiality:** Technical and organisational security measures must be taken by the data controller that are appropriate to the risks, such as against accidental or unlawful destruction or accidental loss, alteration, unauthorised disclosure or access, presented by the processing. Any person acting under the authority of the data controller, including a processor, must not process the data except on instructions from the data controller.

(5) **Rights of access, rectification, deletion and objection:** As provided in Article 12 of Directive 95/46/EC, data subjects must, whether directly or via a third party, be provided with the personal information about them that

an organisation holds, except for requests which are manifestly abusive, based on unreasonable intervals or their number or repetitive or systematic nature, or for which access need not be granted under the law of the country of the data exporter. Provided that the authority has given its prior approval, access need also not be granted when doing so would be likely to seriously harm the interests of the data importer or other organisations dealing with the data importer and such interests are not overridden by the interests for fundamental rights and freedoms of the data subject. The sources of the personal data need not be identified when this is not possible by reasonable efforts, or where the rights of persons other than the individual would be violated. Data subjects must be able to have the personal information about them rectified, amended, or deleted where it is inaccurate or processed against these principles. If there are compelling grounds to doubt the legitimacy of the request, the organisation may require further justifications before proceeding to rectification, amendment or deletion. Notification of any rectification, amendment or deletion to third parties to whom the data have been disclosed need not be made when this involves a disproportionate effort. A data subject must also be able to object to the processing of the personal data relating to him if there are compelling legitimate grounds relating to his particular situation. The burden of proof for any refusal rests on the data importer, and the data subject may always challenge a refusal before the authority.

(6) Sensitive data: The data importer shall take such additional measures (e.g. relating to security) as are necessary to protect such sensitive data in accordance with its obligations under clause II.

(7) Data used for marketing purposes: Where data are processed for the purposes of direct marketing, effective procedures should exist allowing the data subject at any time to 'opt-out' from having his data used for such purposes.

(8) Automated decisions: For purposes hereof 'automated decision' shall mean a decision by the data exporter or the data importer which produces legal effects concerning a data subject or significantly affects a data subject and which is based solely on automated processing of personal data intended to evaluate certain personal aspects relating to him, such as his performance at work, creditworthiness, reliability, conduct, etc. The data importer shall not make any automated decisions concerning data subjects, except when:

(a) (i) such decisions are made by the data importer in entering into or performing a contract with the data subject, and

(ii) the data subject is given an opportunity to discuss the results of a relevant automated decision with a representative of the parties making such decision or otherwise to make representations to those parties, or

(b) where otherwise provided by the law of the data exporter.

Unlike the clauses in the original 2001 decision, the 2004 decision rejects the concept of joint and several liability. Instead, it restricts the parties' liability to actual damage caused by their own breaches, subject to the critical caveat that the data exporter will still be bound by the national provisions in effect in its EC country of establishment.

Where there is an allegation about a data importer, the data subject is obliged to first ask the data exporter to enforce its rights against the data importer. If the data subject makes such a request, the exporter must comply with it within one month of the date of receipt. If the data exporter fails to enforce its rights against the data importer within this one-month period, the data subject is then allowed to proceed against the data importer direct. The main third-party beneficiary rights that are concerned by these liability rules are:

- The data exporter's obligation to use reasonable efforts to determine that the data importer is able to satisfy its legal obligations under the clauses.
- The data exporter's obligation to respond to enquiries from the data subject and the NSA.
- The data exporter's obligation to make the clauses available to the data subject on request.
- The data importer's obligation to put in place appropriate technical, organizational and security measures to guard against loss of or damage to data.
- The data importer's obligation to ensure that none of its local laws may substantially affect the guarantees provided by the clauses.
- The data importer's obligation to process only for the purposes described.
- The data importer's obligation to provide the data exporter with a contact point.
- The data importer's obligation to process in accordance twith he data protection principles in Annex A to the clause, or the laws of the data exporter's country of establishment or a European Commission decision for white list purposes.
- The data importer's obligation not to transfer the data to a third party in a non-adequate country, unless an exception applies.
- The dual obligation to cooperate with resolution of disputes with the data subject or the NSA.

The dispute resolution procedures in this decision are also different from those in the clause approved by the 2001 decision and might be considered to be a much watered down version. The obligations of the data exporter and importer are merely to cooperate with a view to settling disputes in a timely manner and to participating in non-binding mediation. However, they will both abide by a decision of a competent court in the data exporter's country of establishment. This sounds like a strong benefit, but it does not give the data subject any better protection than that offered by the general rules within the DPA and the Human Rights Act 1998.

As with the 2001 decision the clauses survive the termination of any other contracts between the data exporter and the data importer. Likewise, the clauses cannot be varied.

Approved contractual clauses for transfers to data processors in non-adequate countries

On 27 December 2001 the European Commission adopted a second decision[150] under Article 26.4., concerning data transfers to data processors situated in non-adequate countries. Article 1 of this decision says that the standard contractual clauses contained in the annex are 'considered as offering adequate safeguards with respect to the protection of the privacy and fundamental rights and freedoms of individuals'. As with the decisions on data exports, these clauses contain a third-party beneficiary clause. However, again, the precise benefit offered by the third-party beneficiary clause is arguably no greater than the protection offered by the data protection principles and Article 8 of the ECHR.

The data exporter, who will remain the data controller in respect of the data that are transferred to the data processor, carries eight obligations under these clauses. The data exporter warrants and agrees that:

- its processing complies with the relevant national laws;
- it will instruct the data processor to process only upon its instructions;
- it will ensure that the data importer will provide sufficient guarantees of technical and organizational security measures to protect the data;
- it will carry out an assessment of the data importer's security measures in order to determine that they are appropriate;
- it will ensure the data importer's compliance with the security measures;
- it will notify the data subject in advance of any transfers of sensitive personal data;
- it will forward to the relevant NSA the data processor's notification that there are no local laws preventing its compliance with the clauses;
- it will make available to the data subject on request a copy of the clauses and a summary description of the security measures.

The data importer carries seven obligations under the decision. The data importer will:

- process only on behalf of the data exporter in compliance with instructions given by the data exporter;
- confirm that it has no reason to believe that its local laws will prevent its compliance with the clauses;
- confirm that it has implemented the security measures specified in the agreement;

- notify the data exporter of any requests for access to the data received from law enforcement authorities, of any accidental or unauthorized access and of any requests received from the data subject;
- deal promptly with inquiries from the data exporter and will abide by any advice given by the NSA;
- submit to an audit by the data exporter or an independent body following a request from the data exporter;
- make copies of the clauses available to the data subject upon request.

The liability clauses are very different from those in the other decisions; while they do contain a modified joint and several liability clause, the starting point is that the data subject must bring their claim against the data exporter for any damage suffered as a result of any violation of the third-party beneficiary clauses. This means that the data subject can proceed against the data exporter for the data importer's breaches. However, if the data exporter ceases to exist for any reason (such as on dissolution of a company) the data subject is allowed to bring their claims against the data importer. Finally, the liability clauses contain an indemnity clause, which allows the data exporter and the data importer to recover their losses from one another.

The mediation clauses concern only the data importer. Where a data subject brings a claim against a data importer the data subject may refer the dispute to mediation by a third party or by the NSA or to the courts. Where both parties agree, there can be formal arbitration, provided that the data importer's country has ratified the New York Convention on the enforcement of arbitration awards.

Concerning cooperation with the NSA, the clauses state that the data exporter must deposit a copy of the contract with the NSA if requested or if this is required by national data protection laws. In addition, the NSA is given the right to conduct an audit of the data importer's operations.

Once again, the governing law is the law of the Member State in which the data exporter is established and the parties cannot vary the clauses. On termination of the contract the data importer is required to either return all personal data to the data exporter or destroy them, at the data exporter's election.

Other derogations

The other derogations in Article 26.1. are:

- The data subject has given their consent unambiguously to the proposed transfer.
- The transfer is necessary for the performance of a contract between the data subject and the controller, or the implementation of precontractual measures taken in response to the data subject's request.
- The transfer is necessary for the conclusion or performance of a contract concluded in the interest of the data subject between the controller and a third party.

- The transfer is necessary or legally required on important public interest grounds, or for the establishment, exercise or defence of legal claims.
- The transfer is necessary in order to protect the vital interests of the data subject.
- The transfer is made from a register that, according to laws or regulations, is intended to provide information to the public and that is open to consultation either by the public in general or by any person who can demonstrate legitimate interest, to the extent that the conditions laid down in law for consultation are fulfilled in the particular case.

These derogations are very similar to the criteria for making data processing legitimate, contained in Schedule 2 and Schedule 3 of the DPA and the previous discussion applies equally here.

TRANSBORDER DATA FLOWS AND THE DPA

The eighth data protection principle implements the prohibition against the transfer of personal data to non-adequate countries contained in Article 25 of the Data Protection Directive. The eighth data protection principle says:

> **8. Personal data shall not be transferred to a country or territory outside the European Economic Area unless that country or territory ensures an adequate level of protection for the rights and freedoms of data subjects in relation to the processing of personal data.**

The adequacy test set out in Article 25.2. of the Directive is implemented in the interpretation contained in Schedule 1, Part II of the DPA. This says:

> **13. An adequate level of protection is one which is adequate in all the circumstances of the case, having regard in particular to –**
>
> **(a) the nature of the personal data,**
>
> **(b) the country or territory of origin of the information contained in the data,**
>
> **(c) the country or territory of final destination of that information,**
>
> **(d) the purposes for which and period during which the data are intended to be processed,**
>
> **(e) the law in force in the country or territory in question,**
>
> **(f) the international obligations of that country or territory,**
>
> **(g) any relevant codes of conduct or other rules which are enforceable in that country or territory (whether generally or by arrangement in particular cases), and**

(h) any security measures taken in respect of the data in that country or territory.

The interpretation also deals with 'Community findings' under Article 25.4. and Article 25.6. of the Directive. To recap, these articles give the European Commission the power to find that countries outside the EEA do not, or do, provide adequate protection. The effect of the interpretation is to make clear that European Commission decisions on adequacy of third countries are binding within the UK. The interpretation says:

15. – (1) Where –

(a) in any proceedings under this Act any question arises as to whether the requirement of the eighth principle as to an adequate level of protection is met in relation to the transfer of any personal data to a country or territory outside the European Economic Area, and

(b) a Community finding has been made in relation to transfers of the kind in question, that question is to be determined in accordance with that finding.

The derogations found in Article 26 of the Data Protection Directive are found in Schedule 4 to the DPA. This says that the eighth data protection does not apply in the following cases:

(1) The data subject has given his consent to the transfer.

(2) The transfer is necessary –

    (a) for the performance of a contract between the data subject and the data controller, or

    (b) for the taking of steps at the request of the data subject with a view to his entering into a contract with the data controller.

(3) The transfer is necessary –

    (a) for the conclusion of a contract between the data controller and a person other than the data subject which –

        (i)   is entered into at the request of the data subject, or

        (ii) is in the interests of the data subject, or

    (b) for the performance of such a contract.

(4) – (1) The transfer is necessary for reasons of substantial public interest.
     (2) The Secretary of State may by order specify –

    (a) circumstances in which a transfer is to be taken for the purposes of sub-paragraph (1) to be necessary for reasons of substantial public interest, and

(b) circumstances in which a transfer which is not required by or under an enactment is not to be taken for the purpose of sub-paragraph (1) to be necessary for reasons of substantial public interest.

(5) The transfer –

(a) is necessary for the purpose of, or in connection with, any legal proceedings (including prospective legal proceedings),

(b) is necessary for the purpose of obtaining legal advice, or

(c) is otherwise necessary for the purposes of establishing, exercising or defending legal rights.

(6) The transfer is necessary in order to protect the vital interests of the data subject.

(7) The transfer is of part of the personal data on a public register and any conditions subject to which the register is open to inspection are complied with by any person to whom the data are or may be disclosed after the transfer.

(8) The transfer is made on terms which are of a kind approved by the Commissioner as ensuring adequate safeguards for the rights and freedoms of data subjects.

(9) The transfer has been authorised by the Commissioner as being made in such a manner as to ensure adequate safeguards for the rights and freedoms of data subjects.

The eighth and ninth derogations implement the Member State powers set out in Article 26.2. of the Directive, which allows Member States to authorize transfers to non-adequate countries where the data controller adduces adequate safeguards, which can be contained in contractual clauses. This gives the Information Commissioner the power to give approvals, even contractual approvals that are different to those in the European Commission's decisions on model contractual clauses. However, the Information Commissioner's power is weakened by the fact that they are obliged to comply with any decisions of the Commission on derogations. This is the effect of Article 26.3. and Article 26.4. of the Data Protection Directive, implemented by section 54(6) of the DPA:

Where the European Commission makes a decision for the purposes of Article 26(3) or (4) of the Data Protection Directive under the procedure provided for in Article 31(2) of the Directive, the Commissioner shall comply with that decision in exercising his functions under paragraph 9 of Schedule 4 or, as the case may be, paragraph 8 of that Schedule.

The extent of harmonization

Due the importance of the subject matter and the structure of the Data Protection Directive, national laws on transborder data flows can be considered to be the most harmonized of all of the provisions in the Directive. The importance of the structure of the Data Protection Directive cannot be overlooked. It gives significant powers to the EC, which derives assistance from the Article 29 Working Party. The Article 29 Working Party itself consists of the NSAs and representatives from the EC institutions, which means that there is close cooperation between Member States and the EC in the development of rules governing transborder data flows. This is a very dynamic arrangement that has already produced significant results.

The harmonization process is further accelerated in this area as the European Commission has retained for itself many very important powers over the Member States. These powers are:

- The European Commission will inform Member States of any cases where it considers that a third country does not provide adequate protection, which is a highly persuasive authority for the Member States and which helps to shape and mould national positions (Article 25.3.).
- The European Commission may make a finding that a third country does not provide adequate protection. This power is significantly greater that the obligation to inform the Member States of cases where the European Commission considers that a third country does not provide adequate protection, because where a finding of non-adequacy is made (which is a 'Community finding') the Member States are obliged to prevent transfers (Article 25.4.).
- The European Commission also has the sole right to enter into negotiations with countries that it decides are not adequate (Article 25.5.). Again, this gives the European Commission major influence due to it being in control over a heavily political subject.
- The European Commission may make a finding that a third country is adequate (which is another 'Community finding'), which is binding on Member States (Article 25.6.).
- The European Commission may object to authorizations given by Member States under Article 26.2. It if does object, it is required to take 'appropriate measures' and any resulting decision is binding on the Member States (Article 26.3.).
- The European Commission may approve standard contractual clauses. These approvals are binding on the Member States (Article 26.4.).

These powers effectively give the European Commission complete control over the development of laws governing transborder data flows. While the Member States retain residual powers to grant authorizations by way of derogation, to all intents and purposes the European Commission has a right of veto over Member States' decisions.

The Information Commissioner and transborder data flows

The Information Commissioner has issued three authorizations under Schedule 4, paragraph 9 of the DPA.[151] The first authorization, dated 21 December 2001, authorizes exports to data controllers in non-adequate countries where the European Commission's standard contractual clauses are used. The second authorization, dated 18 March 2003, authorizes transfers to data processors in non-adequate countries where the Commission's standard contractual clauses are used. The third authorization, dated 27 May 2005, authorizes data exports to data controllers in non-adequate countries where the European Commission's alternative set of standard contractual clauses are used. The Information Commissioner has not approved the use of any standard contractual clauses other than those adopted by the European Commission.

The Information Commissioner has authorized the use of BCR by General Electric Company. This authorization was made on 15 December 2005.

6 Privacy and Electronic Communications

INTRODUCTION

The right to respect for privacy in communications is afforded legal protection by Article 8 of the ECHR, which identifies a right to respect for correspondence. For these purposes correspondence and communications are synonymous.

In 1997 the EC introduced a specialized Directive on telecommunications privacy,[152] which complemented and built upon the protections within the Data Protection Directive. The object and scope of this Directive was described in Article 1.1. in the following terms:

> This Directive provides for the harmonisation of the provisions of the Member States required to ensure an equivalent level of protection of fundamental rights and freedoms, and in particular the right to privacy, with respect to the processing of personal data in the telecommunications sector and to ensure the free movement of such data and of telecommunications equipment and services in the Community.

The reason for this specialized Directive was explained in its recitals, with particular drivers including the following:

- Advanced digital technologies introduced into the telecommunications sector 'give rise to specific requirements concerning the protection of personal data and privacy of the user' (Recital 3).
- The successful cross-border development of information society services based on new telecommunications services such as ISDN and digital mobile is partly dependent upon the users being confident that their privacy will be respected (Recitals 3 and 4).
- The protection of personal data is an integral component of the common market for telecommunications equipment, networks and services (Recital 5).
- Harmonization of national laws on the protection of personal data is required 'in order to avoid obstacles to the Internal Market for telecommunications' (Recital 8).

- The legitimate interests of subscribers to telecommunications services that are legal persons (companies) require protection (Recital 13).
- The security of telecommunications networks needs to be ensured so as to guarantee confidentiality in communications (Recitals 15 and 16).

The 1997 Directive was a piece of sectoral law making, in the sense that it was targeted at one area only, telecommunications, marking a significant departure from the omnibus approach favoured by the Data Protection Directive. In 2002 the 1997 Directive was replaced by the Directive 'concerning the processing of personal data and the protection of privacy in the electronic communications sector' (DPEC).[153]

THE DIRECTIVE ON PRIVACY AND ELECTRONIC COMMUNICATIONS

The DPEC was introduced as part of the process known as 'convergence', which occurred in 2002. Convergence is the name given to the process whereby the EC widened European telecommunications law to cover all electronic communications, hence the law on telecommunications, the internet and broadcasting was said to have converged (the application of electronic communications law to the broadcasting sector is limited, covering matters such as video on demand services where the broadcaster and the subscriber send and receive electronic communications). The aim of the DPEC is identified in Article 1.1., which says:

> This Directive harmonises the provisions of the Member States required to ensure an equivalent level of protection of fundamental rights and freedoms, and in particular the right to privacy, with respect to the processing of personal data in the electronic communication sector and to ensure the free movement of such data and of electronic communication equipment and services in the Community.

The DPEC expands upon and complements the Data Protection Directive. Importantly, it provides 'for the protection of the legitimate interests of subscribers who are legal persons', which means that companies gain the protection of data protection laws in this specialized area (see Article 1.2.)

Subscribers and users

The protections afforded under the DPEC are enjoyed by 'subscribers' and 'users'. A subscriber may be a living individual or a company, but according to Article 2(a) a user can only be a living individual. The full definition of a user is as follows:

> 'user' means any natural person using a publicly available electronic communications service, for private or business purposes, without necessarily having subscribed to this service.

As this definition makes clear, it does not matter whether a user users a publicly available electronic communications service for private or business purposes. The same is true in the case of subscribers, although, of course, a subscriber can also be a user.

Why there is a distinction between subscribers and users

The DPEC distinguishes between subscribers and users because in a normal household or business environment there may be more than one user of a publicly available electronic communications service, but only one subscriber. In a domestic situation the subscriber can be considered to be the person within the household whose name is on the telephone bill, the satellite TV bill or the ISP bill, while the users might be the entire household.

In a business environment the distinction between subscribers and users is just as easy to understand. The business will be the subscriber to the publicly available electronic communications service and every employee will have the potential to be a user.

Publicly available electronic communications services

The DPEC applies 'to the processing of personal data in connection with the provision of publicly available electronic communications services in public communications networks in the [European] Community' (Article 3.1.). If the electronic communication service is not publicly available, the Directive will not apply. This means that communications over a private network, such as a company intranet, will not be covered by the Directive, because the network is not publicly available. Of course, the Data Protection Directive will still apply if personal data are processed.

The distinction between services and networks

The DPEC makes an important distinction between publicly available electronic communications services and publicly available electronic networks.

The distinction between a service and a network will itself be obvious, but in terms of data protection law the importance of the distinction lies in the fact that most providers of publicly available electronic communications services provide their services over another organization's network (of course, many organizations, like British Telecom and the mobile telephone companies, are both network and service providers). The likelihood of there being separation of control over networks and services presents many difficulties for data protection law.

Security of services

Article 4.1. of the DPEC requires the provider of a publicly available electronic communications service to 'take appropriate technical and organisational measures to safeguard security of its services'. If necessary, the service provider must work 'in conjunction with the provider of the public communications network with respect to network security', pointing to concerns about the separation of control over networks and services.

In terms of the level of security required the service provider must 'ensure a level of security appropriate to the risk presented' and must have regard to the state of the art and the cost of implementing security measures. These obligations mirror the security requirements contained in Article 17 of the Data Protection Directive, implemented in the UK by the seventh data protection principle.

In addition to the obligation to take appropriate technical and organizational measures to safeguard security of the services, the service provider is also under an obligation to inform the subscriber of any particular risk of breach of the network's security (Article 4.2.). Again, this recognizes the difficulties caused by the separation of control over networks and services. If the risk to network security lies outside of the scope of the technical and organizational measures taken by the service provider, the service provider must inform the subscriber of the remedies available to them and provide an indication of their likely cost.

Confidentiality of communications

The purpose of Article 5 of the DPEC is to ensure that Member States protect the confidentiality of communications and the traffic data generated by communications. The key provisions are as follows:

- Member States must prohibit listening, tapping, storage and other kinds of interception or surveillance of communications and related traffic data by a person other than a user without the user's consent (Article 5.1.).

- Member States shall ensure that subscribers and users are provided with comprehensive information about the purpose behind any storage of information by electronic communications networks or the use of networks to gain access to information stored in their terminal equipment (Article 5.3.).

- Member States shall ensure that subscribers and users are provided with the right to refuse the storage of information by electronic communications networks or the use of networks to gain access to information stored in their terminal equipment (Article 5.3.).

Interception and surveillance

The prohibition against the interception and surveillance of communications and related traffic data is not a complete prohibition. There are three exceptions:

- Technical storage of information that is necessary for the conveyance of the communication is permitted, provided that it respects the principle of confidentiality (Article 5.1.).

- The users of the electronic communications services can give their consent to interception and surveillance. Valid consent requires consent from both parties to the communication (Article 5.1.).

- Interception and surveillance can be authorized by law (Article 5.1. and Article 5.2.).

The first exception recognizes the technical need for storage of information during the conveyance of a communication that is particularly prevalent in the 'packet-switched' internet environment. This is discussed in more depth in the section 'Traffic data, retention and deletion' below.

The second exception, interception and surveillance with consent, reflects the basic principle at the heart of the Data Protection Directive, namely that processing pursuant to a valid consent will be lawful.

The third exception, interception and surveillance that is authorized by law, has two components. The first component is that the interception and surveillance is legally authorized in accordance with Article 15(1) of the DPEC. The second component, contained in Article 5.2., applies where the law has authorized the recording of communications and related traffic data when carried out in the course of a lawful business practice for the purpose of providing evidence of a commercial transaction or any other business communication. In the UK provisions have been adopted under the Telecommunications (Lawful Business Practice) (Interception of Communications) Regulations 2000.[154]

Article 15(1) of the DPEC allows Member States to adopt legislative measures to restrict the scope of Article 5 where that constitutes a 'necessary, appropriate and proportionate measure within a democratic society to safeguard national security (i.e. State security), defence, public security, and the prevention, investigation, detection and prosecution of criminal offences or of unauthorised use of the electronic communication system'. In the UK legislative measures have been adopted under the Regulation of Investigatory Powers Act 2000 (RIPA) to allow for interception of communications and to allow access to communications data for law enforcement purposes.

The storage of information and the right to refuse

The right to refuse in Article 5.3. of the DPEC is concerned with the storage of information within a network as well as the use of a network to gain access to information stored in the subscriber's or user's equipment. However, it is not concerned with technical storage, or access for the sole purpose of carrying out or facilitating the transmission of a communication or technical storage or access that is strictly necessary in order to provide an information society service that is explicitly requested by the subscriber or user (an information society service is defined as 'any service normally provided for remuneration, at a distance, by electronic means and at the individual request of a recipient of services'[155]).

In cases where Article 5.3. is engaged the service provider must provide the subscriber or user with clear and comprehensive information about the processing purpose in accordance with the Data Protection Directive. In addition, the subscriber or user must be told about the right to refuse the processing, which is very similar to being given an 'opt-out', meaning that the processing will be lawful until such time as the subscriber or user exercises the right to refuse. The use of cookies, adware and spyware are activities falling within Article 5.3. that the subscriber or user should be given the right to refuse.

Traffic data, retention and deletion

Article 6 of the DPEC is concerned with traffic data. The general rule within Article 6.1. is that traffic data should be erased or made anonymous when it is no longer needed for the purpose of the transmission of a communication. This acts as a prohibition against the retention of data, but there are some exceptions. Traffic data may be retained after the communication has ended for the following purposes:

- billing and interconnection payments (Article 6.2.);
- for the marketing of electronic communications services or for the provision of value added services (Article 6.3.);
- for national security, defence, public security, the prevention, detection and prosecution of crime and unauthorized use of communications systems (Article 6.1. and Article 15.1.).

Of course, even if an exception applies, the traffic data must be erased or made anonymous when the exceptional processing purpose has been completed.

What are traffic data?

Traffic data can be considered to be the by-product of an electronic communication and are defined in Article 2(b) as 'any data processed for the purpose of conveyance of a communication on an electronic communications network or for the billing thereof'. Thus, traffic data is distinguishable from the content of a communication.

Processing for billing and interconnection payments

As an exception to the general rule that traffic data should be erased or made anonymous when it is no longer needed for the purpose of transmission of the communication, Article 6.2. allows for retention of traffic data and its processing for the purposes of subscriber billing and interconnection payments after the communication has been completed, but only up to the end of the period during which the bill may be lawfully challenged or payment pursued. This information needs to be stored for a period to allow calculation of bills and resolution of any disputes about bills.

Processing for marketing purposes and for the provision of value added services

Article 6.3. of the DPEC permits retention and processing of traffic data after the communication has ended for the purposes of marketing electronic communication services or for the purposes of providing value added services, provided that the subscriber or user has given consent. If the subscriber or user has given consent, the duration of the processing can be no longer than is necessary for the marketing purpose and once this time has expired the data must be erased or made anonymous.

Valid consent can only be obtained if the service provider informs the subscriber or user of the types of traffic data that are to be processed and the duration of the processing and this information must be provided before consent is given (Article 6.4.). In addition, the subscriber or user must be given the opportunity to withdraw consent at any time (Article 6.3.).

Processing for the purposes of national security and other matters of national and public importance

Article 6.1. refers to Article 15.1., which has already been mentioned in the context of interception and surveillance of communications. This also allows Member States to adopt legislative measures to restrict the operation of Article 6.1. where the restriction constitutes a necessary, appropriate and proportionate measure within a democratic society to safeguard national security, defence, public security and the prevention, investigation, detection and prosecution of criminal offences and unauthorized use of telecommunications networks. Article 15.1. expressly states that on these grounds Member States may adopt legislative measures providing for the retention of data for a limited period.

In the UK measures have been introduced under the Anti-terrorism, Crime and Security Act 2001 (ATCSA) and measures will soon be harmonized across the EU due to the Communications Data Retention Directive,[156] which amends the DPEC. The Communications Data Retention Directive requires Member States to implement legislation to ensure that traffic data are retained by providers of publicly available electronic communications services and networks. The categories of data to be retained are:

- data necessary to trace and identify the source of a communication;
- data necessary to trace and identify the destination of a communication;
- data necessary to identify the date, time and duration of a communication;
- data necessary to identify the type of communication;

- data necessary to identify the communication device or what purports to be the communication device;
- data necessary to identify the location of mobile communication equipment.

These categories of data are to be retained for 12 months, unless the electronic communication used the internet protocol either wholly or partly, in which case the retention period is six months.

Persons who are allowed to process traffic data

Article 6.5. of the DPEC identifies the persons who are allowed to process traffic data, saying that processing must be restricted to persons acting under the authority of the network and service providers who are responsible for handling billing or traffic management, customer enquiries, fraud detection, marketing of electronic communications services or providing a value added service. The processing that may be done by these persons is restricted to that which is necessary for the purpose involved.

Itemized billing

The privacy issue within itemized billing is straightforward: by reading an itemized bill a third party can obtain the telephone number of a person called by the subscriber. This can compromise the subscriber's privacy, the user's privacy (if not the subscriber) and the privacy of the person called. For these reasons Article 7.1. of the DPEC gives subscribers the right to receive non-itemized bills.

Of course, itemized bills are very important to some subscribers, enabling them to keep track of calling and spending habits. They also have an important role to play in protecting the subscriber from incorrect billing and in furthering a competitive market. Thus, if the subscriber wishes to receive itemized bills, the interests of any users and the called party need to be taken into account. For this reason Article 7.2. requires Member States to apply national provisions in order to reconcile the rights of subscribers wishing to receive itemized bills and the right to privacy of calling users and called subscribers.

Calling and connected line identification

Article 8 is concerned with calling line identification and connected line identification. The difference between these services is as follows:

- Calling line identification shows the telephone number of the caller to the called subscriber.
- Connected line identification shows the telephone number of the called subscriber to the caller.

As with itemized billing the privacy issues are straightforward. First, if calling line or connected line identification services are in use, telephone numbers can be revealed to persons other than the participants of the calls.

Second, if calling line identification is suppressed by the caller, the called subscriber could be connected to a person to whom they did not want to be connected.

The calling subscriber and user's right to prevent calling line identification

Article 8.1. of the DPEC is concerned with the privacy of the calling subscriber and the calling user. If calling line identification is offered, the service provider must also offer the calling subscriber and the calling user a free, simple means for preventing the presentation of the calling line identification. The subscriber must be offered this possibility on a per-line basis while the calling user must have this possibility on a per-call basis.

The called subscriber's right to prevent calling line identification

Article 8.2. of the DPEC is concerned with the privacy of the called subscriber. If the service provider offers calling line identification, it must also offer the called subscriber a free, simple means to prevent the presentation of the calling line identification on incoming calls.

The called subscriber's right to reject incoming calls

Article 8.3. is also concerned with the privacy of the called subscriber. If the service provider offers calling line identification with presentation of the identification taking place before the call is established but the calling subscriber or calling user prevents presentation of the identification, the service provider must provide the called subscriber with a simple means for rejecting the incoming call.

The called subscriber's right to prevent connected line identification

Article 8.4. contains the final protection for the called subscriber. If the service provider offers connected line identification (where the called subscriber's number is presented to the calling subscriber or user) it must also offer the called subscriber a free, simple means for preventing the presentation of connected line identification.

Calling line identification and nuisance or malicious calls

Article 10(a) allows network and service providers to temporarily override the supression of calling line identification when a subscriber receiving nuisance or malicious calls makes a request for the tracing of the number. This is subject to limiting rules for analogue exchanges contained in Article 3.2.

Calling line identification and emergency services

Article 10(b) gives the emergency services the right to override suppression of calling line identification (and any absence of consent to process location data) on a per-line basis. This is also subject to the limiting rules for analogue exchanges.

Digital exchanges and analogue exchanges

The rules in Article 8 of the DPEC apply to subscriber lines connected to digital exchanges. They also apply to subscriber lines connected to analogue exchanges where that is technically possible, provided that it does not require a disproportionate economic effort (Article 3.2.).

Location data

Location data is defined in Article 2(c) as 'any data processed in an electronic communications network, indicating the geographic position of the terminal equipment of a user of a publicly available electronic communications service'. As traffic data can indicate the geographic location of terminal equipment it can also fall within the definition of location data. Article 9 is concerned with the processing of location data, but not traffic data.

The processing of location data

Article 9.1. provides that location data can only be processed where it has been made anonymous, or for the provision of a value added service where the subscribers or users have provided their consent.

Processing for the purposes of value added services

The meaning of value added service is contained in Article 2(9). A value added service is any service 'which requires the processing of traffic data or location data other than traffic data beyond what is necessary for the transmission of a communication or the billing thereof'.

Processing for the provision of value added services is only allowed where the subscriber or user has given consent. The consent must be provided before the processing commences and the service provider must provide information about the processing, which consists of:

- information about the type of location data that will be processed;
- information about the processing purpose;
- information about the duration of the processing;
- information about any transfers to third parties.

The service provider must give subscribers and users the opportunity to withdraw their consent to processing at any time (Article 9.1.). They must also be given free, simple means for temporarily refusing processing (Article 9.2.).

There are also restrictions on the persons who are allowed to process location data. These are persons acting under the authority of the network provider, the service provider or the value added service provider. Their processing must be restricted to what is necessary for the purposes of providing the value added service (Article 9.3.).

Automatic call forwarding

Article 11 of the DPEC is concerned with automatic call forwarding, requiring Member States to ensure that a subscriber is given a free, simple means for stopping automatic call forward to their terminal by a third party.

Directories

Article 12 is concerned with directories of subscribers that are made available to the public, whether printed or electronic. The rules are as follows:

- Subscribers who are individuals should be informed of a directory's purpose prior to being included in it and they should also be told about any further usage possibilities based on search functions embedded in electronic directories (Article 12.1.). Member States are also required to have regard to the legitimate interests of subscribers who are not individuals.
- Subscribers who are individuals should be given the opportunity to determine whether their personal data are to be included in a public directory as well as the right to verify, correct or withdraw their data. No charge will be made to subscribers who decide not to be in a directory or who decide to verify, correct or withdraw an entry (Article 12.2). Member States are also required to have regard to the legitimate interests of subscribers who are not individuals.

Member States are entitled to require additional consents of subscribers for any purpose of a directory that extends beyond a simple search for contact details against a person's name (Article 12.3.).

Unsolicited communications

Article 13 is concerned with direct marketing using electronic communications, specifically the use of automatic calling machines, direct marketing by fax, by email and by telephone. The UK rules are discussed in Chapter 4 of this book.

Remedies, liability and sanctions

Chapter III of the Data Protection Directive, entitled 'judicial remedies, liability and sanctions', discussed in Chapter 7 of this book, also has effect within DPEC because of the provisions of Article 15.2.

UK IMPLEMENTATION OF DPEC

The UK has implemented DPEC through the Privacy and Electronic Communications (EC Directive) Regulations 2003.[157] These regulations were amended by the Privacy and Electronic Communications (EC Directive) (Amendment) Regulations 2004.[158]

There is very little difference between the DPEC and the UK regulations. The main differences are:

- Regulation 9(2), which concerns itemized billing, places a duty on Ofcom to reconcile the rights of subscribers receiving the itemized bills and the right to privacy of calling users and called subscribers. This implements Article 7.2. of the DPEC.

- Regulation 15, which concerns the overriding of suppression of calling line identification when the communication provider is asked to trace a malicious or nuisance call, extends Article 10(b) of the DPEC by making it a requirement that the communications provider is satisfied that this action is necessary and expedient for the purposes of tracing calls.

- Regulation 17, which is concerned with automatic call forwarding, extends Article 11 of the DPEC by imposing an obligation on all communications providers to comply with reasonable requests from subscribers' communications providers for assistance in preventing automatic call forwarding.

- Regulations 25 and 26 are concerned with the Fax Preference Service register and the Telephone Preference Service register respectively. Subscribers, individual or corporate, may register their decision not to receive direct marketing communications with these services. Communications providers are expected to consult the suppression registers.

- Regulation 30 entitles a person who has suffered damage as a result of a contravention of the Regulations to bring a claim for compensation before the courts.

- The enforcement procedures in Part V of the DPA apply with contextual modifications. Ofcom may request the Information Commissioner to take enforcement action, under Regulation 32.

- Regulation 33 places an obligation on Ofcom to provide the Information Commissioner with advice on technical matters for the purpose of the Commissioner's enforcement obligations.

Although DPEC and the UK regulations are very much the same, domestic law on interception of communications and retention of communications data is very much advanced.

REGULATION OF INVESTIGATORY POWERS ACT 2000

Part I of the RIPA, entitled 'Communications', contains two chapters that are of considerable importance to data protection laws. Chapter 1 is titled 'Interception' and Chapter 2 is titled 'Acquisition and Disclosure of Communications Data'.

Part 1 of the RIPA impacts upon the requirements of Article 15.1. of the DPEC, which, to recap, allows Member States to overcome some of the protections of subscribers and users where that is a necessary measure within a democratic society, particularly confidentiality of communications and retention of traffic data.

Interception of communications

RIPA protects the privacy of postal and electronic communications by making it a criminal offence to intercept them in the UK while they are in the course of transmission. The protection offered to postal communications covers only those sent via a public postal service, whereas the protection offered to electronic communications extends to those transmitted over both public and private telecommunication systems. Thus, section 1 of the RIPA actually creates three offences. The first and second offences are in respect of unlawful interception of a communication transmitted via a public postal service or a public telecommunications system. The third offence is in respect of unlawful interception of a communication transmitted via a private telecommunications system.

If there is an interception in the UK of a communication in the course of transmission via a relevant service or system, this will only amount to an offence under either section 1(1)(a) or section 1(1)(b) of the RIPA if three conditions are satisfied. These are:

- the interception must have been intentional;
- it must have been without lawful authority;
- it must not be of a kind that is excluded from criminal liability.

What is an interception?

Curiously, RIPA only provides a definition of interception of communications transmitted by a telecommunications system, with section 2(2) saying:

> **For the purposes of this Act, but subject to the following provisions of this section, a person intercepts a communication in the course of its transmission by means of a telecommunication system if, and only if, he –**
>
> **(a) so modifies or interferes with the system, or its operation,**
>
> **(b) so monitors transmissions made by means of the system, or**
>
> **(c) so monitors transmissions made by wireless telegraphy to or from apparatus comprised in the system,**
>
> **as to make some or all of the contents of the communication available, while being transmitted, to a person other than the sender or intended recipient of the communication.**

Thus, for communications transmitted by a telecommunications system an integral part of the definition is the making of the contents of the communication available to a party other than the sender or recipient. It is suggested that as RIPA is intended to protect information within communications this feature will also be required for the legal definition of interception of sealed postal communications, although merely stopping a postal communication from being delivered may also amount to an 'interception' based on the ordinary dictionary definition of the word.

However, assistance with the meaning of interception of a postal communication is provided by an order[159] made under section 12 of the RIPA, which talks about interception and temporary retention of postal communications. This shows that there is a difference between interception and merely stopping a postal communication. In addition, within the context of interception this order talks about systems for the 'opening, copying and resealing of any postal item', showing that interception requires access to the communication within the envelope.

The meaning of 'in the course of transmission'

The meaning of 'in the course of transmission' seems to be pointing to the period of time that elapses between the sending of a communication and its receipt, but this sense of a period of time elapsing between sending and receipt, while suitable for postal items, emails, faxes and similar electronic communications, does not lend itself well to real-time telephone conversations, where the speaking of words and their hearing by the other party to the call are virtually instantaneous, or new technologies like instant messaging. For this reason section 2(2) of the RIPA says that a communication transmitted by a telecommunications system will be intercepted in the course of transmission if its contents are made available to the interceptor while they are being transmitted. This covers real-time eavesdropping.

Although an interception of a telephone call will enable the interceptor to listen in on a conversation in real time, the interceptor may prefer to record the information and listen to it after the conversation has ended. Section 2(8) of the RIPA deals with this contingency so that an offence will be committed if the contents of a communication are made available to a third party, someone other than the sender and recipient, after the communication has completed its transmission. Section 2(8) says:

> For the purposes of this section the cases in which any contents of a communication are to be taken to be made available to a person while being transmitted shall include any case in which any of the contents of the communication, while being transmitted, are diverted or recorded so as to be available to a person subsequently.

Section 2(7) of the RIPA expands upon the meaning of 'in the course of transmission' for communications transmitted over a telecommunications system to cover situations where, after the communication is sent, it is stored before being received, as happens with emails before they are downloaded. Section 2(7) says:

> For the purposes of this section the times while a communication is being transmitted by means of a telecommunication system shall be taken to include any time when the system by means of which the communication is being, or has been, transmitted is used for storing it in a manner that enables the intended recipient to collect it or otherwise to have access to it.

Public and private services and systems

As far as public postal services are concerned, section 2(1) of the RIPA provides that these must be ones that are offered or provided to the public in any one or more parts of the UK. The service does not need to be offered to all of the public. A substantial section of the public will suffice. A similar formulation is adopted for public telecommunications systems.

A private telecommunication system is one that is attached to a public telecommunications system, provided that the apparatus that makes the connection between the private and public systems is located in the UK. Section 2(1) provides:

> 'private telecommunication system' means any telecommunication system which, without itself being a public telecommunication system, is a system in relation to which the following conditions are satisfied –
>
> (a) it is attached, directly or indirectly and whether or not for the purposes of the communication in question, to a public telecommunication system; and
>
> (b) there is apparatus comprised in the system which is both located in the United Kingdom and used (with or without other apparatus) for making the attachment to the public telecommunication system.

Interception within the UK

A communication will only be protected if the interception takes place in the UK, which means for the purposes of communications transmitted over public services and systems that the interception is 'effected by conduct within the UK'. This means that the conduct that causes the interception must take place in the UK. For communications transmitted over private telecommunications systems there is an additional requirement, namely that the sender or recipient of the communication must be in the UK.

Interception of traffic data

The prohibition against interception of a communication does not include a prohibition against the interception of traffic data (section 2(5)(a) of the

RIPA). Furthermore, if it is necessary to access a communication it order to identify traffic data, that access will not be treated as an unlawful interception (section 2(5)(b) of the RIPA).

The definition of traffic data in RIPA differs from the definition of traffic data in DPEC, as shown in the Table 6.1.

TABLE 6.1   *The meaning of traffic data*

DPEC, Article 2(b)	RIPA, section 2(9)
'Traffic data' means any data processed for the purpose of the conveyance of a communication on an electronic communications network or for the billing thereof	In this section 'traffic data', in relation to any communication, means – (a) any data identifying, or purporting to identify, any person, apparatus or location to or from which the communication is or may be transmitted, (b) any data identifying or selecting, or purporting to identify or select, apparatus through which, or by means of which, the communication is or may be transmitted, (c) any data comprising signals for the actuation of apparatus used for the purposes of a telecommunication system for effecting (in whole or in part) the transmission of any communication, and (d) any data identifying the data or other data as data comprised in or attached to a particular communication.

Intentional interception

The first condition of the offences is that the interceptor must have intended to intercept (sections 1(1)&(2) of the RIPA). This means actual intent, not constructive consent in the sense that the interceptor 'ought to have known', or recklessness.

Lawful authority

The second condition of the offence is that the interception must be without lawful authority. Section 1(5) identifies the conduct that will amount to lawful authority, of which there are only three possibilities. First, conduct will have lawful authority if it is authorized by sections 3 or 4 of the RIPA. Second, conduct will also have lawful authority if it takes place in accordance with an interception warrant granted under section 5 of the RIPA. Third, the exercise of other statutory powers in respect of stored communications data will amount to conduct having lawful authority if the power is exercised to obtain information or to take possession of any property including documents.

Lawful authority – interception without a warrant

Section 3 is titled 'Lawful interception without an interception warrant' and it identifies four situations in which interception without warrant will be considered to lawful. This means that if one of these situations applies, the interceptor cannot be guilty of a criminal offence. It will not be an offence in the following four circumstances:

- If the interceptor has reasonable grounds for believing that the sender and intended recipient have both consented to the interception (section 3(1)).

- If the interceptor has the consent of either the sender or intended recipient and surveillance by way of interception has been authorized under Part II of the RIPA (section 3(2)). Part II of the RIPA is concerned with surveillance of which there are two kinds: (i) directed surveillance; and (ii) intrusive surveillance. Both kinds of surveillance need to be authorized. Intrusive surveillance, where a person's home or vehicle are invaded, is the most serious form of surveillance (a person's home is protected by the right to privacy in Article 8 of the ECHR) and it will only be authorized if it is necessary in the interests of national security, for the purposes of preventing or detecting serious crime, or is in the interests of the economic well-being of the UK (section 32 of the RIPA). Surveillance can be authorized by a wide variety of public authorities.

- If the interception is authorized by the provider of a postal or telecommunications service and it takes place in connection with the provision of the service or the enforcement of laws relating to the service (section 3(3)).

- To intercept a mobile communication if the interception is authorized by a designated person under section 5 of the Wireless Telegraphy Act 1949 and is connected with the issue of licences, the prevention or detection of interference with spectrum or the enforcement of laws relating to interference (section 3(4)). Wireless telegraphy is any form of communication that uses the radio magnetic spectrum, such as voice telephony and data communications over third-generation mobile networks.

The third and fourth situations are concerned more with ensuring good, efficient network operations for wired and wireless networks rather than law enforcement, the focus of the second situation. The first situation has very narrow application.

Lawful authority – foreign interceptions and business interceptions

Section 4 of the RIPA makes foreign interceptions lawful subject to compliance with the regulations issued in 2004.[160] However, for the purposes of domestic data protection laws it is the Telecommunications (Lawful Business Practice) (Interception of Communications) Regulations 2000[161] that are most important. These Regulations will be referred to as the 'Interception and Lawful Business Practice Regulations'.

The Interception and Lawful Business Practice Regulations, which came into force on 24 October 2000, have been made under section 4(2) of the RIPA, which says:

> (2) Subject to subsection (3), the Secretary of State may by regulations authorise any such conduct described in the regulations as appears to him to constitute a legitimate practice reasonably required for the purpose, in connection with the carrying on of any business, of monitoring or keeping a record of –
>
> (a) communications by means of which transactions are entered into in the course of that business; or
>
> (b) other communications relating to that business or taking place in the course of its being carried on.

These regulations permit interception of a communication in the course of transmission by means of a telecommunications system where the interception is carried out with the express or implied permission of the system controller. A system controller is a person with the right to control the operation or use of a telecommunications system. Such interceptions will only be lawful if they satisfy the following conditions:

- The interception is effected solely for the purpose of monitoring or keeping a record of communications relevant to the system controller's business in order to achieve one of the objectives set out in Regulation 3.
- The telecommunications system is provided for use wholly or in part in connection with the business.
- The system controller has made all reasonable efforts to inform every person who may use the system that communications may be intercepted. This does not mean that the system controller needs the consent of users of the system to intercept their communications.

The objectives of the interception as set out in Regulation 3 are as follows:

- The monitoring or keeping of a record is done to: (i) establish the existence of facts; (ii) ascertain compliance with applicable regulatory or self-regulatory practices or procedures; or (iii) ascertain or demonstrate that users of the system are achieving required standards.
- The monitoring or keeping of a record is done in the interests of national security.
- The monitoring or keeping of a record is done for the purposes of preventing or detecting crime.
- The monitoring or keeping of a record is done for the purpose of investigating or detecting unauthorized use of the system.

- The monitoring or keeping of a record is done in order to achieve, or is an inherent part of, the effective operation of the system.
- The monitoring is for the purpose of determining whether the communications are relevant to the system controller's business. This does not permit the recording of communications, however.
- The monitoring is of communications made to a free of charge confidential telephone counselling or support service where users of the service have the option to remain anonymous. Again, this does not permit the recording of communications.

For the purposes of the regulations a business is not confined to the operations of profit-making companies. According to Regulation 2(a) a business includes 'references to activities of a government department, of any public authority or of any person or office holder on whom functions are conferred by or under any enactment'.

Lawful authority – interception with a warrant

Under section 5 of the RIPA the Secretary of State, or the Scottish Ministers, may issue an interception warrant, if one is necessary in the interests of national security, for the purpose of preventing or detecting serious crime, for the purpose of safeguarding the economic well-being of the UK or in order to give effect to the provisions of any international mutual assistance agreement. However, an interception warrant may only be issued where the conduct authorized by the warrant is 'proportionate to what is sought to be achieved' (section 5(2)(b) of the RIPA). Furthermore, when making his decision the Secretary of State must also consider whether the information could reasonably be obtained by other means (section 5(4) of the RIPA).

If the Secretary of State is satisfied that an interception warrant is necessary, the warrant may authorize or require a person to whom it is addressed to do any of the following:

- Intercept a communication in the course of transmission by means of a postal service or a telecommunications system (section 5(1)(a)).
- Make a request for assistance from another country under an international mutual assistance agreement (section 5(1)(b)).
- Provide assistance to another country under an international mutual assistance agreement (section 5(1)(c)).
- Disclose intercepted material and related communications data (communications data includes traffic data, but excludes the content of the communication).

Furthermore, an interception warrant will also authorize the following conduct:

- all such conduct that it is necessary to undertake in order to do what is expressly authorized by the warrant (section 5(6)(a));
- conduct for obtaining related communications data (section 5(6)(b));
- assistance given by any person to the person to whom the warrant is addressed (see section 5(6)(c)).

An interception warrant will only be issued if an application for one is made by a person identified in section 6 of the RIPA. These persons include the Director-General of the Security Services, the Chief of the Secret Intelligence Service, the Director of GCHQ (Government Communications Headquarters), the Director General of the National Criminal Intelligence Service and various chief Police Officers (such as the Commissioner of Police of the Metropolis). If the Secretary of State (or the Scottish Ministers) considers that a warrant should be issued, it will be issued to the person making the application.

Exclusion of criminal liability

Section 1(6) of the RIPA describes the circumstances in which criminal liability will be excluded. These are as follows:

- The interception must be of a communication transmitted over a private telecommunications system.
- The interception is by a person with the right to control the operation or the use of the system, or the interception is by a person with the express or implied consent of the person with the right to control the operation or use of the system.

If criminal liability is excluded, the interceptor can still be sued by the sender or recipient of the communication if the interception is without lawful authority (section 1(3) of the RIPA).

Maintenance of intercept capability

Section 12 of the RIPA allows the Secretary of State to impose obligations on the providers of public postal and telecommunication services for the purpose of securing assistance in relation to interception warrants. This is known as the maintenance of interception capability. In 2002 an order was made under section 12 for these purposes.[162]

Acquisition and disclosure of communications data

Section 21 of the RIPA says that the acquisition and disclosure of communications data will be lawful for all purposes if it is authorized under section 23. Communications data includes traffic data and the full definition contained in section 21(4) is:

communications data means any of the following –

(a) any traffic data comprised in or attached to a communication (whether by the sender or otherwise) for the purposes of any postal service or telecommunication system by means of which it is being or may be transmitted;

(b) any information which includes none of the contents of a communication (apart from any information falling within paragraph (a)) and is about the use made by any person –

(i)   of any postal service or telecommunications service; or

(ii) in connection with the provision to or use by any person of any telecommunications service, of any part of a telecommunication system;

(c) any information not falling within paragraph (a) or (b) that is held or obtained, in relation to persons to whom he provides the service, by a person providing a postal service or telecommunications service.

Under section 22 of the RIPA a designated person within a public authority may authorize another person within the same public authority to obtain communications data. Where the designated person considers that communications data are, or may be, in the possession of a postal or telecommunications operator, the designated person may serve a notice on the operator requiring it to obtain the communication data, if it is not already in the operator's possession, and to disclose the data to the designated person or the authorized person.

Authorizations and notices under section 22 can only be issued if the obtaining of communications data is necessary on one of the following grounds:

- in the interests of national security;
- for the purposes of preventing or detecting crime or preventing disorder;
- in the interests of the economic well-being of the UK;
- in the interests of public safety;
- for the purposes of protecting public health;
- for the purposes of assessing or collecting taxes and similar duties;
- for the purposes of prevention of death or injury in emergency situations;
- for the purposes specified by the Secretary of State in an order that has been approved by both Houses of Parliament.

The designated persons who may grant authorizations and issue notices as well as the relevant public authorities are identified in section 25(1) of the RIPA and in the Regulation of Investigatory Powers (Communications Data) Order 2003.[163]

Of course, having a right of access to communications data will be of little consequence if the data no longer exist. This is why Article 15(1) of the

DPEC allows Member States to override the protections provided by Article 5 (confidentiality of communications) and Article 6 (traffic data) where 'such a restriction constitutes a necessary, appropriate and proportionate measure within a democratic society to safeguard national security (i.e. state security), defence, public security, and the prevention, investigation, detection and prosecution of criminal offences or of unauthorised use of the electronic communications system'. The ATCSA is the overriding measure in the UK as far as the retention of communications data is concerned.

ANTI-TERRORISM, CRIME AND SECURITY ACT 2001

Section 102 of ATCSA requires the Secretary of State to issue a code of practice relating to the retention of communications data by communications providers where this is necessary for (1) the purpose of safeguarding national security or for (2) the purposes of prevention or detection of crime or the prosecution of offenders which may relate directly or indirectly to national security. For these purposes 'communications data' has the same meaning as in RIPA and, to recap, the meaning of communications data extends beyond the meaning of traffic data in DPEC. Before issuing a code of practice the Secretary of State is required to consult the communications industry.

Interestingly, section 102(4) of ATCSA says that 'a failure by any person to comply with a code of practice or agreement under this section which is for the time being in force shall not of itself render him liable to any criminal proceedings'. This means that compliance with a code of practice is voluntary.

On 5 December 2003 the Retention of Communications Data (Code of Practice) Order 2003[164] came into force. This order contains a code of practice entitled 'Voluntary Code of Practice', which prescribes a number of minimum retention periods. This code asks communications providers to retain subscriber information and telephony data for 12 months, SMS and email data for six months and web activity logs for four days. The Voluntary Code of Practice is likely to be superseded by the UK regulations that are introduced to give effect to the requirements of the Communication Data Retention Directive.

RECONCILING RIPA AND ATCSA

The position under the voluntary code of practice is most unsatisfactory, for two reasons. First, the code is voluntary, meaning that it is shrouded by legal uncertainty. Second, although ATCSA allows the Secretary of State to issue a code where that is necessary for the purpose of safeguarding national security or for the prevention or detection of crime impacting upon national security, RIPA allows access to retained communications data for considerably more purposes. Thus, there is an inherent conflict between ATCSA and RIPA. This conflict, while recognized by the Secretary of State, has been very much skirted over by the Voluntary Code of Practice. The foreward to the code says:

> Communications data may be obtained by security, intelligence and law enforcement agencies under the Regulation of Investigatory Powers Act 2000 and other statutory powers. This Code does not deal with these provisions.
>
> The Data Protection Act 1998 requires that personal data are processed lawfully. In retaining communications data for longer than needed for their own business purposes and for the purposes identified in the Act communication service providers will process personal data. The Information Commissioner's Office (ICO) has accepted that such processing will not, on human rights grounds, contravene this requirement of the Act.
>
> However, individual communication service providers must satisfy themselves that the processing is 'necessary' for one of a range of functions. In doing so they are entitled to rely heavily on the Secretary of State's assurance that the retention of communications data for the periods as specified in this Code is necessary for the government's function of safeguarding national security, and on the fact that the Code has been approved by Parliament.
>
> The ICO has though expressed concern about such retained data being acquired for purposes that do not relate to national security. Acquisition of communications data is not addressed in the Act and therefore is not within the proper ambit of this Code.

It may be considered that communications providers are entitled to feel confused by the current state of the law. However, as discussed earlier, in 2005 considerable progress was made towards a harmonized regime for retention and disclosure of communications data as evidenced, which has resulted in the Communications Data Retention Directive.[165] This directive amends the DPEC so as to allow lengthy retention periods for internet and telecommunications data.

7 Enforcing Data Protection Laws

INTRODUCTION

The Data Protection Directive requires strong enforcement measures in order to ensure its harmonized application across the EEA. Thus, in addition to the administrative remedies that may be applied by the national supervisory authorities, the Directive requires Member States to 'provide for the right of every person to a judicial remedy for any breach of the rights guaranteed him by the national law applicable to the processing in question'. The Directive also requires Member States to provide legal mechanisms so that the data subject can recover compensation from the data controller for any damage suffered as a consequence of the data controller's breach of the national laws adopted under the Directive. Finally, the Directive requires Member States to 'adopt suitable measures to ensure the full implementation of [its] provisions', which means that 'sanctions' should be imposed for infringements of national laws.

Of course, data protection laws are enforced in other ways. In addition to enforcement by the national supervisory authority, national courts and by data subjects the Directive creates enforcement roles for the European Commission and for data controllers, both in respect of transborder data flows. The seventh data protection principle in the DPA contains another specialized enforcement role for the data controller, who is required to take appropriate measures to ensure adequate security by data processors.

ENFORCEMENT BY THE DATA SUBJECT

The data subject is endowed with many rights and powers under the DPA that can be properly grouped together as examples of enforcement powers. For example, the right of access under section 7 of the DPA provides the data subject with an invaluable mechanism for securing the data controller's compliance with the DPA. If the data controller fails to comply with a subject access request, or if when complying it reveals evidence of violations of the DPA's provisions, the range of possible outcomes includes:

- The data subject might commence a court action under section 7(9) of the DPA for an order requiring the data controller to comply, or comply fully, with the access request.
- The data subject might exercise their right to object to processing, perhaps on the grounds that it causes substantial and unwarranted

damage and distress, which may create grounds for another court action, such as a claim for compensation under section 13.

• The data subject might make a complaint to the Information Commissioner causing the Information Commissioner to carry out an assessment of the data controller's processing. Alternatively, the Information Commissioner might serve an information notice, which could lead to proceedings before the Information Tribunal or the criminal courts.

Enforcement through rectification, blocking, erasure and destruction of inaccurate personal data

Under section 12A and section 14 of the DPA the data subject may apply to the court for an order that inaccurate personal data be rectified, blocked, erased or destroyed by the data controller. The right to seek these remedies under section 12A arises only in respect of exempt manual data.

Court orders where inaccurate data are required to be rectified etc.

If the court decides to make an order requiring the data controller to rectify, block, erase or destroy inaccurate data it may also order the data controller to notify any third parties to whom the inaccurate data were disclosed of the fact that the data have been so rectified, blocked, erased or destroyed. However, the court will only make this order if it is reasonably practicable for the data controller to notify the third parties.

Court orders where inaccurate data are accurately recorded

There will be occasions when the personal data are inaccurate because the inaccuracies stemmed from the data subject or a third party from whom the data controller obtained the personal data. In cases where the data controller has accurately recorded inaccurate information, the fourth data protection principle will need to be considered.

The interpretation within Schedule 1, Part II of the DPA deals with cases where although the data controller has accurately recorded the information it has received from the data subject or from a third party, there are inaccuracies in the personal data. In these cases the data controller will not be in breach of the fourth data protection principle provided that it took reasonable steps to ensure the accuracy of the data. If the data subject notifies the data controller that the data are inaccurate, the fourth data protection principle will not be breached if the data indicate that the data subject has informed the data controller of the inaccuracy.

In cases such as these the court may order the data controller to supplement the inaccurate data with a statement of the true facts, rather than ordering rectification, blocking, erasure or destruction, but the court can only follow this alternative approach if the data controller took reasonable steps to ensure the accuracy of the data as required by the interpretation to the fourth data protection principle. However, if it transpires that the data controller has not complied with the fourth data protection principle, because it has not taken reasonable steps to ensure the accuracy or because it has failed to indicate that the data subject has notified inaccuracies, the court may order it to do so rather than ordering rectification, blocking, erasure or destruction.

It is worth noting that the data subject's right to seek rectification, blocking, erasure or destruction of inaccurate personal data can also be pursued via the Information Commissioner as an alternative to the court procedure. This is because section 40 of the DPA empowers the Information Commissioner to order rectification, blocking, erasure or destruction through the service of an enforcement notice. If the data subject manages to engage the Information Commissioner in his attempts to secure rectification, blocking, erasure or destruction of inaccurate personal data this can trigger a sequence of events that can, theoretically at least, lead to the criminal prosecution of the data controller.

Orders for rectification where the data subject brings a claim for compensation

If the data subject brings a claim for compensation under section 13 of the DPA the court may also order rectification, blocking, erasure or destruction of inaccurate personal data as well as ordering the data controller to notify any third parties to whom the data have been disclosed, provided that it is reasonably practicable for the data controller to notify third parties.

Enforcement through claims for compensation

Section 13(1) of the DPA entitles the data subject to compensation where they have suffered damage as a result of any contravention of the Act by the data controller. The data subject is also entitled to compensation for distress in two circumstances. The first circumstance is where the data subject has also suffered damage (section 13(2)(a)). The second is where the processing is for the special purposes (section 3), namely for the purposes of journalism or for artistic or literary purposes (section 13(2)(b)). If the processing is not for the special purposes and the data subject has not suffered damage, the data subject will not be entitled to compensation for distress.

The meaning of damage and distress was examined in *Johnson v. Medical Defence Union.*[166] In this case the claimant argued that his reputation had been damaged due to the defendant's unilateral decision to terminate his membership and his insurance cover. He said that this also caused him distress and to incur costs in arranging new insurance cover. The judge, Mr Justice Rimer, held that compensation for damage to reputation is not recoverable under section 13(1), for two reasons. First, he held that section 13(1) is concerned with pecuniary damage only, which he identified to be financial damage or physical damage. Second, he held that such claims should be brought as claims for defamation. For these reasons he felt constrained to dismiss the distress claim too, as he interpreted section 13 to mean that the data subject must sue for compensation for damage in order to recover compensation for distress.

The judge's reasoning on the meaning of damage is unconvincing, but, to be fair to him, he did admit that he did not find the point easy. The first criticism is that there is no convincing authority for the proposition that damage within section 13(1) should be pecuniary, in the sense identified by the judge. Taking the word 'damage' at face value, there seems to be no logical reason to hold that it does not cover damage to reputation if proven to be caused by a breach of the DPA, and the fact that a defamation claim could be pursued is no answer, because the law is fully familiar with the situation where the facts of a case can support more than one cause of action. Furthermore, it is questionable whether the law of defamation actually covers the situation in question, because there was no identified communication of a defamatory statement, oral or written, by the Medical Defence Union to a third party. Second, section 13 does not actually require a data subject to commence a claim for compensation for damage in order to claim compensation for distress. All it requires for a claim for compensation for distress is the suffering of damage (unless section 13(2)(b) applies). Thus, if the facts of the case could have supported a claim in defamation as speculated by the judge, this should have been enough to bring a claim for compensation for distress.

Johnson is interesting for another reason, because it supports the proposition that a data subject need only identify a nominal damages claim to recover relatively substantial compensation for distress. This is because the judge held that he would have awarded £10.50 compensation for pecuniary loss and £5000 compensation for distress had Mr Johnson been able to show that the identified element of unfair processing was causative of these losses (it should be remembered that the judge found that the Medical Defence Union did breach the first data protection principle, but this was not causative of the decision to terminate Mr Johnson's membership and insurance cover).

Mr Justice Rimer's definition of pecuniary damage, which includes physical as well as financial damage, does leave the door open for data subjects to bring distress claims as damages claims. In the field of personal injury law, practitioners are very familiar with the scenario where distress or anxiety is suffered to such an extent that a definition of psychiatric injury is justified. A psychiatric injury is regarded as being a physical injury, so complex distress cases supported by sufficient medical evidence could be brought as damages claims under section 13(1).

It was stated above that there is no convincing authority for the proposition that damage within section 13(1) should be pecuniary in the sense identified by Mr Justice Rimer. However, there are some authorities that would support Mr Justice Rimer. In *Campbell v. Mirror Group Newspapers*[167] the trial judge, Mr Justice Morland, held that damage for the purposes of section 13 'means special or financial damages in contra-distinction to distress in the shape of injury to feelings'. The Information Commissioner also prefers Mr Justice Rimer's definition.[168]

In distinction, the Article 29 Working Party has said:

> It should be borne in mind that 'damage' in the sense of the data protection directive includes not only physical damage and financial loss, but also any psychological or moral harm caused (known as 'distress' under UK and US law).[169]

Enforcement by requesting an assessment

The data subject may request the Information Commissioner to carry out an assessment of a data controller's processing operations by using their powers in section 42 of the DPA. The ability to trigger assessments by the Information Commissioner can be considered to be an enforcement mechanism in its own right as well as being a trigger to other enforcement action by the Information Commissioner, such as the service of an information notice or an enforcement notice.

Section 42 of the DPA allows a person who believes they have been directly affected by processing operations to request the Information Commissioner to assess whether it is likely or unlikely that the processing has been carried out in accordance with the DPA. The Information Commissioner has complete discretion over the manner of the assessment but is required to consider the extent to which the request raises a matter of substance, whether there has been any undue delay in making the request and whether the applicant could make a subject access request under section 7 of the DPA.

ENFORCEMENT BY THE DATA CONTROLLER

The data controller carries a limited number of enforcement obligations, but they are very important in their own right. These concern transborder data flows and the use of data processors.

Transborder data flows

If the data controller wishes to transfer data to a country outside the EEA, it needs to consider the adequacy test, bearing in mind that transfers to non-adequate countries are not allowed unless an exemption applies.

Where the data controller takes advantage of model contractual clauses or the BCR mechanisms to legitimize transfers, it acquires obligations that can be fairly categorized as being akin to enforcement obligations. Taking BCR as an example, the multinational organization needs to show that the rules are binding within the organization as a whole. This requires the organization to enforce the rules within its group, because BCR contain a self-regulatory obligation.

The use of data processors

The seventh data protection principle requires data controllers to take 'appropriate technical and organizational measures' against 'unauthorised or unlawful processing of personal data and against accidental loss or destruction of, or damage to, personal data'. The interpretation within Schedule 1, Part II identifies a series of obligations that the data controller carries in respect of the choice of data processor, which effectively amount to enforcement mechanisms. In appropriate cases the seventh data protection principle will require the data controller to audit the data processor, an activity that many people consider to be synonymous with enforcement.

ENFORCEMENT BY THE EUROPEAN COMMISSION

The European Commission has retained considerable enforcement powers for itself as far as transborder data flows are concerned. For example, the European Commission is able to object to authorizations for data transfers given by Member States where its objection is on justified grounds involving the protection of the privacy and fundamental rights and freedoms of the individual, which effectively gives it a right of veto over Member States (see Article 26.3. of the Data Protection Directive).

ENFORCEMENT BY THE INFORMATION COMMISSIONER

The Information Commissioner is the UK's national supervisory authority as required by Article 28 of the Data Protection Directive and as such is responsible for enforcement of the DPA. According to the DPA the Information Commissioner has the following enforcement powers:

- to carry out assessments, which is exercisable only after the Information Commissioner has received a request from another person, meaning that the Information Commissioner may not carry out an assessment of their own volition;
- to serve information notices, special information notices and enforcement notices;
- to inspect premises and seize property;
- to commence court proceedings;
- to issue authorizations for transborder data flows.

The Information Commissioner has other powers, which are found outside the DPA. The Commissioner can require a credit reference agency to publish a notice of correction on an inaccurate credit file under section 159 of the Consumer Credit Act 1974. They can apply for an injunction under the Unfair Terms in Consumer Contract Regulations 1999, to prevent the continued use of an unfair contract term. They can also serve an enforcement order under section 213 of the Enterprise Act 2002, requiring a person to cease conduct harmful to consumers.

The Information Commissioner's enforcement strategy

In November 2005 the Information Commissioner announced an enforcement strategy at the 2005 Annual Conference of the National Association of Data Protection and Freedom of Information Officers, with the launch of a document entitled 'A Strategy for Data Protection Regulatory Action'.[170] This document shows that the Information Commissioner will not wait for a complaint from a data subject before taking action. In respect of the triggers to an investigation the Information Commissioner says:

The initial drivers will usually be:

- issues of general public concern (including those raised in the media);

- concerns that arise because of the novel or intrusive nature of particular activities;

- concerns raised with us in complaints that we receive;

- concerns that become apparent through our other activities.

The new enforcement strategy identifies the types of situations where enforcement action will be likely and unlikely. These are:

Likely (especially after warning):

- Repeated failure to take adequate security measures.

- Collecting and retaining detailed or sensitive personal information on a 'just in case' basis.

- Inaccurate or long out-dated information which impacts on career prospects.

- Seriously intrusive marketing – e.g. repeated failure to observe Telephone Preference Service requirements.

- 'Professional' breaches of Section 55 (unlawful obtaining) e.g. by private investigation agencies.

- Failure to notify despite reminders.

- Denial of subject access where it is reasonable to suppose significant information is held.

Unlikely:

- 'Accidental' non-compliance with the Data Protection Principles – which is recognised and where effective remedial action is swiftly taken.

- Single non-criminal breaches by small businesses caused by ignorance of requirements.

- Non-compliance which is not particularly intrusive and has not caused significant detriment – e.g. a single mail shot.

- Non-compliance where other pressures – e.g. damage to reputation – may be swifter and more effective than action by a regulator.

- Business vs. business disputes where there is no detriment to customers.

- 'Domestic' breaches of Section 55 (unlawful obtaining) e.g. feuding spouses or work colleagues – except where a significant abuse of trust is involved.

The enforcement strategy is supported by a Regulatory Action Division. The launch of this new division was announced by a press release on 15 June 2005.[171] This division is assisted by a team of investigators and a team of lawyers.

In 2005 the Information Commissioner also issued a series of statements that reveal more information about the enforcement strategy. These show that landlords, private detectives, solicitors and accountants are receiving special attention. For professionals, solicitors,[172] accountants and others, the message seems to be that notification offences will not be ignored. Private detectives need to be very concerned about unlawful obtaining of personal data in breach of section 55 of the DPA.

The Information Commissioner's annual reports to Parliament, required by section 52 of the DPA, also contain very useful information about recent and current regulatory trends. For example in 2005 there were 12 successful prosecutions, eight under section 55 and four under section 21 of the DPA. The largest fine in 2005 was £2,500, with £3,000 costs. The 2004 Annual Report reveals seven successful prosecutions, all under section 55 of the DPA. The largest fine was £10,000, with £5,000 costs. The 2003 Annual Report reveals nine convictions, with most of them being under the Data Protection Act 1984. The convictions under the DPA were mainly for breach of section 55.[173]

Assessments

Assessments at the request of the data subject are governed by section 42 of the DPA. In addition to these powers the Information Commissioner may also, with the data controller's consent, assess a data controller's processing for 'the following of good practice'. This power is contained in section 51(7) of the DPA.

Information and enforcement notices

The rules governing information and enforcement notices are contained in Part V of the DPA, which is titled 'Enforcement'. The Information Commissioner may serve an enforcement notice under section 40 of the DPA where they are satisfied that a data controller has contravened, or is contravening, any of the data protection principles. An information notice under section 41 of the DPA can be served after the Information Commissioner has received a request for an assessment under section 42 of the DPA or where the Information Commissioner reasonably requires any information for the purposes of determining whether the data controller has complied with or is complying with the data protection principles. A special information notice may be served under section 43 of the DPA, again after receipt of a request for an assessment, or when a court claim has been stayed under section 32 of the DPA.

The Information Commissioner may use information notices and enforcement notices in conjunction with one another. For example, an information notice might be used to acquire information that leads the Information Commissioner to conclude that one or more of the data protection principles have been contravened. If this is the case, the information notice might be followed by an enforcement notice. However, it is important to understand that the service of an information notice is not a mandatory prerequisite to the service of an enforcement notice; an enforcement notice can be served without a preceding information notice.

Enforcement notices

Section 40(1) of the DPA says that the Information Commissioner may only serve an enforcement notice where they are satisfied that the data controller has contravened, or is contravening, any of the data protection principles. Of course, the Information Commissioner will need reliable evidence before they can come to the conclusion that the data controller has failed to comply with the DPA, which may come from the data subject or another person or in response to an information notice or in exercise of a search warrant. If the Information Commissioner does not have sufficient evidence to justify an enforcement notice, the data controller can expect to have it cancelled.

A very important consideration for the Information Commission is whether the contravention complained of has caused, or is likely to cause, any person damage or distress, which echoes the court's responsibility in applications brought under section 10 of the DPA. The suffering of damage or distress is clearly an aggravating factor and in serious cases it is inevitable that the Information Commissioner will act.

The essence of an enforcement notice is that it requires the data controller to do things, or stop doing things, which may include stopping processing. Thus, where an enforcement notice requires the data controller to do something, or not do something, it will either ask the data controller to take 'specified steps', or to refrain from taking specified steps. Thus, if the notice does not specify the steps to be taken, or not to be taken, it will be invalid.

The notice must state the time for compliance in that it must provide a deadline for when the data controller is required to refrain from taking steps. Where an enforcement notice tells the data controller to refrain from processing, it must also make it clear whether the prohibition against processing relates only to a specific purpose or only to processing done in a specific manner. Again, the time for compliance must be clear.

An enforcement notice must give the data controller sufficient information about the Information Commissioner's reasoning behind their conclusion that there has been a contravention of the data protection principles. The notice must identify the data protection principles alleged to have been contravened and it must include the Information Commissioner's reasons.

Unless the case is one of urgency, the time for compliance with an enforcement notice cannot be less than 28 days calculated from the date on which the notice was served on, or given to, the data controller. This period is specified in the Information Tribunal (Enforcement Appeals) Rules 2000[174] and it constitutes the time period for bringing an appeal against a notice. If the Information Commissioner considers that the case is one of urgency and that a shorter deadline is required, the enforcement notice must state this, giving the Information Commissioner's reasons. However, the deadline for compliance with an enforcement notice cannot be less than seven days beginning with the day on which the notice is served.

Enforcement notices and inaccurate data

An enforcement notice may require a data controller to rectify, block, erase or destroy inaccurate data and any other data that contains an expression of opinion that appears to the Information Commissioner to be based on inaccurate data. This power complements the court's powers under section 14 of the DPA.

If personal data are inaccurate, the Information Commissioner also needs to consider whether the data controller has accurately recorded inaccurate data provided by the data subject or a third party (it will be recalled that this scenario is also addressed by section 14 of the DPA and by the interpretation to the fourth data protection principle). If the data controller has accurately recorded inaccurate information, the Information Commissioner has two options. First, the enforcement notice may require the data controller to rectify, block, erase or destroy the inaccurate data and any related opinion. Second, the enforcement notice may require the data controller to take the steps required by the interpretation to the fourth data protection principle and additionally, if the Information Commissioner thinks fit, it may require the data controller to supplement the inaccurate data with a statement of the true facts approved by the Information Commissioner.

The steps that are required by the interpretation to the fourth data protection principle are discussed in Chapter 3, but to recap, the data controller must take reasonable steps to ensure the accuracy of data received from the data subject or a third party and must ensure that if the data subject notifies it of an inaccuracy, that the data indicate this fact.

Finally, in cases of inaccuracy the enforcement notice may require the data controller to notify third parties to whom the data have been disclosed that the data have been rectified, blocked, erased or destroyed. Such a requirement may only be imposed where it is reasonably practicable to require the data controller to notify third parties and in considering whether it is reasonably practicable the Information Commissioner will have regard to the number of third parties to be notified.

Cancellation and variation of enforcement notices

Section 41 of the DPA prescribes the circumstances in which the Information Commissioner may cancel or vary an enforcement notice. In summary, the Information Commissioner may cancel or vary an enforcement notice if they consider that all or any of its provisions need not be complied with in order to ensure compliance with the data protection principles concerned. In these circumstances the enforcement notice may be cancelled or varied by the Information Commissioner giving written notice to the person on whom the enforcement notice was served.

Under section 41(2) of the DPA a data controller may apply to the Information Commissioner to have an enforcement notice cancelled or varied on the grounds that there has been a change in circumstances resulting in it not being necessary to comply with the notice fully or in part in order to ensure compliance with the data protection principles concerned. A request under these powers must be made in writing and only after expiry of the time for bringing an appeal, which is 28 days, calculated from the date on which the enforcement notice was served on, or given to, the data controller.

The power to cancel or vary does not apply to information notices or special information notices.

Information notices and special information notices

Information notices and special information notices are discussed in Chapter 2 of this book.

Appeals to the Information Tribunal

Section 48 of the DPA is concerned with appeals against enforcement notices and both kinds of information notice. Appeals against these notices are made to the Information Tribunal.

In addition to an appeal against the service of a notice, or as an alternative, a data controller may appeal to the Information Tribunal under section 48(2), against the refusal by the Information Commissioner to vary or cancel an enforcement notice following a request under section 41(2) of the DPA. An appeal can also be made under section 48(3), against the abridgement of time for compliance with a notice (in cases of urgency the Information Commissioner may reduce the 28-day time period for compliance with a notice to seven days). Finally, under section 48(4) a data controller may appeal a determination made by the Information Commissioner under section 45 that the processing is not for, or not only for, the special purposes or is not with a view to the publication of previously unpublished journalistic, literary or artistic material.

Orders that the Information Tribunal may make

Where the data controller makes an appeal against the service of a notice the Information Tribunal is required by section 49(1) of the DPA to address two considerations. First, it needs to consider whether the notice is in accordance with the law. This will require the Information Tribunal to examine whether the notice is properly served and whether it contains the correct information. Second, the Tribunal needs to consider whether the Information Commissioner ought to have exercised their discretion to serve a notice differently. When considering these matters the Information Tribunal is entitled to review determinations of fact upon which the notice was based.

If the Tribunal is satisfied that the notice is not in accordance with the law, or that the Information Commissioner should have exercised their discretion differently, it has two options. First, it can allow the appeal, which will result in the cancellation of the notice. Second, it may substitute the notice or the Information Commissioner's decision with a different notice or decision, provided that it is one that the Information Commissioner could have made. If the Tribunal is not satisfied that the notice is not in accordance with the law, or that the Information Commissioner should have exercised their discretion differently, it must dismiss the appeal.

Where an appeal is brought against the Information Commissioner's refusal to cancel or vary an enforcement notice the Information Tribunal may cancel it, or vary it, where it considers that it 'ought' to do so.

Where an appeal is brought against the Information Commissioner's decision to shorten the time for compliance with a notice the Tribunal may direct that the notice will have effect as if it did not contain the abridgement of time or that the abridgment of time will not have effect in relation to specific parts of the notice.

Where an appeal is brought against the Information Commissioner's decision that the processing is not for the special purposes, or is not done with a view to the publication of previously unpublished journalistic, literary or artistic material, the Information Tribunal may cancel the Information Commissioner's decision.

Appeals from the Information Tribunal

If the data controller is still dissatisfied after the Information Tribunal has given its decision, it may appeal to the court. In England, Wales and Northern Ireland the appeal lies to the High Court of Justice. In Scotland the appeal lies to the Court of Session. Appeals from the Information Tribunal can only be brought on a point of law by the data controller or the Information Commissioner.

Failure to comply with a notice

Section 47 of the DPA makes it a criminal offence to fail to comply with an enforcement notice, an information notice or a special information notice. The only defence that is available is that the data controller exercised all due diligence to comply. Of course, the data controller bears the burden of proof on the defence.

It is also an offence to make a false statement in purported compliance with an information notice or a special information notice. The offence is committed where the data controller knows that the statement is false, or is reckless as to the truth.

The power to enter and seize

Section 50 of the DPA gives the Information Commissioner the power to enter premises where they consider that there has been a breach of the data protection principles, or where they consider that an offence has been committed. The power is described in detail in Schedule 9 of the DPA.

The need for a warrant

The Information Commissioner may only enter premises where they have obtained a warrant from a judge. A judge will only issue a warrant if the Information Commissioner provides information that satisfies the judge that:

- There are reasonable grounds to suspect either: (i) that a data controller has contravened, or is contravening, any of the data protection principles; or (ii) that an offence under the DPA has been committed. The Information Commissioner must provide their evidence on oath.
- Evidence of the contravention or the offence will be found on the premises that the Information Commissioner wishes to enter.

It is important to note that execution of warrants is not confined to premises owned by the data controller or under the data controller's control. They can be directed to any premises, provided that the Information Commissioner overcomes the hurdle of satisfying the court that evidence will be found on the premises concerned.

If the court is satisfied that a warrant should be granted, it will draw up a document, the warrant itself, which will be taken by the Information Commissioner's officers to the premises concerned when they go to 'execute' the warrant.

Warrants and prior warning

The court will not grant a warrant if the Information Commissioner has not given the occupier seven days' written notice demanding access to the premises. If the Information Commissioner has given the required notice, the court will not grant a warrant unless:

- The demand for access has been unreasonably refused or, if access was granted, the occupier unreasonably refused to allow the Information Commissioner to do any of the things that can be authorized by a warrant granted by the court.
- After the refusal the Information Commissioner has notified the occupier of their intention to seek a warrant and the occupier has been given an opportunity to make representations to the court.

This rule does not apply in cases of urgency, however, or where written notice would defeat the purpose of the warrant, perhaps through the destruction or concealment of evidence.

Things authorized to be done by a warrant

A warrant allows the Information Commissioner's officers to do the following things:

- Enter the premises identified in the warrant.
- Search the premises.
- Inspect, examine, operate or test any equipment found on the premises that is used, or intended to be used, to process personal data. Occupiers who are subject to a search can therefore expect their computers to be accessed by the officers.
- Seize any documents or other material found on the premises that may be evidence of a contravention of the principles or the commission of an offence.

The warrant entitles the Information Commissioner to do these things at any time within seven days of the date of the warrant. If the Information Commissioner fails to act upon the warrant, it will expire. The Information Commissioner must return all warrants to the court after they have been executed, or after they have expired.

Execution of warrants

The warrant must be executed at a reasonable hour, unless that would mean that evidence would not be found, in which case the warrant may be executed at any time, such as in the middle of the night when the occupier is unprepared. The occupier must be shown the warrant when it is executed and be given a copy of it, unless they are not present at the time, in which case a copy of the warrant must be left at the premises.

The person executing the warrant is entitled to use reasonable force, if this is necessary. Indeed, it is an offence for anyone to obstruct the execution of a warrant or to fail without reasonable excuse to give assistance to the person executing it.

If anything is seized during execution, the occupier is entitled to a receipt, but only if they ask for one. Items that are seized may be kept by the Information Commissioner for as long as is necessary, but the occupier is entitled to copies of documents seized if they ask for copies before the officers leave, subject to the proviso that if the person executing the warrant considers that providing copies would cause undue delay during execution they need not provide copies.

Exemptions

The powers conferred by a warrant are not exercisable in respect of personal data to which the national security exemption in section 28 of the DPA applies, nor are they exercisable in respect of communications between a professional legal adviser and their client in connection with the giving of legal advice about the client's obligations, liabilities and rights under the DPA, or in connection with any legal proceedings concerned with the DPA.

If the occupier objects to inspection or seizure of any material on the grounds that either of these exemptions applies, the person exercising the warrant is entitled to request a copy of the material with the controversial parts removed.

CRIMINAL PROCEEDINGS

In theory any breach of the data protection principles can result in criminal proceedings against the data controller, because of the provisions of section 47 of the DPA, which says that a person who fails to comply with an enforcement notice, an information notice or a special information notice is guilty of an offence. However, as far as these offences are concerned the data controller always has a 'second chance', because if a notice is complied with, section 47 is not engaged.

The DPA does create a series of criminal offences that do not require the Information Commissioner to go through the notice procedure before prosecution. In these cases the Information Commissioner may commence criminal proceedings if he considers that he has sufficient evidence to prove beyond reasonable doubt that the data controller is guilty. These criminal offences are as follows:

- notification offences by virtue of sections 21 and 22 of the DPA;
- failure to provide information under section 24;
- obstruction of inspection of overseas information systems under section 54A;
- unlawful obtaining, disclosure or sale of personal data under section 55;
- enforced subject access under section 56;
- Information Commissioner offences under section 59;
- Information Tribunal contempt offences under Schedule 6, paragraph 8;
- Obstruction of warrant offences under Schedule 9.

Who can be prosecuted?

Under this series of offences a variety of people can be prosecuted. Under sections 21 and 22 of the DPA only a data controller can be prosecuted, because it is only a data controller who has the obligation to notify. Conversely, under sections 54A, 55 and 56 of the DPA and under Schedule 6 and Schedule 9 any person can be prosecuted, meaning that the offences are not limited to data controllers. The offences under section 59 can only be committed by the Information Commissioner, or by a past or current member of staff or agent of the Information Commissioner.

Criminal liability of directors etc.

Section 61 contains a very important provision for corporate bodies, as it makes directors, managers, secretaries and similar officers personally liable for criminal offences committed by their organizations where they have consented to the offence or connived in it or if the offence was committed due to their negligence. This means that the DPA pierces the corporate veil.

Who can bring a prosecution?

The Information Commissioner is the primary prosecuting authority, but criminal proceedings can also be commenced by the Director of Public Prosecutions and by any other person with the consent of the Director. In Northern Ireland the additional prosecuting authority is the Director of Public Prosecutions for Northern Ireland.

Penalties

Offences under section 54A and Schedule 9, paragraph 12 can only be tried in the Magistrates' Court. All of the other offences, including notice offences, can be tried in either the Magistrates' Court or in the Crown Court, depending upon seriousness. The maximum fine in the Magistrates' Court is currently £5,000, but in the Crown Court fines are unlimited. At the date of publication of this book the Department of Constitutional Affairs is conducting a public consultation on proposals made by the Information Commissioner for the introduction of custodial sentences of up to two years imprisonment for breaches of section 55 of the DPA.

Notification offences

Section 21(1) of the DPA makes it an offence for a person to process personal data without having first notified in accordance with section 17(1). This is a strict liability offence, meaning that if a data controller fails to notify when required to do so, it will be convicted. There is no due diligence defence.

Section 21(2) makes it an offence to fail to notify changes to processing, in breach of section 20. The combined effect of section 20 and the Data Protection (Notification and Notification Fees) Regulations 2000[175] is to make it a requirement to keep notifications accurate and up to date, or as section 20(2) prefers, 'current'. Thus, the data controller is required to notify the

Information Commissioner of any respect in which an entry on the register of notifications becomes inaccurate or incomplete. The notification of the inaccuracy must be given as soon as possible and not later than 28 days after the date when the entry on the register became inaccurate or incomplete. Unlike the offence in section 21(1) there is a due diligence defence for offences under section 21(2). Section 21(3) says that 'it shall be a defence for a person charged with an offence under [section 21(2)] to show that he exercised all due diligence to comply with the duty'.

Section 22(6) of the DPA will make it a criminal offence to carry out 'assessable processing' in breach of section 22(5). Section 22 of the DPA describes assessable processing as 'processing which is of a description specified in an order made by the Secretary of State as appearing to him to be particularly likely to cause substantial damage or substantial distress to data subjects, or otherwise significantly to prejudice the rights and freedoms of data subjects'. At the date of publication of this book the Secretary of State has not made any orders under section 22.

Failure to provide information

Section 24(4) of the DPA makes it an offence for a data controller who has not notified to fail to comply with a request for 'the relevant particulars'. Relevant particulars form the bulk of the information that a data controller would supply as registrable particulars when notifying for the purposes of section 17 of the DPA. Section 24(5) contains a due diligence defence saying 'it shall be a defence for a person charged with an offence under [section 24(4)] to show that he exercised all due diligence to comply' with a request.

Obstruction offences

Sections 54A, Schedule 6, paragraph 8 and Schedule 9, paragraph 12 all contain obstruction offences.

Section 54A was inserted into the DPA by section 81 of the Crime (International Co-operation) Act 2003 and it gives the Information Commissioner a right of inspection over any personal data recorded in the Schengen information system, the Europol information system and the Customs information system. These multi-jurisdictional information systems are the products of international governmental agreements. They are particularly sensitive because they are concerned with transborder data flows of information required for law enforcement purposes, with obvious consequences for personal privacy. Section 54A(6) makes it an offence for any person to intentionally obstruct the Information Commissioner or to fail without reasonable excuse to give reasonable assistance during an inspection.

Schedule 6 is concerned with appeals from notices heard by the Information Tribunal. Paragraph 8 creates an offence of contempt of the Information Tribunal, replicating the offence of contempt of court. If the Tribunal finds that a person is in contempt it may 'certify the offence' to the High Court, or the Court of Session in Scotland. Certification then places the High Court, or the Court of Session, in control of the contempt proceedings.

The offence in Schedule 9, paragraph 12 is the offence of obstructing a warrant. To recap, it is an offence for any person to intentionally obstruct the execution of a warrant or to fail without reasonable excuse to give the person executing the warrant such assistance as they may reasonably require.

Unlawful obtaining, disclosure and sale of personal data

There have been more successful prosecutions under section 55 of the DPA than under all the other sections combined, although it has to be added that the overall number of successful prosecutions is low.

A frequently occurring theme within section 55 prosecutions is the 'blagging' of personal data by private detectives, often in the course of the tracing debtors or investigating claimants in insurance claims. While not a term of art, 'blagging' is commonly recognized as being the underhand obtaining of personal data, often from public authorities, by private detectives who conceal or misrepresent their true identity or their purpose. In almost every case the blagging is done by telephone. This kind of activity is prosecuted with vigour by the Information Commissioner because it encapsulates every kind of serious contravention of the DPA.

Section 55 offences are not limited to the blagging of personal data by private detectives operating at the outer parameters of lawfulness. Preventing unlawful access to personal data is a logistical problem for most businesses and this includes data misuse by employees who may be tempted to offer their employer's data to criminals, or to use it for their own interests or for the interests of their acquaintances. Newspaper reports draw attention to these problems from time to time and among other things they have highlighted the problem of workers at an Indian call centre offering a journalist access to information relating to customers of UK banks and police officers misusing the Police National Computer.

Unlawful obtaining and disclosure of personal data

Section 55 creates four offences. These are:

- **Obtaining or disclosing of personal data**: A person is guilty of an offence if they knowingly or recklessly obtain or disclose personal data, or the information contained in personal data, without the consent of the data controller (section 55(1)(a)).
- **Procuring a disclosure of personal data**: A person is guilty of an offence if they knowingly or recklessly procure the disclosure to another person of the information contained in personal data, without the consent of the data controller (section 55(1)(b)).

- **Sale of personal data**: A person is guilty of an offence if they sell personal data that they have obtained in contravention of sections 55(1)(a)&(b) (section 55(4)).
- **Offering to sell personal data**: A person is guilty of an offence if they offer to sell personal data that they have obtained in contravention of sections 55(1)(a)&(b) (section 55(5)).

All of the offences focus on two forms of processing, which are obtaining and disclosing. The essence of each offence is basically the same: a person has knowingly, or recklessly, obtained or disclosed personal data without the data controller's consent. This breaks down into three elements:

- Has personal data been obtained or disclosed?
- If so, was the processing done with the data controller's consent?
- If so, was the processing done knowingly or was it the result of recklessness?

Has personal data been obtained or disclosed?

The obtaining of personal data is directly relevant to offences under section 55(1)(a) (obtaining or disclosing personal data), section 55(4) (sale of personal data) and section 55(4) (offering to sell personal data). The question whether personal data has been obtained involves two separate issues of fact. The first is whether the data are personal data, presumably in the sense described by the Court of Appeal in *Durant v. Financial Services Authority*.[176] The second issue is whether personal data have been obtained by the defendant.

As the Information Commissioner is the primary prosecuting authority for the purposes of section 55, it follows that the Commissioner carries the burden of proving that personal data have been obtained by the defendant. If the Information Commissioner cannot prove these facts, the defendant must be acquitted. The standard of proof is beyond reasonable doubt.

The fact of disclosure of personal data is relevant to all of the offences and, as with obtaining, the question of whether there has been a disclosure is a question of fact upon which the Information Commissioner bears the burden of proof.

Was the processing done with or without the data controller's consent?

The significance of the focus of section 55 on the data controller's consent should not be overlooked, because it shows that the DPA treats more seriously the unlawful obtaining of data from data controllers rather than from data subjects. Thus, a determined person can 'blag' personal information from the data subject without fear of prosecution (although a notice offence could ultimately be committed).

Consent is not defined in the DPA, but the Data Protection Directive gives assistance with the meaning of 'data subject's consent', which it defines as 'any freely given specific and informed indication of his wishes by which the data subject signifies his agreement to personal data relating to him being processed'. There is no reason to think that a similar formulation cannot be applied for the meaning of the data controller's consent.

In many cases the defendant may argue that consent was obtained, in the sense that they spoke to the data controller and asked for the personal information that is at the centre of the prosecution. If in such a case the defendant disguised their true identity, a 'blag' in every sense of the word, the data controller's consent will be negated because the data controller was duped.

Was the processing done knowingly or recklessly?

The Information Commissioner will need very good quality evidence to prove that the defendant knowingly processed the data, but very often there is an abundance of evidence left behind by the criminal, particularly as a result of ignorance about the realities surrounding the deletion of electronic files and the monitoring of communications. The Information Commissioner will need to prove that the defendant actually knew that the obtaining or disclosure had occurred and that they actually knew that this was without the data controller's consent.

The concept of recklessness is well known to the criminal law. The classic definition was in the case of *R. v. Lawrence*[177] where Lord Diplock said:

> Recklessness on the part of the doer of an act presupposes that there is something in the circumstances that would have drawn the attention of an ordinary prudent individual to the possibility that his act was capable of causing the kind of serious and harmful consequences that the section that created the offence was intended to prevent, and that the risk of those harmful circumstances occurring was not so slight that an ordinary prudent individual would feel justified in treating them as negligible. It is only when this is so that the doer of the act is acting 'recklessly' if, before doing the act, he either fails to give any thought to the possibility of there being any such risk or, having recognised that there was such a risk, he nevertheless does on to do it.

This definition points to the following issues:

- The circumstances as a whole need to be considered.
- The circumstances must cause an ordinary, prudent individual to consider that there is more than a negligible risk that the harm at the heart of the offence could be caused.
- If there is more than a negligible risk of harm, the defendant will have acted recklessly if they do the act in question without giving any consideration to the possibility of there being a risk, or having appreciated the risk they continue to do the act in question.

Procuring disclosure to another person

A person is guilty of an offence under section 55(1)(b) if they knowingly or recklessly procure the disclosure to another person of the information contained in personal data without the data controller's consent. The essence of this offence is that the defendant causes, or brings about, the disclosure of personal information to a third party.

Sale of personal data

The final offences in section 55, the sale of personal data that have been unlawfully obtained (section 55(4)) and offering to sell personal data that have been unlawfully obtained (section 55(5)) are prohibitions against commercial dealing and will have particular resonance in industries where a person is paid for providing information, such as in the private detective industry. The meaning of offering to sell is assisted by section 55(6), which says that 'an advertisement indicating that personal data are or may be for sale is an offer to sell the data'. Of course, a person guilty of an offence under sections 55(4) and 55(5) will also be guilty of unlawfully obtaining data under section 55(1)(a) and, depending on the facts, unlawfully disclosing under section 55(1)(b) or procurement of a disclosure under section 55(1)(b).

Exemptions

By reason of section 55(8), the offences do not apply where personal data are processed for national security purposes (section 28(1)(c)) or where the personal data consist of manual data recorded by public authorities (section 33A(1)(f)). This second exemption is of particular importance in 'blagging' cases, as public sector data controllers are often the target of dupers. In a prosecution for unlawful obtaining or disclosure from a public authority the Information Commissioner will have to provide evidence of the processing operations at the public authority so that the court can determine whether or not an exemption applies.

Defences

Section 55(2) contains a series of defences. These are:

> (a) The obtaining, disclosing or procuring –
>   (i)   was necessary for the purpose of preventing or detecting crime, or
>   (ii) was required or authorised by or under any enactment, by any rule of law or by the order of a court.
> (b) He acted in the reasonable belief that he had in law the right to obtain or disclose the data or information or, as the case may be, to procure the disclosure of the information to the other person.
> (c) He acted in the reasonable belief that he would have had the consent of the data controller if the data controller had known of the obtaining, disclosing or procuring and the circumstances of it, or
> (d) In the particular circumstances the obtaining, disclosing or procuring was justified as being in the public interest.

The prevention and detection of crime defence requires the processing to be necessary, meaning that the obtaining, disclosure or procurement of the data must have been essential to the processing purpose, namely the prevention or detection of crime. This defence is consistent with the crime and taxation exemption in section 29 of the DPA, which exempts most of the first data protection principle and section 7 (the right of access) if their application would be likely to prejudice the prevention or detection of crime, the apprehension or prosecution of offenders or the assessment, or collection of any tax or duty. It is also consistent with the rules in the Data Protection (Processing of Sensitive Personal Data) Order 2000,[178] which allows non-consensual processing of personal data for, among other things, the prevention or detection of crime.

In many cases the law enforcement agency will take advantage of the exemption within section 29(3) of the DPA and will approach the data controller direct to obtain personal data, but there will be occasions when an open approach will be counterproductive, perhaps because the data controller is also under investigation, or for fear that an open approach might lead to a person being tipped-off, or evidence being destroyed. Thus, section 55 provides a defence for these situations.

The second defence, that the processing was required or authorized by an enactment, rule or law or order of the court does not contain a necessity element, but it will require the defendant to prove that a legal authority for his actions applied.

The third defence, that the defendant held a reasonable belief of a legal right to process the data, is subject to an objective test, namely that the defendant's belief will not be regarded as being reasonable if it is objectively unreasonable. The same point is made with the fourth defence.

The final defence is a public interest defence. This defence could well apply where the defendant is revealing an illegal act and there were no other routes open to obtaining or disclosing the personal data.

Enforced subject access

Section 56 of the DPA contains prohibitions against the compulsory production of 'relevant records', which include: (i) criminal records obtained by a data subject from the police; (ii) certain records from the Secretary of State; and (iii) records from the Department of Health and Social Services for Northern Ireland following a subject access request under section 7.

In summary, section 56(5) creates two offences. The first is for contravention of section 56(1). The second is for contravention of section 56(2). These are strict liability offences, meaning that intention and knowledge are irrelevant to a conviction. However, there are two defences.

Relevant records

A relevant record is a record consisting of information about a data subject obtained from one of the three data controllers identified above. In order to qualify as a relevant record, the record needs to have been obtained by the data subject using his right of access in section 7 of the DPA. By definition such information is sensitive personal data within the meaning of section 2 of the DPA.

This definition of a relevant record is very important, because the offences both concern the supply or production of relevant records by 'another person' or by a 'third party'. When these concepts are merged it becomes apparent that the offences are very specialized, extending to the rare cases where a data controller participating or contemplating participating in a relationship with a second person asks a third person to supply sensitive personal data.

Types of relevant records

A table in section 56 identifies the following types of relevant records:

- convictions and cautions where they are obtained from police chief officers and chief constables, from the Director General of the National Criminal Intelligence Service, from the Director General of the National Crime Squad or from the Secretary of State;
- records relating to the Secretary of State's functions concerning the detention of young persons following a conviction;
- records relating to the Secretary of State's functions relating to prisons;
- records relating to the Secretary of State's functions concerning National Insurance and state benefits;
- records relating to the Secretary of State's functions under Part V of the Police Act 1997; these concern the issuing of criminal conviction certificates and criminal records certificates.

Personal data that falls within paragraph (e) of the definition of data in section 1(1) of the DPA, that is, recorded information held by a public authority that does not fall in to any of the other categories, cannot be a relevant record for the purposes of section 56 (section 56(6A)).

A record that contains no data, sometimes called an empty record, will fall within the prohibitions due to section 56(9) of the DPA, which says that 'a record which states that a data controller is not processing any personal data relating to a particular matter shall be taken to be a record containing information relating to that matter'.

Employment situations

Section 56(1) is concerned with employment and similar situations. It prohibits a person from requiring another person to supply or produce a relevant record in three situations:

- In connection with the recruitment of another person as an employee, which means that a prospective employer is not allowed to ask a prospective employee or a third party to supply or produce a relevant record. By definition the third party cannot be a prospective employee.
- In connection with the continued employment or another person, which means that an employer is not allowed to ask an employee or a third party to supply or produce a relevant record.

- In connection with a contract for the provision of services, which covers situations akin to employment situations, such as where a business hires a subcontractor or temporary worker, applying where there is a contract for the provision of services by the one person to another. In these situations the recipient of the service cannot ask the service provider or a third party to supply or provide a relevant record.

Section 56(10) defines the meaning of 'employee'. An employee is an individual who works under a contract of employment as defined by section 230(2) of the Employment Rights Act 1996 or who holds any office and it is irrelevant whether a salary is paid.

Provision of goods, facilities and services

Section 56(2) is concerned with situations where a person provides goods, facilities or services to the public or to a section of the public. It does not matter whether the goods, facilities or services are provided for payment or not, meaning that charities and public bodies are affected just as much as companies.

The prohibition in section 56(2) is against making the provision conditional upon the supply or production of a relevant record. Again, the person receiving the goods, facilities or services could be asked to supply or produce a relevant record or a third party could be asked.

Defences

There are two defences available under section 56(3). These are:

- The imposition of the requirement to supply or produce a relevant record was required or authorized by or under an enactment, a rule of law or by court order.
- The imposition of the requirement to supply or produce a relevant record was justified as being in the public interest.

Section 56(4) makes it clear that the public interest defence is limited in one very important respect, namely that a person is not allowed to take advantage of the public interest defence just because the supply or production of a relevant record would assist in the prevention or detection of crime. This is because Part V of the Police Act 1997 contains a legal framework for obtaining information about a person's criminal record and convictions. Persons wishing to take advantage of the Police Act 1997 must proceed through the Criminal Records Bureau.

Information Commissioner offences

Section 59(3) of the DPA makes it an offence for any person to knowingly or recklessly disclose information in contravention of section 59(1). Section 59(1) is concerned with unlawful disclosures of certain types of information by the Information Commissioner and persons working for them. The ingredients of the offence are:

- There must be disclosure of information that: (i) has been obtained by, or furnished to, the Information Commissioner under, or for the purposes of, the DPA or the Freedom of Information Act; (ii) relates to an identified or identifiable individual or business; (iii) is not at the time of the disclosure, or at any time before, available to the public from other sources.
- The person making the disclosure is the Information Commissioner, a past Information Commissioner, a member of the Information Commissioner's staff or an agent of the Information Commissioner.
- The disclosure must be made without lawful authority.
- The person making the disclosure must do so knowing that it is a contravention of section 59(1) or must be reckless as to whether the disclosure is in contravention of section 59(1).

Lawful authority

The absence of lawful authority for the disclosure is a vital component of the offence. Section 59(2) identifies the only circumstances in which disclosure will be with lawful authority:

- The disclosure is made with the consent of the individual or of the person carrying on the business.

- The information was provided for the purpose of its being made available to the public under any provision of the DPA or the Freedom of Information Act.

- The disclosure necessary for the purposes of (i) any functions under the DPA or the Freedom of Information Act; or (ii) any Community obligation.

- The disclosure is made for the purposes of any legal proceedings.

- The disclosure is necessary in the public interest, having regard to the rights and freedoms or legitimate interests of any person.

8 Compliance

INTRODUCTION

A person or organization addressing data protection compliance for the very first time can be forgiven for thinking that they are facing an impossibly daunting task and a common initial comment is 'I do not know where to start'. Of course, the only logical response is 'start at the beginning' and this means working out first of all whether or not the DPA applies. As discussed in Chapter 1 the key considerations are:

- Is the data controller established in the UK or, if not, is the data controller established outside the EEA?
- Is the data controller processing data in the context of its UK establishment or, if established outside the EEA, is the data controller using processing equipment in the UK other than merely for the purpose of transiting data through the UK?
- Are the data that are processed personal data?
- Does an exemption apply?

If the DPA does apply, the data controller will need to prioritize matters within its compliance strategy, to ensure that the most serious matters are dealt with first. This means carrying out an assessment of risk with the data controller trying to determine, as accurately as possible:

- the nature of the risks to which they or their organization are exposed;
- the probability of the risks turning into realities;
- the consequences if the risks do indeed turn into realities;
- the actions to be taken to prevent the risks turning into realities.

Many data controllers, particularly those in the private sector, need to be persuaded that compliance with the DPA is worth the effort, which may or may not be an odd state of affairs given that compliance is required as a matter of law. Thus, many commentators, including the Information Commissioner, have pointed to other factors that they hope will encourage errant data controllers to take their responsibilities seriously. Arguments that have been advanced in the name of encouraging compliance include the following:

- **Reputation**: The reputation argument says that the errant data controller's good reputation will be damaged by its failure to comply with the DPA. Data subjects who are clients and customers will eventually turn their backs on these data controllers. Potential clients and customers will not want to deal with data controllers with bad reputations. Nor will other data controllers.

- **Reduction of risk**: The reduction of risk argument says that DPA compliance will also bring the data controller into compliance with other laws and regulations, thereby reducing the overall level of risk within the organization. This is because DPA compliance requires the data controller to examine its entire range of operations, a process that can reveal the presence of concealed 'smoking guns', such as evidence of discrimination or harassment within the workplace. DPA compliance also overlaps with other regulatory frameworks, for instance money laundering, so there are incidental benefits.

- **Efficiency**: The efficiency argument says that DPA compliance will make the data controller's operations generally more efficient. It is now being appreciated that there is substantial strength in this argument. For instance, the inevitable proliferation of electronic data in a non-compliant organization leads to higher data storage and management costs and lengthens data search and retrieval times. The financial cost of long-term storage of data is a real problem for businesses and public authorities.

All of these justifications for compliance have substantial merit, but the focus of this chapter is the core compliance challenges presented by the DPA.

PRIORITIZATION OF ACTION

For all data controllers, whether new to DPA compliance or seasoned hands, the prioritization of actions within a compliance strategy is a necessity and, obviously, the most serious threats to the data controller's interests need to be addressed first. The natural order of priority is as follows:

- criminal offences;
- data subject action;
- enforcement action by the Information Commissioner.

Criminal offences

Most data controllers are exposed to a risk of criminal prosecution, with the most likely criminal offences being under either section 21(1) or section 21(2), namely failure to notify or failure to keep notifications accurate and up to date. A critical compliance goal is the accurate measurement of the size of the risk. If the data controller has never addressed DPA compliance before, then there is a high probably that it is guilty of an offence under section 21(1), for non-notification, although it will be remembered that exemptions do apply. If the data controller has notified but has failed to keep on top of compliance, it must be exposed to a risk of prosecution for breach of section 21(2). Thus, the data controller will wish to move very quickly to a position of comfort, namely it will wish to satisfy itself (and its directors and other officers, if it is a company) that criminal proceedings are not a possibility or are unlikely.

Fortunately, the risk of prosecution for an offence under section 21(1) can be quickly eliminated, because notification is a relatively quick, simple and cheap process that takes advantage of a series of very broad templates created by the Information Commissioner. When these templates are considered the data controller will soon discover that the Information Commissioner is seeking to extract only basic, generalized information with the result that most data controllers should be able to successfully notify with only a modicum of effort and with only a basic understanding of the DPA's requirements. Furthermore, data controllers can use the Information Commissioner's notification telephone helpline, which promises advice along the way.

Eliminating the risk of prosecution under section 21(2) requires the data controller to keep on top of any changes in its processing operations and, if there are any, to notify them speedily to the Information Commissioner. Section 21(2) is subject to a due diligence defence, which most data controllers should be able to avail themselves of by taking advantage of the notification helpline run by the Information Commissioner; if the data controller gives the Information Commissioner a fair account of any changes in processing it should be able to rely upon the advice given over the notification helpline. Likewise, reliance upon legal advice can support a due diligence defence.

Data subject action

The risk of the data subject taking action against the data controller comes second in the natural order of priority for the simple reason that the data subject's actions in terms of seriousness do not carry the immediate ramifications of a criminal prosecution. However, the data subject has the ability to cause considerable disruption to the data controller's processing activities, particularly through exercise of the right of access within section 7 of the DPA.

The risk of data subject action can itself be prioritized. In order of seriousness, the data subject's ability to commence legal proceedings for compensation for damage or distress must rank higher than, say, the data subject's right to demand the cessation of processing for direct marketing purposes. Of course, the data controller must recognize that there is a very fine line between the exercise of the data subject rights and court action, because the exercise of the data subject rights can be a precursor to court action.

Enforcement action by the Information Commissioner

Enforcement action by the Information Commissioner has been ranked third in the order of priority, but only just. The deciding factor that places the risk of data subject action above Information Commissioner action is merely that the individual data subject is inherently more focused on the protection of his own rights and so is more incentivized than the Information Commissioner to protect them. Thus, the data subject, rather than the Information Commissioner, is likely to be the first person to realize that their rights are affected by processing. However, this is a very fine point indeed. Furthermore, the data controller must not overlook the fact that the mishandling of Information Commissioner action can soon elevate the situation in seriousness, as the Information Commissioner has the option of commencing criminal proceedings if enforcement action does not achieve the results that they desire.

STAGE 1 – GATHERING INFORMATION ABOUT DATA

A data controller cannot hope to be complaint with the DPA if it does not understand its own processing operations, a point that has the greatest resonance in large organizations where personal data is gathered from a variety of sources and is subjected to a variety of processing operations and for a variety of different purposes. Thus, the initial stages of a compliance strategy are always dominated by the following key questions:

- What personal data are being processed?
- Whose personal data are being processed?
- Why are personal data being processed?
- How are personal data being processed?

The first question causes the data controller to identify the categories of information being processed, which will enable the data controller to deal with the critical issue of whether the data are sensitive personal data or not.

The second question focuses the data controller on the identities of the data subjects. The third question focuses the data controller on the purpose of the processing. The fourth question focuses the data controller on the manner of the processing. Collectively these second, third and fourth questions represent the essence of the definition of data controller contained in section 1(1) of the DPA, which, to recap, is:

> 'data controller' means . . . a person who (either alone or jointly or in common with other persons) determines the purposes for which and the manner in which any personal data are, or are to be, processed.

Of course, these questions are also at the heart of the DPA's transparency provisions and are essential to satisfying the data controller's obligations under the first data protection principle, under the second data protection principle, under Part III of the DPA (notification) and under section 7 (the right of access). Table 8.1 shows the interface between these obligations illustrating the overall importance of the second to fourth questions dominating the initial stage of compliance.

TABLE 8.1   *Transparency and the supply of information*

	Information to be supplied by the data controller
The first data protection principle	The purpose or purposes for which data are intended to be processed Having regard to the processing purpose(s) any further information that is necessary to enable the processing to be fair
The second data protection principle	A statement of the processing purpose
Registrable particulars	A description of the personal data being processed and the categories of data subjects to which they relate A description of the purpose(s) for which the personal data are being, or are to be, processed A description of any recipients The names of countries outside the EEA to where the data are to be processed
Subject access	The purposes for which the personal data are to be processed The recipients or classes of recipients to whom the data are to be disclosed The information constituting personal data Information about the source of the data

The data protection officer

The data controller cannot hope to be compliant with the DPA without nominating a person to take overall responsibility for the compliance process. This person can be called the data protection officer. The data protection officer is responsible for driving the compliance process forward and for ensuring that all interfaces between the data controller and the data subject, third parties and the Information Commissioner are compliant with the DPA. In summary, these key interfaces are:

- **The data controller–data subject interface**: There are three parts to this interface: (i) the provision of the information required by the first and second data protection principles; (ii) dealing with the exercise of the data subject rights; and (iii) dealing with court action commenced by the data subject.

- **The data controller–third parties interface**: There are two parts to this interface: (i) dealing with data processors; and (ii) dealing with data importers in countries outside the EEA.

- **The data controller–Information Commissioner interface**: Again, there are three parts to this interface: (i) the provision of the registrable particulars; (ii) dealing with enforcement action; and (iii) dealing with court action commenced by the Information Commissioner.

Where the data controller is established outside the EEA its obligation to nominate a representative is equivalent to the appointment of a data protection officer.

The data protection officer's role is a critical one and the data controller should ensure that it is accompanied with the powers that are necessary to enable the officer to fulfill their duties. A particularly sensitive issue is the fact that the data protection officer's role is necessarily cross-departmental. Thus, the data protection officer will need sufficient authority over departmental heads. Of course, the data protection officer should aim to build a cross-departmental consensus and with this in mind many data protection officers chair committees of departmental representatives constituted solely for compliance purposes.

What personal data are being processed?

The aim of this question is to cause the data controller to identify personal data by category, with the broad purpose being to determine whether data are sensitive or not. How this question is tackled and the methodology used depends upon the nature and identity of the data controller and the nature and identify of the person who is responsible for compliance within the data controller's organization, but a process akin to an audit is basically unavoidable. How detailed the audit needs to be depends upon the data controller's circumstances.

Unlike the other three questions, the data controller does need to identify the categories of data with real precision, because of the importance associated with whether data are sensitive or not. The resulting list will provide the foundations for the more detailed work to come.

Dealing with Durant

It could be said that the case of *Durant v. Financial Services Authority*[179] has not made DPA compliance any easier. The deeper the data controller examines the Court of Appeal's focus and biographical significance concepts, the more unsatisfactory they seem to become. Of course, the data controller cannot escape the current state of the law and at some point it does become necessary to apply the Court of Appeal's reasoning in order to determine whether data are personal data. This creates its own difficulties, particularly deciding at what stage the Durant concepts should be applied.

It is very tempting to apply the *Durant* concepts right at the very beginning of the compliance process; after all, if data are not personal data, the DPA will not apply and the data controller will be spared the trouble of the entire compliance exercise. However, while this is tempting, in most cases it would be a mistake for the data controller to try to apply *Durant* at the initial stages of the compliance process because if the concepts are incorrectly applied at the beginning, the data controller could abandon the compliance process leaving itself completely vulnerable in the event of subsequent enforcement action. Furthermore, it should be understood that the law can change.

Whose personal data are being processed?

Again, how this question is tackled as well as the methodology used depends upon the nature and identity of the data controller and the nature and identity of the person who is responsible for compliance, but an obvious starting point is to identify all the categories of persons with whom the data controller comes into contact during the course of its daily operations. Within a corporate environment a typical, basic list will include some or all of the following categories of persons:

- staff;
- customers;
- suppliers;
- professional advisers;
- public servants;
- miscellaneous.

This list of data subjects can be checked against the lists contained in the Information Commissioner's notification templates, available on the Information Commissioner's website. Examples are shown in Table 8.2.

The aim at this stage is not to identify each and every individual whose personal data are processed but, rather, to create a framework around which a compliance strategy can be built. As a result of this, the categories of persons identified at this stage will be deliberately general, loose and fluid. An overly rigid approach to definitions at the beginning of a compliance strategy can be counterproductive, as the aim of the exercise is to advance the data controller down the path of compliance, not to bog down the data controller with technical legal issues.

Why are personal data being processed?

Identification of the processing purpose satisfies a multitude of compliance issues. Using the terminology preferred by this book, the processing purpose needs to be identified in order to satisfy the rules about transparency and as part of the general rules on lawfulness. By definition the processing purpose needs to be established to satisfy the following specific requirements:

- Fair processing as required by the first data protection principle. The interpretation for the first data protection principle requires the data controller to inform the data subject of the purpose or purposes for which the data are to be processed, as part of the prescribed information. Furthermore, the interpretation states that the data subject should not be deceived or misled as to the processing purpose or purposes.
- The second data protection principle says that personal data shall be obtained only for one or more specified and lawful purposes and shall not be further processed in any manner incompatible with that purpose or those purposes.

TABLE 8.2   *Categories of data subjects from the Information Commissioner's templates*

Template	Data subjects
N.858 – General, unclassified N.801 – Legal, solicitors	• Complainants, correspondents and enquirers
	• Customers and clients
	• Suppliers
	• Advisers, consultants and other professional experts
	• Relatives, guardians and associates of the data subject
	• Staff including volunteers, agents, temporary and casual workers
N.896 – Ombudsman/regulatory body	• Complainants, correspondents and enquirers
	• Customers and clients
	• Suppliers
	• Members of the public
	• Offenders and suspected offenders
	• Relatives, guardians and associates of the data subject
	• Staff including volunteers, agents, temporary and casual workers
	• Those inside, entering or in the immediate vicinity of the area under surveillance
	• Witnesses

- The third data protection principle says that personal data shall be adequate, relevant and not excessive in relation to the purpose or purposes for which they are processed.
- The fifth data protection principle says that personal data processed for any purpose or purposes shall not be kept for longer than is necessary for the purpose or purposes.
- Notification requires the data controller to provide the Information Commissioner with a description of the purpose or purposes for which the personal data are being, or are to be, processed.
- The right of access entitles the data subject to a description of the purposes for which the data are being processed.
- Processing for direct marketing purposes is subject to the data subject's right to object.
- The processing purpose determines whether any exemptions apply.

As with the categories of data subjects, the categories of processing purposes need only be expressed in general terms at the initial stages of a compliance strategy. Again, the Information Commissioner's notification templates provide an excellent starting point for identification of common categories of processing purposes, but this is not the only reference point. The DPA itself identifies many specific processing purposes, which are generally stated for the purpose of exemptions.

How are personal data being processed?

The issue here is whether data are processed by equipment operating automatically or whether the processing is manual. The extremely wide meaning of processing means that identifying how personal data are being processed is arguably the most difficult of the four initial questions. As the meaning of processing covers everything from the initial obtaining or collecting of data right through to its final deletion or destruction, it follows that the data controller needs to identify all of the people who have access to the data and all of the equipment used to process it. So, when tackling this question the data controller needs to ask itself 'how do we obtain, capture or collect personal data?' The methods used to obtain personal data form part of the interfaces between the data controller and the data subject.

A technique for dealing with this question is to trace information flows through the organization, starting with the point of capture, with the findings being represented in diagrammatic form within a flow chart. The data controller should be able to identify precisely how the data are captured and what happens to it afterwards. Figure 8.1 shows a possible flow of data following capture through a website.

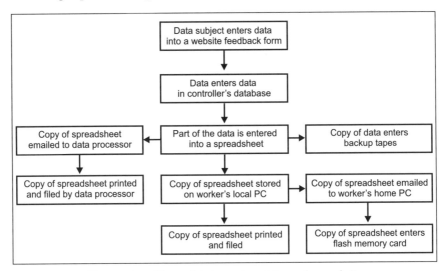

FIGURE 8.1 *Flow of data captured through a website*

When tracing the flow of data through the organization the data controller should be very conscious of the fact that electronic data is easily copied and that multiple copies of the same data may exist at the same time. The data controller should take particular care with portable storage media and portable storage devices and the propensity for the temporary storage of data to become permanent.

Alarms bells – transfers and recipients

During these initial stages the data controller should keep a careful lookout for any transfers of data out of the organization, whether to a recipient, within Europe or abroad. The key point, of course, is that once data leaves the data controller's possession direct control over it is lost. If data is transferred out of the organization in a disorganized, non-compliant fashion, it is almost inevitable that the data controller will fall foul of any enforcement action commenced either by the data subject or the Information Commissioner.

Drawing the information together

At conclusion of the initial work the data controller should possess a comprehensive body of information. At this point the data controller should draw the information together. Depending on the data controller's preference the information can be gathered together in tabular form. Table 8.3 provides an illustration of how things might appear at this stage within a financial services organization.

TABLE 8.3 *Processing within a financial services organization*

What personal data are being processed?	Whose personal data are being processed?	Why are personal data being processed?	How are personal data being processed?
Name and address = non-sensitive	Workers	Employment	By computer and manually
Sickness record = sensitive	Workers	Employment	By computer and manually
Name and address = non-sensitive	Customers	To assess loan application	By computer, via website
Salary = non-sensitive	Customers	To assess loan application	By computer, via website
Age = non-sensitive	Customers	To assess loan application	By computer, via website
Occupation = non-sensitive	Customers	To assess loan application	By computer, via website

STAGE 2 – LAWFULNESS AND THE CRITERION FOR LEGITIMACY

After the initial work has been completed the data controller will possess a comprehensive body of information that will enable it to tackle the important issues of lawfulness and legitimacy. To recap, as well as complying with the DPA the data controller's processing must also be generally lawful, so the task here is to weed out anything that is obviously unlawful. In most cases the data controller's investigations will not reveal anything that is generally unlawful and in any event it is highly unlikely that a generally unlawful data controller will bother with DPA compliance.

In all probability the data controller will spend the bulk of its time at this stage identifying the Schedule 2 criterion for legitimacy and the additional Schedule 3 condition if sensitive personal data are being processed. These conditions need to be mapped to each processing operation. Using the pattern within the previous table, at the end of this stage of the compliance process the data controller should be able to present the information shown in Table 8.4.

TABLE 8.4 *Processing within a financial services organization, with criterion for legitimacy*

What personal data are being processed?	Whose personal data are being processed?	Why are personal data being processed?	How are personal data being processed?	Is processing generally lawful?	Criterion for legitimacy
Name and address = non-sensitive	Workers	Employment	By computer and manually	Yes	Schedule 2: consent & contractual necessity
Sickness record = sensitive	Workers	Employment	By computer and manually	Yes	Schedule 2: consent & contractual necessity Schedule 3: employment law necessity
Name and address = non-sensitive	Customers	To assess loan application	By computer, via website	Yes	Schedule 2: consent & contractual necessity
Salary = non-sensitive	Customers	To assess loan application	By computer, via website	Yes	Schedule 2: consent & contractual necessity
Age = non-sensitive	Customers	To assess loan application	By computer, via website	Yes	Schedule 2: consent & contractual necessity
Occupation = non-sensitive	Customers	To assess loan application	By computer, via website	Yes	Schedule 2: consent & contractual necessity

STAGE 3 – IMPLEMENTING COMPLIANCE MECHANISMS

The next stage within the compliance process is to implement compliance mechanisms, with the strategy being to serve two broad aims. The first aim, naturally, will be to make the data controller fully compliant with the DPA. The second aim will be to ensure that the data controller remains fully compliant with the DPA. Of course, the key compliance issues for the data controller during this stage of the compliance process will reflect the order of priority mentioned earlier, namely:

- criminal offences;
- data subject action;
- enforcement action by the Information Commissioner.

The primary criminal offences are notification offences and section 55 offences. To recap, compliance with the notification obligations of the DPA should not cause the data controller too much trouble if the initial information gathering process is conducted in a diligent fashion. The key mechanisms that are discussed here are those aimed at preventing action by the data subject and other enforcement action by the Information Commissioner.

Supplying the data subject with information

The data controller–data subject interface is the most dynamic interface of the three mentioned earlier and it is imperative that the data controller implements mechanisms to ensure that the data subject is provided with sufficient information at each interface. Typical interfaces include websites, product order forms, job applications forms and over the counter in office and shop premises. Less obvious interfaces include networking events, trade fares, temporary concessions in supermarkets and shopping centres and CCTV systems.

The mechanisms for supplying information to the data subject are not complex, revolutionary or extraordinary but are the mundane stuff of ordinary business and ordinary life, namely contracts, notices and similar documentation. However, DPA compliance has generated its own terminology and the 'privacy statement' is now regarded as a norm of DPA compliance.

Privacy statements

Regular users of the internet will be familiar with privacy statements. Compliant websites will usually contain a hyperlink to such documents. A good quality privacy statement contains all of the information that needs to be supplied to the data subject under data protection law and should not confine itself to a structure based on individual provisions of the DPA. Consequently, it may be fair to regard the privacy statement as an amalgamated strategy for compliance with the data controller's obligations under the first and second data protection principle, under Part III of the DPA (notification) and under section 7. A good quality privacy statement includes the following information:

- the data controller's name and contact details, or the name and contact details of the data controller's nominated representative (typical contact details consist of a postal address, an email address, a telephone number and a fax number);
- the data controller's notification reference number;
- a description of the personal data collected by the data controller;
- a description of the processing purposes;
- a statement about retention periods;

- a statement about how data will be kept accurate and up to date;
- a statement about the data controller's security measures;
- a description of any recipients or transfers;
- information about the data controller's direct marketing activities;
- information about the data controller's use of cookies and similar devices, including information about how the data subject can decline to accept them;
- information about how the data subject can exercise the right to object;
- information about the data controller's policy in respect of subject access, such as whether a fee is charged;
- the Information Commissioner's contact details.

It is important to note that privacy statements are not recognized by the DPA or the Data Protection Directive. Rather, they are a pragmatic combined solution, or part solution, to the various information supply obligations placed upon the data controller. Of course, the data controller must appreciate that if it publishes a privacy statement, it must adhere to its contents. Failure to do so will attract a charge that the data subject has been deceived or misled, in breach of the first data protection principle.

Privacy statements lend themselves perfectly to the online environment, where there are no physical space constraints. In the offline environment, where there are space constraints, they are less useful, but this does not mean that they do not have a role to play. For example, an application form, say for a loan, may contain a statement that refers to the privacy statement, such as: 'We are data controllers under the Data Protection Act and we will process your personal data in accordance with our privacy statement, a copy of which can be obtained from our website or by telephoning our helpline.'

This process of referring to a privacy statement is perfectly acceptable for the purposes of the first and second data protection principles. As discussed in Chapter 2 of this book, the prescribed information required by the first data protection principle need only be made 'readily available' to the data subject, rather than physically supplied to the data subject, and because the second data protection principle can be satisfied by a notice given for the purposes of the first data protection principle a reference to a privacy statement will be sufficient for all purposes. Of course, the data controller must focus on the fact that the privacy statement must be 'readily available', because if it is not readily available the data controller will be in breach of the first data protection principle.

Company documents

Where the data subject is a member of the data controller's staff, the prescribed information required by the first data protection principle and the description of the processing purposes required by the second data protection principle can both be supplied through ordinary company documents, such as the company handbook and on notices of the staff notice board.

Particular care should be taken with monitoring of staff communications. While permitted by the Telecommunications (Lawful Business Practice) (Interception of Communications) Regulations 2000,[180] staff must be warned that this may occur. The Information Commissioner's 'Employment Practices Code'[181] provides detailed advice and guidance.

Of course, one very valuable advantage open to the data controller where the data subject is a member of staff that is not open in other data controller–data subject relationships is the regularity of contact and because of this it is very hard to see how a data controller in an employment situation can fail to find an opportunity to supply all of the information required by the DPA.

Scripts

The data controller must ensure that the data subject is supplied with the prescribed information at every interface and because some interfaces will take the form of meetings or conversations, in shops for instance, the data controller needs to satisfy itself that its staff are working to scripts at appropriate times. In a controlled environment, such as a telephone call centre, it is relatively easy to work to a script but in more fluid environments, such as sales meetings, the data controller is totally at the mercy of its representatives.

Consequently, where scripts are to be used the data controller should ensure that all relevant members of staff are provided with a physical copy of the script and receive training in how to deliver it and why adhering to it is a necessary requirement within the workplace.

Other notices – CCTV

The use of CCTV systems poses its own difficulties, because these systems can acquire data about persons who are total strangers to the data controller. Mere passers-by are unlikely to consider whether a data controller has a privacy statement. Indeed, very often they will either not be aware that CCTV systems are in operation, or they will have no idea who the data controller is.

Following the decision of the Court of Appeal in *Durant v. Financial Services Authority* the Information Commissioner published guidance on the application of the DPA to CCTV systems.[182] The Commissioner's view is that fixed systems that are used for general security and deterrent purposes that capture passers-by are not regulated by the DPA in light of *Durant*. On a logical level the Information Commissioner is right, but this assumes that the decision in *Durant* is right. *Durant* did not consider CCTV or image data and it is possible that the focus and significant biography concepts will need to be modified or supplemented. Thus, for now there remains considerable doubt about how to apply the decision in *Durant* to the CCTV environment and the distinction that the Information Commissioner makes between fixed and moveable CCTV systems might not be safe. If all CCTV systems must comply with the DPA, the prescribed information and the information about the processing purpose must be made readily available to the data subject.

Conventional thinking has it that the best way of satisfying the information supply obligations of the DPA where they concern CCTV is through a prominent notice at eye level situated in the vicinity of each camera in the system. These notices are often bright yellow in colour with large black type stating that a CCTV system is in use, that it is in use for the purposes of preventing or detecting crime and that the use is regulated by the DPA. The data controller's name and contact telephone number are also given. This approach to DPA compliance probably amounts to making readily available to the data subject the information required by the first and second data protection principles.

Obtaining consent

If the data controller chooses to rely upon consent as the criterion for legitimacy under Schedule 2 and/or Schedule 3, it will need to consider very carefully how it will obtain consent of sufficient quality that can be proved in the event of enforcement action. Of course, the supply of the prescribed information and the statement of the processing purpose are both prerequisites to the obtaining of consent with the result that privacy statements, company documents, scripts and other notices have an important role to play within the obtaining of consent. However, their mere existence does not provide a guarantee that valid consent will be obtained. Perhaps the most vital component is understanding what does and what does not amount to valid consent.

Consent through conduct

The overall circumstances of a particular transaction between the data controller and the data subject very often result in a conclusion that the data subject has consented to the data controller's processing operations. So, if a data subject completes and returns a loan application form that refers to a comprehensive, readily obtainable privacy statement, the data controller will be entitled to think that it has acquired the data subject's consent.

In the example under consideration, the completion and return of a loan application form, the data controller has ordered its systems in such a fashion that valid consent is obtained, but it has not specifically asked the data subject for consent. This demonstrates that for the purposes of DPA compliance the structure and order of the system is just as important as what is actually said by the parties, which should encourage data controllers to think about their systems in as wide a sense as possible. If this point is considered within the context of an online environment, the data controller should be able to structure its website so that the data subject is guided through a sequence of hyperlinks prior to submitting personal data that can only lead a reasonable, objective observer to conclude that consent of the requisite nature and quality required by the DPA has been obtained. Simple statements such as 'By clicking here I acknowledge that I have read the privacy statement' are very useful compliance mechanisms.

Contracts

Of course, if the data controller is able to design its systems so that the data subject is effectively guided down a particular route, it should be able to take the final logical step and obtain contractual consent for its processing operations. So, the final hyperlink on a compliant website may say something to the effect of: 'By clicking here I accept and agree the terms of use for this website.'

If the data controller chooses to rely upon contractual consent, it must ensure that the contract explains the data controller's processing operations or incorporates by reference another document, perhaps a privacy statement, in which its processing operations are explained. If the contract fails to do either, valid consent will not be obtained.

There is one final point about contractual consent that is worth noting, because a data controller might observe that for the purposes of non-sensitive data there is no advantage in obtaining contractual consent because if a contract exists between the data controller and the data subject, or if the parties intend to enter into contract, the data controller can rely upon the contractual necessity criterion for legitimacy. Such an observation is accurate, but two points arise. First, the contractual necessity criterion contains the complex element of necessity, which is missing from the consent criterion. Second, if sensitive personal data are to be processed, the contractual necessity criterion cannot be relied upon for general contracts, such as contracts for the supply of goods or services. Consequently, if the data controller and the data subject are in a true contractual relationship and sensitive personal data are to be processed, in most cases the data controller will have to acquire explicit consent, which is obtained most easily in contractual form.

Opt-ins and opt-outs

A variant of contractual consent is the use of opt-ins and opt-outs, which are as common in paper application forms as they are in the online environment. For many purposes an opt-out will suffice for the obtaining of consent. However, where the processing is for direct marketing purposes, or where the data are sensitive personal data, an opt-in is the preferred solution.

Contracts generally

For DPA compliance purposes contracts are not limited to obtaining the data subject's consent. They are also required to regulate the data controller's relationships with its own staff, with data processors, with data importers situated in non-adequate countries, for satisfying the data controller's obligations under the fourth data protection principle and for relationships with third-party suppliers of data.

The fourth data protection principle

The fourth data protection principle requires personal data to be accurate and, where necessary, kept up to date. Thus, there are two compliance objectives for the data controller. The requirement for accuracy arises in all cases, unlike the requirement to keep personal data up to date. For the purposes of creating a compliance strategy these obligations coupled with the interpretation identify two basic questions for the data controller, which are:

- Will the personal data be processed only once, or will they be processed more than once?
- Who supplied the personal data to the data controller?

If the personal data are to be processed only once, it is only the obligation that 'personal data shall be accurate' that is engaged. If the data are to be processed more than once, the obligation to keep them 'up to date' will also be engaged, but only if it is 'necessary'. The likelihood of the second obligation being engaged depends upon the nature of the data that are processed, the period of time over which they are processed and the identity of the supplier.

Of course, when considering the first question the data controller must keep in mind the very broad meaning of processing, which covers everything from the initial collection of personal data right through to its final deletion or destruction. The consequence of this broad meaning is that in the vast majority of cases personal data will be processed more than once. This means that most data controllers will need to include a process within their compliance strategies that causes them to consider whether or not it is necessary to keep personal data up to date. If this process of consideration leads to a conclusion that it is necessary to keep personal data up to date, then, of course, the data controller will need to implement a process for so doing.

EXAMPLES

(1) A data controller collects personal data through a user-editable form on an ecommerce website that sells books. When the data subject clicks the Send button at the foot of the form the data are transmitted to a database. This act of collection is the first act of processing. At a later date the data controller retrieves the data from the database in order to complete the order, the second act of processing. In this scenario the data controller will have considered the requirements of the fourth data protection principle during the design of its website and its order processing system and it will have concluded that the requirement to keep data up to date is not engaged; orders are processed quickly and there is no prospect of the data becoming inaccurate.

(2) The data controller is a GP who routinely prescribes drugs for their patients. Before prescribing a drug the GP will need to be sure that the patient's personal data are accurate. In the case of repeat prescriptions the GP will always be under an obligation to keep personal data up to date, to take account of any medical changes.

The identity of the person supplying the personal data is of fundamental importance to the implementation of compliance strategies under the fourth data protection principle, because of the wording of the interpretation. The reason why the identity of the supplier of the information is important is because it affects the duty of accuracy. There are only two sources of the data controller's information:

- the data subject;
- a third party.

In respect of the personal data supplied by the data subject or by a third party, the primary compliance obligation is to ensure that the data are accurately recorded, not that they are accurate, but there are still duties concerning accuracy all the same; in terms of ascertaining the accuracy of the data supplied, the data controller's duty is to take 'reasonable steps to ensure the accuracy'. The interpretation says that the reasonableness of the steps to be taken must be measured by reference to the processing purpose(s). This means that in some cases the steps to be taken will be nominal. In other cases the data controller will need to take significant steps.

EXAMPLE

The data controller is a dating agency that matches people by reference to their tastes and preferences. Two data subjects are matched based on indications of similar interests and after both declaring that they are non-smokers. In fact, one of the data subjects is a smoker and the other complains about the mismatch. In this case the data controller has acquired the personal data from the data subjects and in giving the data subjects the opportunity to admit or deny smoking the agency has taken reasonable steps to ensure the accuracy of the information provided.

In terms of compliance strategies, particular caution should be taken where the data are supplied by a third party, because the data controller is at least one step further removed from the data subject (the third party might have obtained the information from another third party). The fact that data are obtained from a third party does not automatically lead the data controller to a situation where it is under a duty to verify the accuracy (because it is the nature of the processing purposes that determine the reasonableness of the steps to be taken), but it does put the data controller on notice.

It is the very complexity of the issues within the fourth data protection principle that point to a contractual solution. Where contracts are used during the process of collection of data from the data subject the data controller should consider including a term about accuracy, whereby the data subject warrants: (i) that the data supplied are accurate; and (ii) that they will inform the data controller if any inaccuracies are discovered at a later date. Such contractual solutions may insulate the data controller from compensation claims based on the processing of inaccurate data. As regards data collected from a third party, a contract should also be used containing terms about accuracy together with a right of indemnity for any losses suffered by the data controller or the data subject as a result of the processing of inaccurate data.

Third party suppliers of data

The data controller should also insist upon a written contract whenever a third party supplies it with personal data. These contracts will contain provisions about data accuracy. In addition, they should contain such clauses as are necessary to ensure that the transfer of the personal data from the third party to the data controller is lawful.

Data transfers between data controllers are common, everyday occurrences, which is hardly surprising given that one of the dual aims of data protection is the maintenance of data flows. Thus, data controllers in all fields of economic activity, public sector, private sector and the not-for-profit sector, should be well used to contracts governing the supply of data. However, one area that has been especially problematic in recent years is the economic activity known as list broking, which involves the data controller purchasing a list of contact information to be used for direct marketing purposes. Data controllers considering purchasing mailing lists should ensure that the seller of the list has obtained verifiable consents to the transfers from the data subjects on the list. This is known as permission-based marketing.

The seventh data protection principle – relationships with staff

The seventh data protection principle requires the data controller to take reasonable steps to ensure the reliability of staff who have access to personal data. Necessary ingredients within a compliance strategy for this obligation include the training of staff, the taking up of references and appropriate staff contracts. Staff contracts should contain provisions pursuant to which members of staff agree only to process personal data pursuant to a specific authorization given by the data controller, in the manner specified by the data controller and for the purpose specified by the data controller. These contracts should also specify the consequences for breaches of the processing provisions. Finally, the data controller may wish to include a provision enabling it to obtain an indemnity from staff in the event that their breaches of the processing conditions result in the court awarding the data subject compensation.

The seventh data protection principle – relationships with data processors

The role of contracts within this area of compliance is specifically recorded within the interpretation to the seventh data protection principle, which says that data controller–data processor relationships must be carried out under a contract that is made or evidenced in writing. A comprehensive contract for compliance with this part of the seventh data protection principle will include the following elements:

- The data processor will act only on instructions from the data controller.
- The data processor will cease processing at the data controller's instruction.
- The data processor will implement appropriate technical and organizational measures to guard against unauthorized or unlawful processing of personal data and against accidental loss or destruction of, or damage to, personal data.
- The data processor will cooperate fully with the data controller throughout the existence of the relationship to enable the data controller to be sure that the processor has implemented necessary security safeguards and to enable the data controller to be sure that the processing is being done pursuant to the data controller's instructions. The data controller may wish to specify a right of entry into the data processor's premises coupled with a right of inspection and a right of audit.
- The data processor will indemnify the data controller for any loss or damage suffered by the data controller as a result of the processor's breach of contract, to include an indemnity in respect of any compensation payable by the data controller to the data subject.
- The data processor will carry sufficient insurance to cover the indemnities.
- At termination of the relationship the data processor will cooperate fully with the data controller to ensure that all personal data are deleted, erased or destroyed, or returned to the data controller. Again, the data controller may wish to specify a right of entry into the data processor's premises coupled with a right of inspection and a right of audit.

The final three elements are not specified by the interpretation to the seventh data protection principle, but, rather, they are included as a matter of commercial good sense.

The eighth data protection principle – data transfers and data exports

The role of contracts within the compliance process for data transfers and data exports to non-adequate third countries is specifically mentioned within the Data Protection Directive and the DPA. To recap, the European Commission and the Information Commissioner have approved model contractual clauses for the transfers of personal data to data processors and data controllers established in non-adequate third countries.

Training staff

The data controller must train its staff to ensure compliance with all of the data protection principles. In environments where staff are not trained comprehensive breaches of the DPA are easily discovered. The nature of the training will vary from organization to organization and will depend very much on the staff concerned, but three common patterns are discernable within the compliant organization.

Management

DPA compliance is driven by the data controller's management. If the management does not understand the concepts within data protection, they will not be able to enforce a compliance strategy within their organization. Board members and department heads should consider undergoing training, which includes instilling an understanding of the aims, theories and philosophies of data protection.

A further incentive to the comprehensive training of management is the fact that they can be personally prosecuted for criminal offences under the DPA committed with their consent, connivance or neglect.

Staff working at the interfaces

Members of staff working at the interfaces require training on the compliance issues pertinent to their roles. While they do not necessarily require training on the aims, theories and philosophies of the DPA, they do need to understand the mechanics of the data protection principles, the data subject rights and the Information Commissioner's powers.

Other staff

All other members of staff need basic training on the core elements of data protection focusing on the fact that personal data needs to be respected and that processing in breach of the DPA can result in penalties.

Information technology

The data controller needs to pay special attention to the compliance issues involved in the use of IT. The primary issue within the use of IT is that its very existence motivated organizations such as the Council of Europe, the EC and the OECD to create data protection laws in the first place, so a compliance strategy that fails specifically to address the use of IT is going to be fatally flawed putting the data controller in breach of the DPA. Many issues arise within this element of compliance, with three requiring particular attention.

IT and data proliferation

The ease by which electronic data can be copied, reproduced and replicated is one of the primary concerns at the heart of all data protection laws, because uncontrolled data proliferation poses security problems, accuracy problems, retention problems and other problems. Copying, reproduction and replication are all acts of processing and the ease by which these processing operations can be performed has shaped all of the data protection principles. For example, the requirement of the third data protection principle that personal data be 'not excessive' is obviously addressing, in part, the ability of IT to do these things. The requirement of the fourth data protection principle that personal data be kept up to date is a further example of the same point.

Of course, the ease by which electronic data can be copied provides part of its value to data controllers and the compliance objective is not to eradicate copying. Instead, the compliance objective is to put the data controller in control of copying so that the possibility of uncontrolled proliferation of data is eradicated from the organization. Naturally, control can be asserted via the IT itself, but control over IT is not solely an IT issue, hence why DPA compliance also involves education of the data subject and the data controller's staff, the use of contracts and other legal devices and the implementation of mechanisms for handling interventions by the data subject, the Information Commissioner and the courts.

During the first stage of compliance the data controller is advised to examine how personal data flows through its organization, an exercise that is bound to reveal multiple instances of copying, reproduction and replication. Obvious incidences include the transfer of data to portable storage devices, to portable storage media and to local computers.

The essential compliance goals to prevent data proliferation are:

- identification of all acts of copying;
- recording of all acts of copying;
- cessation of all acts of copying at the appropriate time;
- deletion of all copies at the appropriate time.

The final two goals cannot be achieved if the data controller fails to identify and record all acts of copying.

EXAMPLE

The data controller implements a policy for regular deletion of personal data from its database. However, the data controller fails to implement a policy for the deletion of data from backup tapes, local PCs or from portable storage media. After the end of the processing purpose and despite the deletion, policy data are retained, putting the data controller in breach of the fifth data protection principle. After the end of the processing purpose the data subject makes an access request under section 7 of the DPA. The data controller checks its database, finds no data and responds by saying that it is not processing personal data. However, personal data are retained in backup tapes and so on, so the data controller's response puts it in breach of section 7 and in breach of the sixth data protection principle.

IT and security

The seventh data protection principle deals specifically with IT from the perspective of security of personal data. The data controller's obligations as far as technical security measures are concerned are to keep abreast of technological developments and to implement appropriate solutions measured against the harm that might result from a security breach. These obligations cannot be satisfied if the data controller fails to review its IT compliance strategy regularly.

IT and the data subject rights

The data controller's IT strategy should always take account of the data subject rights. Of course, this means avoiding data proliferation, but the issue is much broader than this.

Suppose the data subject exercises the right to object to processing for direct marketing purposes. If this is the only processing operation concerning the data subject, it will follow that deletion of the data subject's personal data from the data controller's systems will satisfy the data subject's objections. However, if direct marketing is only one of a range of processing purposes relating to the data subject, the data controller will need a different IT strategy, such as a direct marketing suppression list that processes personal data only for the purpose of satisfying the right to object.

Likewise, if the Information Commissioner or the court requires cessation of a particular processing activity, the data controller's IT strategy needs to be flexible enough to permit a sufficiently rapid response (the court may impose a tight deadline). Data proliferation will naturally slow down the process but even where the phenomenon of data proliferation has been eradicated the data controller will still require an IT facility that enables compliance with a request or order for cessation of processing within a short time frame.

The need for an IT strategy that permits a rapid response is further highlighted by the right of access within section 7. The data controller is given a short period of time to respond, generally 40 days, and this demands electronic search, location and retrieval systems that also take account of the fact that the response period is short and covers all issues within the context of the right of access, such as the data controller's consideration of the implications of *Durant v. Financial Services Authority*, the taking of legal advice, the seeking of third-party consent to disclosure of information, the redaction of documents and so on. Subject access is such a complex issue that problems are inevitable if the data controller's IT strategy has overlooked DPA compliance issues.

Compliance strategies for dealing with exercise of the data subject rights

The data controller's compliance strategy needs to pay special attention to the data subject rights, as failure to properly comply with an access request or a data subject notice can trigger a chain reaction leading to enforcement action by the Information Commissioner or legal action by the data subject. The key compliance goals for the data controller are:

- Identifying that a data subject has exercised their rights. A subject access request must be in writing. A data subject notice is required for the valid exercise of the right to object.
- Coordinating the organization so that a suitable response can be given.

- Maintaining an opportunity for the data controller to take legal advice.
- Providing a suitable response.

Identifying that a data subject has exercised their rights

As the DPA does not prescribe a format or mechanism for the exercise of the data subject rights, it follows that all persons working at the interfaces between the data controller and the data subject need to be trained in how to recognize when the data subject has exercised their rights. The fact that the DPA does not prescribe a format or mechanism for the exercise of the data subject rights does not prevent the data controller from guiding the data subject down a particular path, however, but it needs to be understood that this legitimate strategy is not binding on the data subject.

EXAMPLE

The data controller explains in its privacy statement that the data subject may make an access request under section 7 of the DPA by completing an online form on the data controller's website. This is perfectly lawful and will certainly streamline the data controller's procedures. However, if the data subject prefers to send an access request by post, they are perfectly entitled to do so.

It follows therefore that the absence of a prescribed format or mechanism for the exercise of the data subject rights means that the data controller is vulnerable to the data subject directing its rights at any one of potentially hundreds of different interfaces, such as any of the email addresses used by the data controller. If the data controller does not attempt to guide the data subject down a particular path, the data controller may receive a request for access (section 7 of the DPA), or a data subject notice requesting cessation of processing (sections 10, 11, 12 and 12A), or for written particulars (section 24) by post, by fax, by email or by any other form of electronic communication capable of retention for subsequent reference.

The best that the data controller can hope to do is to train its staff in understanding what constitutes a valid exercise of a data subject right, so that they can look out for relevant requests. Staff need to understand that a valid exercise of a data subject right is one that it is in writing and that contains certain core information, namely the identity of the data subject and either a request for information about processing or a request for cessation of processing. If a member of staff receives a request that satisfies these key requirements, they must understand that they must forward it to the data protection officer without delay.

Coordinating the organization so that a suitable response can be given

Training staff to recognize when a data subject right has been validly exercised forms part of this compliance goal, but it is not the only component. The data controller's organization needs to work as a unit if the data subject is to be given a sufficient response, which means coordinating actions across the organization.

If the data subject's right to prevent processing likely to cause substantial, unwarranted distress is taken as an example (section 10 of the DPA), it will be seen that the data controller is required to consider a series of complex issues. These are:

- Does the right apply? The issue here is whether the criterion for legitimacy relied upon for the processing of personal data (not sensitive personal data) is consent, contractual necessity or data subject vital interests, because if one of these applies, the right to prevent processing likely to cause substantial, unwarranted distress does not apply.
- If the right applies, will damage or distress be caused to the data subject or to another person?
- If the right applies and damage or distress will be caused to the data subject or to another person, is the distress substantial and unwarranted?
- If the right applies and substantial and unwarranted distress will be caused to the data subject or another person, will the data controller comply with the request or will it refuse to comply?

The data controller needs to consider all of these interlinked issues before the expiry of 21 days from the date of receipt of the data subject's request, which is the deadline for responding. Many departments and many people may need to be involved in the process, but if the data controller fails to put in place a strategy for coordinating its actions and its response across its entire organization, the chances of it failing to provide a sufficient response within the allotted time frame are increased.

Maintaining an opportunity for the data controller to take legal advice

A compliance strategy cannot eliminate the possibility that the data controller may need to take legal advice following the exercise of a data subject right. The key point here is that the data controller's coordinated strategy must contain enough slack for legal advice to be sought and received before the expiry of the relevant deadline. A sensible contingency will be no less than seven days, although this could be reduced if the data controller identifies its lawyer as part of its compliance strategy rather than sourcing one after the exercise of a data subject right.

Providing a suitable response

The range of responses open to the data controller following exercise of a data subject right are many and various, but they can only fall into one of four categories. These are:

- The data controller complies in full.
- The data controller complies in part.
- The data controller refuses to comply.
- The data controller fails to respond.

The difference between the third and fourth categories is very important. In the case of the fourth category the data controller fails to give any response whereas in the case of the third category the data controller does respond, with its response being that it will not comply. The second and third categories should only apply where the data controller has reasons that are good enough to withstand the scrutiny of the Information Commissioner or the court. The fourth category must always be avoided, because this is the greatest indicator of a non-compliant environment and could well trigger a much more serious response from the data subject or from the Information Commissioner, if they are involved.

The second category really has two parts to it. The data controller may comply only in part because it has good reasons not to comply in full (perhaps in the case of subject access under section 7 the data controller has decided that information should be withheld because disclosure would affect a third party's rights), or it may comply only in part because it is not entirely sure what its position should be at the expiry of the deadline for compliance, perhaps because it is still waiting for legal advice or perhaps because there is a fault in its coordination of its organization. If it is the second, the data controller is best advised to explain this to the data subject. A genuine confusion or uncertainty that prevents the data controller from complying in full may discourage the data subject, or the Information Commissioner, from precipitous action. However, if the confusion or uncertainty is a symptom of a non-compliant environment, the data subject, or the Information Commissioner, may not look favourably upon the data controller's position.

Compliance strategies for dealing with the Information Commissioner

The Information Commissioner takes a very pragmatic approach to DPA compliance, as evidenced by their current enforcement strategy.[183] Serious breaches can expect to be met with a strong response; petty breaches will not.

The Information Commissioner is in an unusual position and the dynamics of their powers and their position need to be fully appreciated. On the one hand, the Information Commissioner is there to encourage good practice in data processing, which sometimes involves them or their officers chivvying data controllers along in a 'good cop' style. On the other hand, the Information Commissioner is the prosecuting authority and the 'good cop' style can easily turn into a 'bad cop' style when they consider that an example needs to be set. Furthermore, the data controller needs to appreciate that the Information Commissioner works through their staff and officers. Their individual styles and tolerance levels are as multiple and as varied as can be found in any organization and the outcome must depend in part upon who is actually dealing with a particular case.

The message for data controllers is therefore a simple one: they should treat approaches from the Information Commissioner seriously. Correspondence should not go unanswered. Telephone calls should be returned. An aggressive stance is always counterproductive, but a firm stance is not. A conciliatory approach right from the outset could pay dividends. Of course, if the circumstances warrant, the data controller may wish to be formally represented by a solicitor. This is advisable if a criminal prosecution is possible.

Handling initial enquiries

The Information Commissioner can be motivated to contact a data controller in a variety of circumstances. For example, they might have received a request for an assessment from a data subject (section 42 of the DPA), they might be investigating special purposes processing following the stay of court proceedings (section 32 of the DPA) or they might be examining processing within a particular sector of the economy reflecting the public interest at the time. It does not follow that all initial enquiries from the Information Commissioner will turn out bad for the data controller. Indeed, the evidence contained in the Information Commissioner's annual reports to Parliament shows that only a small percentage of initial enquiries result in criminal proceedings.

The data controller should treat initial enquiries in a professional manner, responding to enquiries as previously mentioned. The data controller's aim after receipt of an initial enquiry should be to find out as much information as possible, so that it can make a proper determination as to the best strategy to adopt. In most cases initial enquiries from the Information Commissioner will remain just that.

Handling the service of notices

The Information Commissioner is highly unlikely to serve an enforcement notice, an information notice or a special information notice without having a prior communication with the data controller, although in cases of urgency or exceptional seriousness these may be served without prior communications. It therefore follows that most data controllers will not be taken by surprise by the receipt of a notice.

Of course, the service of a notice is much more serious than an initial enquiry, by a high order of magnitude, because non-compliance with a notice can result in the commencement of criminal proceedings. Consequently, the data controller must have a compliance strategy for the handling of notices. This strategy will be built around two points. First, these notices may start a chain reaction leading to a criminal prosecution as already mentioned. Second, the data controller has only a short amount of time to comply with a notice, or to appeal a notice, with the default period being 28 days. As with the exercise of a data subject right, the data controller needs to ensure that it has built into its systems sufficient slack to enable coordination of actions across its entire organization and to take legal advice, if required.

Finally, if the data controller considers that it wishes to comply with a notice but requires longer than 28 days, it should ask the Information Commissioner for more time. The Information Commissioner is unlikely to refuse a reasonable request if it is made before the expiry of the deadline. Of course, a request for more time should be reasoned.

Handling investigations

The Information Commissioner may wish to carry out an investigation in contemplation of the commencement of criminal proceedings and the first time that the data controller may appreciate that an investigation is underway is when it receives a surprise visit from investigators acting under a warrant. A surprise visit is always going to be very unsettling, but the data controller must be alive to the issues. These are:

- The investigators must provide the data controller with a copy of a warrant.
- The investigators must provide a receipt for any documents that are seized, if the data controller requests one.
- Although the data controller is under an obligation to give assistance during the exercise of a warrant, this does not extend to answering questions about processing activities. The Information Commissioner does not have the power of arrest and interviews with the data controller may only take place with the data controller's consent. The data controller is perfectly within its rights to say that it requires an opportunity to take legal advice before considering whether to answer questions about processing.
- Interviews must be conducted under caution and must be tape-recorded. Everything that the data controller says under caution is admissible in evidence.

Handling criminal prosecutions

The criminal process is about obtaining justice and the Information Commissioner bears the burden of proof. The criminal process is an adversarial process and the data controller is entitled to test the Information Commissioner's case. However, the handling of contested criminal prosecutions does need specialist legal advice.

In terms of compliance strategies, the key point is merely a reminder of what has already been stated, namely that the data controller is perfectly within its rights to seek legal advice. If legal advice is sought, the data controller should focus on the following matters, to assist its lawyer:

- The data controller should write everything down and the sooner the better. The lawyer will wish to obtain a chronological account of what has happened. This will include information about conversations, particularly with the Information Commissioner's investigators.

Typically, the lawyer will be looking to see whether the investigators complied with the law concerning the exercise of warrants, whether they complied with the law about cautions and whether they gave balanced information about their powers.

- Collate all of the documentary evidence. The lawyer will need to see copies of all correspondence passing between the Information Commissioner and the data controller. The lawyer will want to see a copy of the warrant, a copy of the receipt for evidence seized and a copy of the court summons if one has been received.

- The lawyer will need names and contact details for all relevant witnesses.

Remaining fully compliant with the DPA

The data controller needs to ensure that it has a process for the regular review of its processing operations. This is required not only to ensure that no offences are committed under section 21(2) of the DPA (failure to keep a notification accurate and up to date), but to satisfy the data protection principles generally. For example, if the data controller's processing operations change or modify so that they can no longer be said to be compatible with the purpose for which the data were originally obtained, the second data protection principle will be breached. The following additional principles also require the data controller to implement a compliance strategy that contains a regular review process:

- **The third data protection principle**: The requirement that personal data shall be 'adequate, relevant and not excessive' cannot be satisfied by a once-and-for-all review of the data controller's processing operations.

- **The fourth data protection principle**: Again, the requirement that personal data shall be 'accurate and, where necessary, kept up to date' behoves the data controller to implement a process of review.

- **The fifth data protection principle**: This says that personal data shall not be kept for longer than is necessary for the processing purpose. Obviously, the data controller needs to know when the processing purpose has concluded in order to be able to satisfy the fifth data protection principle. This requires a process of review.

- **The seventh data protection principle**: The data controller's obligation to take appropriate technical and organizational measures to guard against accidental loss or destruction of, or damage to, personal data contains a requirement to keep abreast of the state of technological developments. Likewise, the obligation to ensure the reliability of employees cannot be satisfied by a once-and-for-all review.

Again, how the data controller goes about keeping its operations under review is a matter for the data controller. Some will require regular periodic audits by independent auditors. Other will rely upon the data protection officer remaining on top of changes.

Notes

1. Guidelines for the Regulation of Computerized Personal Data Files, adopted by General Assembly resolution 45/95 of 14 December 1990.
2. Recommendation of the Council of the OECD concerning Guidelines Governing the Protection of Privacy and Transborder Flows of Personal Data, 23 September 1980.
3. Council of Europe Convention on the Protection of Individuals with Regard to Automatic Processing of Personal Data, 28 January 1981.
4. Directive of the European Parliament and of the Council of 24 October 1995 on the protection of individuals with regard to the processing of personal data and on the free movement of such data, 95/46/EC.
5. S.D. Warren and L.D. Brandies (1890) The right to privacy, *Harvard Law Review*, 4(5).
6. *A v. B & C* [2002] EWCA Civ 337, 11 March 2002.
7. *Peck v. United Kingdom*, European Court of Human Rights, 28 January 2003.
8. *Campbell v. Mirror Group Newspapers*, [2004] UKHL 22, 6 May 2004.
9. *Von Hannover v. Germany*, European Court of Human Rights, 24 June 2004.
10. *Douglas v. Hello! Ltd (No 2)*, [2005] EWCA Civ 595, 18 May 2005.
11. Council of Europe Recommendation 509 on human rights and modern scientific and technological developments, 31 January 1968.
12. Council of Europe Resolution (74) 29 on the protection of the privacy of individuals vis-à-vis electronic data banks in the public sector, 20 September 1974.
13. Council of Europe Resolution (73) 22 on the protection of the privacy of individuals vis-à-vis electronic data banks in the private sector, 26 September 1973.
14. Council of Europe Resolution (74) 29 on the protection of the privacy of individuals vis-à-vis electronic data banks in the public sector, 20 September 1974.
15. Recommendation of the Council of the OECD concerning Guidelines Governing the Protection of Privacy and Transborder Flows of Personal Data, 23 September 1980.
16. Council of Europe Convention on the Protection of Individuals with Regard to Automatic Processing of Personal Data, 28 January 1981.
17. Commission of 29 July 1981 relating to the Council of Europe Convention for the protection of individuals with regard to automatic processing of personal data (81/679/EEC).
18. Commission proposal for the Data Protection Directive, 1990.

19. Directive of the European Parliament and of the Council of 24 October 1995 on the protection of individuals with regard to the processing of personal data and on the free movement of such data, 95/46/EC.
20. Commission's first report on the implementation of the Data Protection Directive, 15 May 2003.
21. *Campbell v. Mirror Group Newspapers*, [2004] UKHL 22, 6 May 2004.
22. *Douglas v. Hello! Ltd (No 2)*, [2005] EWCA Civ 595, 18 May 2005.
23. *A v. B & C* [2002] EWCA Civ 337, 11 March 2002.
24. *Bodil Lindqvist v. Åklagarkammaren i Jönköping*, (Case C-101/01) [2004] 1 CMLR 20 ECJ.
25. Directive of the European Parliament and of the Council of 15 December 1997 concerning the processing of personal data and the protection of privacy in the telecommunications sector 97/66/EC.
26. Directive of the European Parliament and of the Council of 12 July 2002 concerning the processing of personal data and the protection of privacy in the electronic communications sector (Directive on privacy and electronic communications), 2002/58/EC.
27. Directive 2006/24/EC of the European Parliament and of the Council of 15 March 2006 on the retention of data generated or processed in connection with the provision of publicly available electronic communications services or of public communications networks and amending Directive 2002/58/EC.
28. Article 29 Working Party Working Document on Genetic Data, WP 91, 17 March 2004.
29. Article 29 Working Party Opinion 5/2004 on unsolicited communications for marketing purposes under Article 13 of Directive 2002/58/EC, 27 February 2004.
30. Article 29 Working Party Opinion 2/2003 on the application of the data protection principles to the Whois Directory, 13 June 2006.
31. Article 29 Working Party Opinion 4/2003 on the level of protection ensured in the US for the transfer of passengers' data, 13 June 2003.
32. *Durant v. Financial Services Authority* [2004] EWCA Civ 1746, 8 December 2003.
33. Commission's first report on the implementation of the Data Protection Directive, 15 May 2003.
34. *Bodil Lindqvist v. Åklagarkammaren i Jönköping*, (Case C-101/01) [2004] 1 CMLR 20 ECJ.
35. *Durant v. Financial Services Authority* [2004] EWCA Civ 1746, 8 December 2003.
36. Recommendation of the Council of the OECD concerning Guidelines Governing the Protection of Privacy and Transborder Flows of Personal Data, 23 September 1980.
37. *Smith v. Lloyds TSB Bank Plc* [2005] EWHC 246 (Ch), 23 February 2005.
38. *Campbell v. Mirror Group Newspapers* [2003] EWCA Civ 1372, 14 October 2002. This is the judgement of the Court of Appeal.

39. *Johnson v. Medical Defence Union* [2006] EWHC 321 (Ch), 3 March 2006.

40. *Durant v. Financial Services Authority* [2004] EWCA Civ 1746, 8 December 2003.

41. *Durant v. Financial Services Authority* [2004] EWCA Civ 1746, 8 December 2003.

42. Information Commissioner (2006) The 'Durant' case and the impact of the Data Protection Act 1998, available www.ico.gov.uk.

43. Information Commissioner (2005) A strategy for data protection regulatory action, available www.ico.gov.uk.

44. Data Protection (Processing of Sensitive Personal Data) Order 2000, SI 2000/417.

45. *Johnson v. Medical Defence Union* [2006] EWHC 321 (Ch), 3 March 2006.

46. *CNN Credit Systems Ltd v. The Data Protection Registrar*, Data Protection Tribunal, 15 February 1991.

47. *Campbell v. Mirror Group Newspapers* [2003] EWCA Civ 1372, 14 October 2002.

48. *Smith v. Lloyds TSB Bank Plc* [2005] EWHC 246 (Ch), 23 February 2005.

49. *Johnson v. Medical Defence Union* [2004] EWHC 347 (Ch), 20 February 2004.

50. *Harper v. The Information Commissioner* [2005] EA/2005/0001, 14 November 2005. This case can be downloaded from the Information Tribunal website: www.informationtribunal.gov.uk.

51. *Skjevesland v. Geveran Trading Co Ltd* [2002] EWCA Civ 1567, 30 October 2002.

52. Article 29 Working Party Working Document on determining the international application of EU data protection law to personal data processing on the Internet by non-EU based web sites, WP 56, 30 May 2002.

53. Information Commissioner (n.d.) Data Protection Act 1998 legal guidance, available www.ico.gov.uk.

54. Information Commissioner (n.d.) Data Protection Act 1998 legal guidance, available www.ico.gov.uk.

55. *Innovations (Mail Order) Ltd v. The Data Protection Registrar*, Data Protection Tribunal, 29 September 1993.

56. *Linguaphone Institute Ltd v. The Data Protection Registrar*, Data Protection Tribunal, 14 July 1995.

57. *British Gas Trading Ltd v. Data Protection Registrar*, Data Protection Tribunal, 24 March 1998.

58. *Midlands Electricity Plc v. The Data Protection Registrar*, Data Protection Tribunal, 7 May 1999.

59. *Johnson v. Medical Defence Union* [2006] EWHC 321 (Ch), 3 March 2006.

60. Information Commissioner (n.d.) Data Protection Act 1998 legal guidance, available www.ico.gov.uk.
61. *Johnson v. Medical Defence Union* [2006] EWHC 321 (Ch), 3 March 2006.
62. Information Commissioner (n.d.) Data Protection Act 1998 legal guidance, available www.ico.gov.uk.
63. Data Protection (Conditions under Paragraph 3 of Part II of Schedule 1) Order 2000, SI 2000/186.
64. Data Protection (Conditions under Paragraph 3 of Part II of Schedule 1) Order 2000, SI 2000/186.
65. *CNN Credit Systems Ltd v. The Data Protection Registrar*, Data Protection Tribunal, 15 February 1991.
66. *Infolink Ltd v. The Data Protection Registrar*, Data Protection Tribunal, 28 February 1992.
67. *Credit and Data Marketing Services Ltd v. The Data Protection Registrar*, Data Protection Tribunal, 15 October 1991.
68. *Innovations (Mail Order) Ltd v. The Data Protection Registrar*, Data Protection Tribunal, 29 September 1993.
69. *Linguaphone Institute Ltd v. The Data Protection Registrar*, Data Protection Tribunal, 14 July 1995.
70. *British Gas Trading Ltd v. Data Protection Registrar*, Data Protection Tribunal, 24 March 1998.
71. *Midlands Electricity Plc v. The Data Protection Registrar*, Data Protection Tribunal, 7 May 1999.
72. Directive of the European Parliament and of the Council of 12 July 2002 concerning the rocessing of personal data and the protection of privacy in the electronic communications sector (Directive on privacy and electronic communications), 2002/58/EC.
73. Data Protection (Notification and Notification Fees) Regulations 2000, SI 2000/188.
74. Information Commissioner (2001) Notification handbook – A complete guide to notification, available www.ico.gov.uk.
75. Information Commissioner (2001) Notification exemptions – A self assessment guide, available www.ico.gov.uk.
76. Data Protection (Fees under section 19(7)) Regulations 2000, SI 2000/187.
77. Data Protection (Notification and Notification Fees) Regulations 2000, SI 2000/188.
78. Data Protection (Notification and Notification Fees) Regulations 2000, SI 2000/188.
79. *Durant v. Financial Services Authority* [2004] EWCA Civ 1746, 8 December 2003.
80. Information Commissioner (n.d.) Data Protection Act 1998 legal guidance, available www.ico.gov.uk.

81. Information Commissioner (n.d.) Data Protection Act 1998 legal guidance, available www.ico.gov.uk.

82. *Durant v. Financial Services Authority* [2004] EWCA Civ 1746, 8 December 2003.

83. *Smith v. Lloyds TSB Bank Plc* [2005] EWHC 246 (Ch), 23 February 2005.

84. Data Protection (Subject Access) (Fees and Miscellaneous Provisions) Regulations 2000, SI 2000/191.

85. Data Protection (Subject Access) (Fees and Miscellaneous Provisions) Regulations 2000, SI 2000/191.

86. Data Protection (Subject Access) (Fees and Miscellaneous Provisions) Regulations 2000, SI 2000/191.

87. Data Protection (Subject Access) (Fees and Miscellaneous Provisions) Regulations 2000, SI 2000/191.

88. *Durant v. Financial Services Authority* [2004] EWCA Civ 1746, 8 December 2003.

89. Consumer Credit (Credit Reference Agency) Regulations 2000, SI 2000/290.

90. Freedom of Information and Data Protection (Appropriate Limit and Fees) Regulations 2004.

91. *Johnson v. Medical Defence Union* [2004] EWHC 2509 (Ch), 9 November 2004.

92. Information Tribunal (Enforcement Appeals) Rules 2000, SI 2000/189.

93. The Data Protection (Subject Access Modification) (Health) Order 2000, SI 2000/413.

94. The Data Protection (Subject Access Modification) (Education) Order 2000, SI 2000/414.

95. The Data Protection (Subject Access Modification) (Social Work) Order 2000, SI 2000/415.

96. Data Protection (Designated Codes of Practice) (No 2) Order 2000, SI 2000/1864.

97. Information Commissioner (2005) Data protection good practice note – Subject access and employment references, available www.ico.gov.uk.

98. 'New guidance clarifies students' rights to exam information', Information Commissioner press release, 2 August 2005; Information Commissioner (2005) Data protection good practice note: Individuals' rights of access to examination records, available www.ico.gov.uk.

99. Data Protection (Miscellaneous Subject Access Exemptions) Order 2000, SI 2000/419.

100. Information Commissioner (n.d.) Data Protection Act 1998 legal guidance, available www.ico.gov.uk.

101. *Community Charge Registration Officer Of Rhondda Borough Council v. Data Protection Registrar*, Data Protection Tribunal, 11 October 1990.

102. *Community Charge Registration Officer of Runnymede Borough Council v. Data Protection Registrar, Community Charge Registration Officer*

of *South Northamptonshire District Council v. Data Protection Registrar* and *Community Charge Registration Officer of Harrow Borough Council v. Data Protection Registrar*, Data Protection Tribunal, 27 October 1990.

103. *The Chief Constables of West Yorkshire, South Yorkshire and North Wales Police v. The Information Commissioner*, Information Tribunal, 12 October 2005.

104. *The Chief Constables of West Yorkshire, South Yorkshire and North Wales Police v. The Information Commissioner*, Information Tribunal, 12 October 2005.

105. Information Commissioner (2005) The Employment Practices Code, available www.ico.gov.uk.

106. Information Commissioner (n.d.) The Employment Practices Code: Supplementary guidance, available www.ico.gov.uk.

107. Telecommunications (Lawful Business Practice) (Interception of Communications) Regulations 2000, SI 2000/2699.

108. European Commission Decision of 27 December 2001 on standard contractual clauses for the transfer of personal data to processors established in third countries, under Directive 95/46/EC, (2002/16/EC).

109. Information Commissioner's authorization under Section 54(6) and Schedule 4, paragraph 9 of the DPA, 18 March 2003.

110. Information Commissioner (n.d.) Data Protection Act 1998 legal guidance, available www.ico.gov.uk.

111. Information Commissioner (n.d.) Data Protection Act 1998 legal guidance, available www.ico.gov.uk.

112. *Bodil Lindqvist v. Åklagarkammaren i Jönköping*, (Case C-101/01) [2004] 1 CMLR 20 ECJ.

113. Data Protection (Processing of Sensitive Personal Data) Order 2000, SI 2000/417.

114. Data Protection (Processing of Sensitive Personal Data) Order 2000, SI 2000/417.

115. Data Protection (Processing of Sensitive Personal Data) (Elected Representatives) Order 2002, SI 2002/2905.

116. *R (on the application of Alan Lord) v. The Secretary of State for the Home Department* [2003] EWHC 2073, 1 September 2003.

117. Data Protection (Processing of Sensitive Personal Data) Order 2000, SI 2000/417.

118. Directive of the European Parliament and of the Council of 12 July 2002 concerning the processing of personal data and the protection of privacy in the electronic communications sector (Directive on privacy and electronic communications), 2002/58/EC.

119. Information Commissioner (n.d.) Data Protection Act 1998 legal guidance, available www.ico.gov.uk.

120. Privacy and Electronic Communications (EC Directive) Regulations 2003, SI 2003/2426.

121. Directive of the European Parliament and of the Council of 12 July 2002 concerning the processing of personal data and the protection of privacy in the electronic communications sector (Directive on privacy and electronic communications), 2002/58/EC.
122. *Innovations (Mail Order) Ltd v. The Data Protection Registrar*, Data Protection Tribunal, 29 September 1993.
123. *Linguaphone Institute Ltd v. The Data Protection Registrar*, Data Protection Tribunal, 14 July 1995.
124. *British Gas Trading Ltd v. Data Protection Registrar*, Data Protection Tribunal, 24 March 1998.
125. *Midlands Electricity Plc v. The Data Protection Registrar*, Data Protection Tribunal, 7 May 1999.
126. Information Commissioner (2005) Data protection good practice note – Electronic mail marketing, available www.ico.gov.uk.
127. Article 29 Working Party Working Document on transfers of personal data to third countries, applying Articles 25 and 26 of the EU data protection directive, WP 12, 24 July 1998.
128. Available at www.export.gov/safeharbor/.
129. European Commission Decision of 26 July 2000 pursuant to Directive 95/46/EC of the European Parliament and of the Council on the adequacy of the protection provided by the safe harbour privacy principles and related frequently asked questions issued by the US Department of Commerce (2000/520/EC).
130. European Commission Decision of 26 July 2000 pursuant to Directive 95/46/EC of the European Parliament and of the Council on the adequate protection of personal data provided in Switzerland (2000/518/EC).
131. European Commission Decision of 26 July 2000 pursuant to Directive 95/46/EC of the European Parliament and of the Council on the adequate protection of personal data provided in Hungary (2000/519/EC).
132. European Commission Decision of 20 December 2001 pursuant to Directive 95/46/EC of the European Parliament and of the Council on the adequate protection of personal data provided by the Canadian Personal Information Protection and Electronic Documents Act (2002/2/EC).
133. European Commission Decision of 30 June 2003 pursuant to Directive 95/46/EC of the European Parliament and of the Council on the adequate protection of personal data in Argentina.
134. European Commission Decision of 21 November 2003 on the adequate protection of personal data in Guernsey (2003/821/EC).
135. European Commission Decision of 28 April 2004 on the adequate protection of personal data in the Isle of Man (2004/411/EC).
136. Aviation & Transport Security Act, 19 November 2001.

137. European Commission Decision of 14 May 2004 on the adequate protection of personal data contained in the Passenger Name Record of air passengers transferred to the US Bureau of Customs and Border Protection (2004/535/EC).

138. Council Decision of 17 May 2004 on the conclusion of an agreement between the European Community and the US on the processing and transfer of PNR data by Air Carriers to the United States Department of Homeland Security, Bureau of Customs and Border Protection (2004/496/EC).

139. Article 29 Working Party Opinion 1/2004 on the level of protection ensured in Australia for the transmission of Passenger Name Record data from airlines, 16 January 2005.

140. Article 29 Working Party Opinion 1/2005 on the level of protection ensured in Canada for the transmission of Passenger Name Record and Advance Passenger Information from airlines, 19 January 2005.

141. *European Data Protection Supervisor v. Council of the European Communities*, [2006], Case C-317/04.

142. *European Data Protection Supervisor v. Commission of the European Communities*, [2006] Case C-318/04.

143. Article 29 Working Party Working Document 74, Applying Article 26(2) of the EU Data Protection Directive to Binding Corporate Rules for international data transfer.

144. Article 29 Working Party Working Document Setting Forth a Co-Operation Procedure for Issuing Common Opinions on Adequate Safeguards Resulting From 'Binding Corporate Rules', WP 107, 14 April 2005.

145. Article 29 Working Party Working Document establishing a model checklist application for approval of Binding Corporate Rules, WP 108, 14 April 2005.

146. European Commission Decision of 15 June 2001 on standard contractual clauses for the transfer of personal data to third countries, under Directive 95/46/EC (2001/497/EC).

147. European Commission Decision of 27 December 2004 amending Decision 2001/497/EC as regards the introduction of an alternative set of standard contractual clauses for the transfer of personal data to third countries (2004/915/EC).

148. Article 29 Working Party Working Document on transfers of personal data to third countries, applying Articles 25 and 26 of the EU data protection directive, WP 12, 24 July 1998.

149. Article 29 Working Party Opinion of 27 December 2004 amending Decision 2001/497/EC as regards the introduction of an alternative set of standard contractual clauses for the transfer of personal data to third countries.

150. European Commission Decision of 27 December 2001 on standard contractual clauses for the transfer of personal data to processors established in third countries, under Directive 95/46/EC (2002/16/EC).
151. The authorizations are available on the Information Commissioner's website: www.ico.gov.uk.
152. Directive of the European Parliament and of the Council of 15 December 1997 concerning the processing of personal data and the protection of privacy in the telecommunications sector 97/66/EC.
153. Directive of the European Parliament and of the Council of 12 July 2002 concerning the processing of personal data and the protection of privacy in the electronic communications sector (Directive on privacy and electronic communications), 2002/58/EC.
154. Telecommunications (Lawful Business Practice) (Interception of Communications) Regulations 2000, SI 2000/2699.
155. Directive 98/34/EC of the European Parliament and of the Council of 22 June 1998 laying down a procedure for the provision of information in the field of technical standards and regulations.
156. Directive 2006/24/EC of the European Parliament and of the Council of 15 March 2006 on the retention of data generated or processed in connection with the provision of publicly available electronic communications services or of public communications networks and amending Directive 2002/58/EC.
157. Privacy and Electronic Communications (EC Directive) Regulations 2003, SI 2003/2426.
158. Privacy and Electronic Communications (EC Directive) (Amendment) Regulations 2004, SI 2004/1039.
159. Regulation of Investigatory Powers (Maintenance of Interception Capability) Order 2002, SI 2002/1931.
160. Regulation of Investigatory Powers (Conditions for the Lawful Interception of Persons outside the United Kingdom) Regulations 2004, SI 2004/157.
161. Telecommunications (Lawful Business Practice) (Interception of Communications) Regulations 2000, SI 2000/2699.
162. Regulation of Investigatory Powers (Maintenance of Interception Capability) Order 2002, SI 2002/1931.
163. Regulation of Investigatory Powers (Communications Data) Order 2003, SI 12003/3172.
164. Retention of Communications Data (Code of Practice) Order 2003, SI 2003/3175.
165. Directive 2006/24/EC of the European Parliament and of the Council of 15 March 2006 on the retention of data generated or processed in connection with the provision of publicly available electronic communications services or of public communications networks and amending Directive 2002/58/EC.

166. *Johnson v. Medical Defence Union* [2006] EWHC 321 (Ch), 3 March 2006.
167. *Campbell v. Mirror Group Newspapers Limited* [2002] EWHC 499 (QB), 27 March 2002. This is the High Court judgement.
168. Information Commissioner (n.d.) Data Protection Act 1998 legal guidance, www.ico.gov.uk.
169. Article 29 Working Party Working Document: Judging industry self-regulation: when does it make a meaningful contribution to the level of data protection in a third country? 14 January 1998
170. Information Commissioner (2005) A strategy for data protection regulatory action, available www.ico.gov.uk.
171. 'New division gets tough with businesses over personal information', Information Commissioner press release, 15 June 2005.
172. 'One third of solicitors likely to be in breach of Data Protection Act', Information Commissioner press release, 12 August 2005.
173. The Information Commissioner's annual reports are available from www.ico.gov.uk.
174. Information Tribunal (Enforcement Appeals) Rules 2000, SI 2000/189.
175. Data Protection (Notification and Notification Fees) Regulations 2000, SI 2000/188.
176. *Durant v. Financial Services Authority* [2004] EWCA Civ 1746, 8 December 2003.
177. *R. v. Lawrence* [1982] AC 510
178. Data Protection (Processing of Sensitive Personal Data) Order 2000, SI 2000/417.
179. *Durant v. Financial Services Authority* [2004] EWCA Civ 1746, 8 December 2003.
180. Telecommunications (Lawful Business Practice) (Interception of Communications) Regulations 2000, SI 2000/2699.
181. Information Commissioner (2005) Employment Practices Code, available www.ico.gov.uk.
182. Information Commissioner (2004) CCTV systems and the Data Protection Act – Good practice note on when the Act applies, available www.ico.gov.uk.
183. Information Commissioner (2005) A strategy for data protection regulatory action, available www.ico.gov.uk.

Index

BCS Products and Services

Other products and services from the British Computer Society, which might be of interest to you include:

Publishing

BCS publications, including books, magazine and peer-review journals, provide readers with informed content on business, management, legal, and emerging technological issues, supporting the professional, academic and practical needs of the IT community. Subjects covered include Business Process Management, IT law for managers and transition management. **www.bcs.org/publications**

BCS Professional Products and Services

BCS Group Membership Scheme. BCS offers a group membership scheme to organizations who wish to sign up their IT workforce as professional members (MBCS). By encouraging their IT professionals to join BCS through our group scheme organizations are ensuring that they create a path to Chartered Status with the post nominals CITP (Chartered IT Professional). **www.bcs.org.uk/forms/group**

BCS promotes the use of the **SFIA*plus***™ IT skills, training & development standard in a range of professional development products and services for employers leading to accreditation. These include **BCS IT Job Describer, BCS Skills Manager** and **BCS Career Developer**. **www.bcs.org/products**

Qualifications

Information Systems Examination Board (ISEB) qualifications are the industry standard both here and abroad, and with over 100,000 practitioners now qualified, it is proof of their popularity. They ensure that IT professionals develop the skills, knowledge and confidence to perform to their full potential. There is a huge range on offer covering all major areas of IT. In essence, ISEB qualifications are for forward looking individuals and companies who want to stay ahead – who are serious about driving business forward. **www.iseb.org.uk**

BCS Professional Examinations are internationally recognised and essential qualifications for a career in computing and information technology (IT). At their highest level, the examinations are examined to the academic level of a UK university honours degree and acknowledge practical experience and academic ability. **www.bcs.org/exams**

European Computer Driving Licence™ **(ECDL)** is the internationally recognised computer skills qualification which enables people to demonstrate their competence on computer skills. ECDL is managed in the UK by the BCS.

ECDL Advanced has been introduced to take computer skills certification to the next level and teaches extensive knowledge of particular computing tools. **www.ecdl.co.uk**

Networking and Events

BCS's Specialist Groups and Branches provide excellent professional networking opportunities by keeping members abreast of latest developments, discussing topical issues and making useful contacts. **www.bcs.org/bcs/groups**

The Society's programme of social events, lectures, awards schemes, and competitions provides more opportunities to network. **www.bcs.org/events**

Further Information

This information was correct at the time of publication, but could change in the future. For the latest information, please contact:

The British Computer Society
First Floor, Block D
North Star House
North Star Avenue
Swindon
SN2 1FA, UK

Telephone: 0845 300 4417 (UK only) or + 44 1793 417 424 (overseas)
E-mail: customerservice@hq.bcs.org.uk
Web: www.bcs.org